WATER-WiSE
PLANTS FOR THE
SOUTHWEST

NAN STERMAN, MARY IRISH, JUDITH PHILLIPS, AND JOE LAMP'L

EDITED BY DIANA MARANHAO

COOL
SPRINGS
PRESS

Growing Successful Gardeners™

BRENTWOOD, TENNESSEE

Published by Cool Springs Press
P.O. Box 2828
Brentwood, TN 37024

Cataloging-in-Publication data available

EAN: 978-1-59186-468-4

First Printing 2010

Printed in the United States of America
10 9 8 7 6 5 4 3 2 1

Project Editor: Diana Maranhao
Editor: Nan Sterman
Art Director: Marc Pewitt

WATER-WISE
PLANTS FOR THE
SOUTHWEST

FOREWORD

The Southwest encompasses a broad geographical region spanning six states—Arizona, California, Nevada, New Mexico, Texas, Utah—that includes USDA Cold Hardiness Zones 5 through 11. Gardeners living in the higher zones may experience long growing seasons, where the changes between fall and winter temperatures are subtle, and the spring and summer seasons seem to flow slowly together. In the winter months, the differences between gardening in Zones 5 through 11 become the most apparent. In Zones 5 through 7, the lowest temps range from minus 20 to 0 degrees F, early autumn nighttime frosts are a common occurrence, and winters are sometimes accompanied by snowfall. In contrast, Zones 8 through 11 feature a temperate 40 degrees F, so winter frosts and snowfall are uncommon. Knowing the zone you live in is key to selecting the plants that can grow in your winter conditions. Even better, zone awareness helps you as a gardener to determine how and when to plant, as well as the seasonal maintenance tasks that are necessary to keep the plants healthy and thriving throughout the year.

The soil in your garden is probably the single most important factor for determining which plants survive and which thrive. Soil has a direct effect on a plant's roots, for it is through the roots that a plant takes in moisture, and along with it, essential nutrients. The textures of Southwest soils range from sandy and fast-draining to clayey and waterlogged. Most of these soils have an alkaline pH, best dealt with by selecting alkaline-tolerant plants. Always keep in mind the adage "the right plant for the right place."

For gardeners in the arid Southwest, water conservation and the use of Xeriscaping remain at the forefront of gardening strategies. For some of us, our annual precipitation falls in the winter months when plants are dormant or growth is slowed, and the moisture requirements are therefore lower. Desert regions experience occasional summer monsoons, but, for the most part, supplemental watering must be applied during the hottest months of the year to keep plants alive. Efficient irrigation systems and the right amount of water at the right time are the keys to getting plants off to a good start so they can ultimately survive in the Southwest on natural rainfall. Because learning when and how to water and how much water to apply will assure you of the results you want, we have devoted an entire section to this topic in the back of the book.

After having worked in the horticulture industry and lived and gardened in Southern California (USDA Zone 9) for over twenty years, I wasn't prepared for the gardening challenges that awaited me at my new home in southern Utah (USDA Zone 5). Not only had the plant materials changed, but the climate was very different due to the different elevations (from below sea level to almost 5000 feet), high summer temperatures, cold winters (temperatures sometimes in single digits), and winds in the high desert. Choosing the proper plants for a desert region based upon the plant's ability to survive (once established) on whatever rainfall that Mother Nature provides is a challenge. Few references have the information you need to plan your water-wise garden in the Southwest.

That is why I am delighted that Cool Springs Press decided to provide gardeners living in the Southwest within such a broad zone range a book tailored just for Southwest gardeners, something to take the guesswork out of making plant selections that satisfy the region's unique criteria. *Water-Wise Plants for the Southwest* provides detailed descriptions of more than 150 water-wise plants—enough to landscape even the largest gardens—with diversity in size, leaf and bark texture, flower, and form to create gardens that burst with color and interest at all seasons. These are the workhorse plants of the Southwest, plants that require nothing more than adequate space to live in, that are not picky about the soil in which they grow, and that are water-wise to boot.

In compiling this resource, I went straight to the experts. Who better to help make sensible water-wise plant choices and to give tips and techniques for managing our gardens than the horticulturists who live, grow, and write about their gardens firsthand? Some of our best and brightest garden writers have contributed tried and true water-wise plant selections from their region, providing information on how to deal with the soils in the Southwest, how and when to irrigate, and when it's necessary to fertilize or to prune.

For gardeners in the Mediterranean region of the Southwest, **NAN STERMAN**, author of *California Gardener's Guide: Volume II*, provides plants, companion plants, and other information. For those living in arid desert regions, **MARY IRISH**, author of *Arizona Gardener's Guide*, suggests plants that are proven to be tough and durable in a desert setting, and also gives valuable tips for gardening in a low desert climate. **JUDITH PHILLIPS**, author of *New Mexico Gardener's Guide*, recommends water-wise plants for gardening in high desert and dry mountainous regions, an area long known for its drought-tolerant designs. And rounding out the team is **JOE LAMP'L**, author of *The Green Gardener's Guide*, who offers excellent advice for watering, irrigation systems, and water conservation techniques for the Southwest gardener.

DIANA MARANHAO

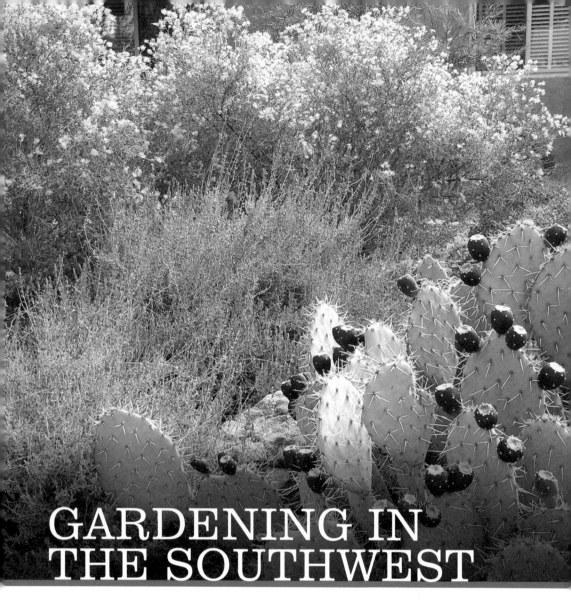

GARDENING IN THE SOUTHWEST

DIANA MARANHAO

When my husband and I moved from a Mediterranean climate in southern California to the high desert of southern Utah, we had no way of knowing what challenges laid before us. Our goal was to create gardens, an orchard, and a vineyard that would eventually support us throughout the year. Both of us, professionals in the horticulture industry, had confidence in our education and skills, so we dove in headfirst and started planting our favorite vegetables, fruits, and flowers on a sunny, warm spring weekend in April. We quickly learned that while we still lived in the Desert Southwest region, spring planting at an elevation of almost 5000 feet isn't the same as planting at sea level. Spring does not make its appearance here until May. Needless to say, we lost a few of our plants that first year. While the list of differences in growing here (USDA Zone 5) as opposed to growing in Southern California (USDA Zone 9) has grown by leaps and bounds, there still remains some basic similarities.

SOUTHWEST USDA COLD HARDINESS ZONES

This book is written for gardeners in Arizona, California, Nevada, New Mexico, Texas, and Utah. The USDA assigns each area a numerical gardening zone. Arizona's low desert USDA Zone 9 has winter temperatures rarely falling below freezing. The state's higher elevation region is Zone 6, where temperatures hit minus 10 degrees F or lower. In parts of northeastern Nevada, low temperatures range from minus 10 degrees to as low as minus 25 degrees, whereas the rest of the state rarely falls below freezing. California has perhaps the broadest range of USDA Zones within its boundaries. In Zone 4, winter temperatures can plummet to 20 to 25 degrees below zero. In coastal Southern California (Zone 11), on the other hand, winter temperatures rarely fall below 40 degrees F. New Mexico and Utah, with their vast ranges of elevations, span Zones 4 through 8, with large central portions of the states at Zones 6 and 7. The entire state of Texas typically experiences freezing and below freezing temperatures in winter. So no matter where you live in the Southwest, this book should address your gardening situation. Consult pages 30 through 33 to find your Cold Hardiness Zone.

MARY IRISH, author of *Arizona Gardener's Guide*, explains how microclimates and other variables affect interpreting the Cold Hardiness Zone Map:

With each zone, local changes in topography can create microclimates that may be one zone warmer or colder. Plants that are rated for one zone may well be grown in a colder zone if your site is warmer than the average for the zone, or if they are provided overhead protection, or if they are planted facing south. In addition, large urban areas are much warmer than other areas at their elevation or the surrounding areas.

NAN STERMAN, author of *California Gardener's Guide: Volume II*, describes cold hardiness in this way:

Cold hardiness is a term that describes the minimum temperature that a plant is likely to survive. Keep in mind that cold hardiness temperatures are estimates, rather than hard and fast rules, and that there is tremendous variability. After a few hours at its coldest temperature, a plant may sustain some leaf or stem damage, or it may die back to the ground altogether, yet it will still resprout in spring. After many hours at its coldest temperature or several nights at the coldest temperature, the same plant may die completely.

JUDITH PHILLIPS, author of *New Mexico Gardener's Guide*, lives and gardens in New Mexico and talks about the challenges of gardening in an unpredictable climate:

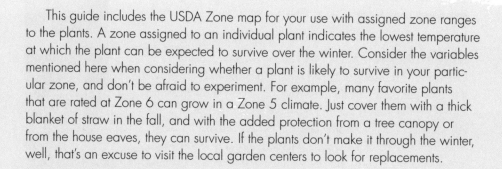

To a Southwestern gardener, altitude has enormous significance. Every 1000-foot gain in altitude yields a 3-degree drop in temperature, and at least a few inches' increase in annual precipitation. Cold-hardiness zones based on potentially lowest temperatures are difficult to apply to New Mexico because there may be episodes of minus 20 degrees Fahrenheit that last only a few hours and occur only once in a decade. This unpredictability affects plants much differently than would a routine occurrence or longer spells of comparable cold. To survive anywhere in our state, plants need at the very least to adapt to 40-degree swings in daily temperatures. The lack of substantial cloud cover and a humidity level that is commonly less than 25 percent at 5 p.m. cause heat to dissipate quickly at night. In summer, this rapid cooling makes life after sundown a refreshing reward for having endured the day's heat. In spring and autumn, it may sound a death knell for plants that can't make the transition.

This guide includes the USDA Zone map for your use with assigned zone ranges to the plants. A zone assigned to an individual plant indicates the lowest temperature at which the plant can be expected to survive over the winter. Consider the variables mentioned here when considering whether a plant is likely to survive in your particular zone, and don't be afraid to experiment. For example, many favorite plants that are rated at Zone 6 can grow in a Zone 5 climate. Just cover them with a thick blanket of straw in the fall, and with the added protection from a tree canopy or from the house eaves, they can survive. If the plants don't make it through the winter, well, that's an excuse to visit the local garden centers to look for replacements.

SOUTHWEST RAINFALL

Gardening in the Southwest means living with minimal annual precipitation. Most parts of the region get only 4 to 10 inches of rain a year. Though parts of central and northern California can get upwards of 30 inches per year, that precipitation is all between November to March. There is little to no measureable rainfall in the warmest months of the year—April through October—a very stressful situation for plants from parts of the world where rain falls year-round.

Our rainfall patterns (or lack thereof) have produced record drought for the last several decades. What rain you do receive might fall at the coolest time of the year when the plants have slowed their growth and need less water, rather than in the heat of the summer when the plants are flourishing and desperately need it. In desert areas, monsoonal summer rains arrive so quickly that the precious moisture runs off in flash floods that erode the soil. Gentle winter rains or snowfall are welcomed, but they cannot be counted on to sustain plantings throughout the winter months. Selecting water-wise plants is the best solution to being able to garden in the Southwest. Once established, they will survive on the natural rainfall, whenever that should come.

MARY IRISH (AZGG) describes her home state of Arizona as a land of challenges:

Arizona presents many obvious challenges for gardeners, especially for recent arrivals. Soils do not appear as fertile as they were in a previous home, and rocks are a way of life, a fact that is daunting to some gardeners. The skies are clear and the abundant sunshine makes a welcome change, but rain is just a dream in some seasons, and there never seems to be very much of it even in the best of times. What becomes clearer the longer you garden here is that the soils are absolutely fine for plants that are well adapted to them, rocks are one of the treasures of a well-designed garden, shade is a great partner, especially in the lower zones to give your plants relief from that constant sunshine, and while you can't count on rain, you absolutely must be able to rely on your irrigation system.

NAN STERMAN (CAGG) living and growing in Southern California, discusses gardening in a Mediterranean climate where the rainy period is concentrated from November through March. The rest of the year is hot and dry—perfect for people who like to sunbathe or do outdoor sports, but terribly stressful for plants from rainier parts of the world. Since California is so large and geographically diverse, gardeners there find themselves in micro-climates that differ from region to region:

Coastal gardens are bathed in cool moist air, fog, and ocean breezes that flow inland along bays, estuaries, and lagoons. Because of the ocean's buffering capacity, coastal gardens have the mildest growing conditions; these frost-free gardens are warmer in winter and cooler in summer. Though the ocean is a huge reservoir of water, plants growing right along the beach are subject to significant stress from intense sun (which can alternate with summer fog and often a thick marine layer), constant wind, and salt spray. Wind and salt spray diminish quickly as you move away from the beach.

Inland valleys (and associated foothills) have little ocean influence. Instead they are hot, sunny, and dry in all but the winter rainy season. Even then, valleys receive far less rain than the coast. Temperature variations are greater, with winter frost more common in northern valleys and less common in southern valleys. Central Valley air is hot and dry in summer with average August temperatures well into the 90s. Winters are cool and damp with average January temperatures in the 30s. The Central Valley is known for dense, thick tule fog that blankets the ground in fall and winter. The Sacramento Valley gets more rain and frost than the drier San Joaquin Valley, where winter temperatures seldom dip below freezing.

Low desert regions are east of Southern California's mountains and include the Coachella Valley, Anza Borrego desert, and parts of the Imperial Valley. Desert air is dry and hot, peaking with average August temperatures over 100 degrees F and midwinter temperatures in the 40s. Annual rainfall is 6 inches or less. Intermediate and high deserts refer to the desert areas above 1000 feet elevation, primarily those along Highway 395 down the backside of the Sierra Nevada Mountains, from north of Bishop, and south through the Mojave Desert to the vicinity of Twentynine Palms. Summers are cooler than those in low deserts and winters are much colder.

Therein lies some of the challenges of gardening in a diverse Southwest climate. While each region has its own particular set of climate parameters, gardeners in the Southwest are joined together under one shared goal—to garden and grow in the arid Southwest while still preserving our most precious natural resource—water. The number one rule then, is to select plants that naturally grow in dry, arid climates. Water-wise plant selection is key to making the whole system work. Start with the right plant in the right place, and you are most of the way to creating your water-wise dream garden.

PLANTING AND GROWING IN SOUTHWEST SOILS

"Dirt is what you get our of your vacuum cleaner. Soil is what gardeners dig in," the saying goes. It really is all about the soil. No matter what you grow or where you grow it, the soil dictates how a plant grows, how strong it is, and how well it survives.

It is virtually impossible to change soil chemistry, and it takes an immeasurable amount of work and product to alter soil texture. You might be able to temporarily affect a soil's pH, but this can only be done by some pretty radical means (such as siting acid-loving plants in an alkaline soil by planting them entirely in a backfill of peat moss). But, eventually the plant's rootball will exceed the amended area, and the plant's roots will end up in the native alkaline soil. The same holds true for the old habit of amending the backfill soil when planting. By amending the backfill soil, you'll create a fluffy, organic medium for the plant's home. Eventually, though, those roots will reach far beyond the hole you dug, and will have to make their way through whatever native soil you have. Sometimes they can't survive the transition.

So, what's the best solution? Choose plants that grow happily in their dry, but well-draining native soil, and *grow them in similar, well-draining soils*. Select plants that actually prefer alkaline soils and there is no need to amend the soil. Choose water-wise plants that are not "thirsty" and needy in terms of nutrients or water. You will work a lot less, and the plants are perfectly happy to live on whatever they can get out of the soil and out of the atmosphere.

MARY IRISH (AZGG) describes how to deal with the classic Southwestern alkaline soil:

While each zone in the state has its own distinct soils, it can be said that the soils in Arizona are alkaline, often thin with low humus content, and often just as rocky. It is time-consuming and often impossible to correct the composition of any soil, especially its pH. On the other hand, it is impossible to correct the inherent physiology of plants, including their preference for or ability to survive in soils of varying composition and pH. Plants that love the acid soils of forests and bogs are not well suited to the basic soils of Arizona. They become chlorotic quickly, they often live much shorter lives, and in many cases, they just refuse to flower and grow with the same vigor they would in a more congenial soil. It is much easier and less frustrating to look for and grow plants that are content with the soils that are found in your garden.

JUDITH PHILLIPS (NMGG) explains how to work with Southwestern soils:

Because of the pervasive dryness and intense sunlight, the soils lack organic matter. New Mexico soils are rich in calcium and other mineral salts, and moderately to strongly alkaline because there isn't enough rainfall to leach out mineral salts or to break down organic matter that would mellow mineral concentrations. Regardless of elevation, climatic conditions conspire to keep soils high in pH and low in humus.

Sand absorbs water quickly and also loses it rapidly to evaporation. Immediately after rain or irrigation, water fills the pore spaces in the soil. As plants absorb moisture and evaporation dries the soil surface, the absent water is replaced with air, restoring the soil's oxygen balance.

Clay is the most difficult soil to garden because it absorbs water slowly and stays sticky-wet too long for many plants. It is difficult to know when to water because while the clay still feels damp, plants may begin to wilt from reverse osmosis. Adding insult to injury, concentrations of salt crust collect on the surface where the clay drains most slowly, making gardening nearly impossible.

Many of the plants profiled in this book are described as preferring "well-drained soil." Plant roots require oxygen as well as water to thrive, and good drainage is the healthful balance of moisture and air in the soil. When soil pore spaces are consistently filled with water or are compacted, oxygen levels in the soil become too low to support root growth. New transplants fail to root out, and the roots of established plants die, causing the plants to decline.

Many of the plants described in this book have adapted to dry climates and need no compost added to the soil. Drought-adapted plants are the camels of horticulture and can flourish under the most extreme conditions of intense sunlight, heat, and wind. These chronic xerics will decline in soils enriched with organic matter. Just as too much water in the soil can deprive drought-adapted plants of oxygen, too much organic matter can be harmful to plants that have evolved to thrive in gritty, mineral-rich soils.

If there is little to be done to change our soils, then what is the best way to prepare a site for a plant so that it will thrive? The answer lies in preparation. As you work the soil with your hands, you are increasing the number of pore spaces that are the means for getting moisture and nutrients down into the soil so that a plant's roots can use them.

JUDITH PHILLIPS (NMGG) continues her explanation:

All plants benefit from having generous holes dug: Dig only as deep as but several times the diameter of the rootball of the transplant. All plants need permeable soil to establish their roots. I hope that this universal imperative to loosen the soil echoes through your mind as you dig, urging you to chip away a little further. This is hard work, but think of how it feels to wear shoes a size too small, and work a little harder. Your plants will thank you with vigorous growth that will make you both look good.

NAN STERMAN (CAGG) gives some easy detailed steps to follow for planting water-wise plants from nursery containers:

• Water the plant in its pot thoroughly the day before you intend to plant. Dig a hole just as deep as the pot is tall and 1½ to 2 times as wide as the pot.

• Fill the hole with water and allow it to drain completely.

• Most of the plants in this book are planted best into native, unamended soils. Add a few handfuls of worm castings to the bottom of the hole. Refill the bottom of the hole with enough soil so the plant will sit at the same level it was in the pot. When planting natives, set plants an inch higher than they were in their pots. Step on the soil in the bottom of the hole to pack it down.

• Lay the pot on its side and squeeze the sides gently to loosen the plant from the pot. Grab the plant at the base of the trunk of trees and shrubs and carefully pull it from the pot. Check the roots. If they circle the rootball, gently loosen them unless they require minimum root disturbance. Remove any roots that are broken or dead.

• Set the plant into the hole. Refill with soil, tamping it as you go to eliminate air pockets. Before you reach the top, water the soil to settle it, then continue adding soil. Make a watering basin.

• Apply 3 or 4 inches of mulch to the soil surface, making sure that the mulch covers the entire rootball area. To make sure no mulch touches the plant, stop the mulch at least 3 inches away.

DESIGNING WITH WATER-WISE PLANTS

As you read this book and see the comprehensive list of water-wise plants available for Southwest gardens, you may find yourself wandering down some new garden paths. I have found that even with all the challenges of growing plants in the high desert of southern Utah, my plant palette has grown by leaps and bounds, along with my design style. Numerous plants have joined my list of favorites as I continue to learn about new water-wise plants that grow here.

MARY IRISH (AZGG) shares her experience:

Using plants that demand little in the way of supplemental irrigation is not a sentence to boredom—far from it. The diversity of plants, whether native or from similar regions around the world, is astounding.

When I left the Gulf Coast and moved to Arizona, I imagined that I would have to begin entirely from scratch. I was certain that I would not recognize anything, and nothing I had grown would be part of my gardens in the West. While some of those imaginings were true, others were just myths, and I was delighted and surprised by how many outstanding new plants were added to my garden. I would never have predicted that the most interesting, exhilarating, and satisfying garden I had ever designed would be the one at my desert home.

Whether you are gardening in the higher zones and have a short, but intensely colorful growing season, or in the low zones with their year-round growing season, the selection of well-adapted plants for Arizona gardens is large and diverse.

The low zones offer the most diversity in plant choices. In these zones, frost is only a brief consideration, and temperatures rarely plunge lower than the mid-twenties.

Most of Zone 1, Yuma and the interior urban areas of Phoenix, are virtually frost-free. Here, a gardener can take advantage of the tropical and subtropical summer-flowering shrubs such as red bird of paradise, hibiscus, and yellowbells, as well as the vast numbers of flowering trees, shrubs, and perennials from the Sonoran and Chihuahuan deserts such as palo verde, cascalote, dalea, Texas sage, and chuparosa.

Although the range of choice in succulents is greatest in the warm, low zones, a group of succulents exists for gardens in every zone, and the use of these plants is what sets many Arizona gardens apart from gardens elsewhere. In the higher zones, agaves, yuccas, and some species of cacti are easily mixed with evergreens and summer-flowering perennials. In the mid zones, the symmetry of desert spoon, the sculptural highlights of ocotillo, and the beauty of some of the hardier ice plants open up the choices even more. In addition to all of these, the low zones can showcase the mighty, treelike saguaro, countless prickly pears, cholla, hedgehog cactus, winter-flowering aloes, tiny dudleya, elegant sansevieras, and spectacular winter-flowering aloes to create tremendous interest and contrast to the garden.

These plants not only add texture, contrast, and striking form to the Arizona garden, they also give them a distinctive style. What's more, liberal use of these plants not only helps the water bill, but gives a garden a gentle nudge toward the surrounding natural landscapes.

Mediterranean plants lend themselves to many different styles of gardening and bring water-wise benefits with them.

NAN STERMAN (CAGG) explains it this way:

Rather than fight the peculiarities of our climate, I encourage you to grow with them. These pages include beautiful Mediterranean climate plants, many native to California and others native to other Mediterranean regions. These plants are so well adapted to our growing conditions that they thrive with little irrigation once established. They are also adapted to our poor soils and grow at a rate that won't overwhelm you with the need to prune (unless you plant them in too small a space). Better yet, pests tend to ignore them. In other words, if you are looking for a great beauty with little maintenance, Mediterranean climate plants are the way to go.

JUDITH PHILLIPS (NMGG) describes the water-wise style of gardening:

Gardening is ultimately about beauty, and realizing the need to conserve water in New Mexico has led us to begin to cultivate many styles of beauty as we diversify the garden palette. Instead of working so hard to change the desert to suit plants from wetter climates, we're being selective and gardening with the many plants that meet us halfway.

Water-efficient xeric plants can be used lavishly or with great restraint to create any number of garden styles. We can choose to celebrate the desert, temper it a bit, or do both in different parts of the garden. Our gardens are dynamic mirrors of our evolving relationship to our world. We can make lush oases that use surprisingly little water, or pay tribute to the prairie with a dramatic sweep of ornamental grasses. We can build a rock garden that makes us feel 10,000 feet high, or plant a soothing meditation garden that draws us inward.

Water-Wise Plants for the Southwest gives you an extensive list of plant choices. The selections were made based upon recommendations of our authors, all experts on gardening in the Southwest. Once you make the decision to design your gardens the water-wise way, your next challenge could be trying to fit all of your favorites into your garden space! This guide does not list all of the drought-tolerant plants available. Make regular visits to your local garden centers and botanical gardens to see the newest species and cultivars available. Tour water conservation and demonstration gardens for inspirational design techniques, companion planting ideas and examples of how mature plants perform in the landscape. The possibilities for water-wise gardening are endless. Once you start down the water-wise path, you'll wonder how you ever gardened any other way.

WATER-WISE GARDENING

"Could you help me plant one of those *Zero-scapes*?" this question might make you chuckle, or it might make you think "I want one of those!" (This is a phrase heard from college students in horticulture who are not exactly sure what the correct word or practice—Xeriscape—actually represents. I have also heard this request from homeowners who want a garden but who live under the constant worry of having no water to keep it alive. *Zero-scape* is a word coined by landscapers for a landscape laid out in a blanket of white gravel, with a lone cactus (surrounded by red scalloped edging) struggling to protect itself from the harsh reflective sun and from having absolutely no water touch its roots. The correct word is *Xeriscape*, pronounced ZEER-uh-scape, which comes from the Greek word *xeros*, meaning

In the Southwest, low-water-use plants such as blue grama grass and desert willow trees use 73.4 percent less water than high-water-use plants such as Kentucky bluegrass. Converting a 5000-square-foot traditional landscape to Xeriscape in Albuquerque can save at least 50 percent of landscape water— and sometimes as much as 75 percent (depending upon the types of plants chosen). That's a potential savings of 74,680 gallons of water per year per home.

dry. Nowadays, we use other expressions, such as water-wise landscaping, dry landscaping, or low-water-use landscaping to clarify the practice. They all mean the same thing.

Water-wise landscaping involves a healthy, lush landscape that includes plants that grow here naturally (natives), as well as plants that grow in climates similar to ours. Water-wise landscaping helps us create an environment where low-water-use plants are allowed to grow into their natural forms and sizes and where they live in harmony with other plants of similar needs. Learning to use the principles of water-wise gardening is quite easy, and more important, it brings immense pleasure to know that you are creating a healthy, thriving landscape while still conserving water.

NAN STERMAN (CAGG) lists these principles of water-wise landscaping:

• Start with a plan based on a water-efficient approach. The concept of clustering plans based on water need, for example, means that low-water plants are in one part of the garden and watered by one set (zone) of sprinklers, bubblers, or drip emitters.

• Install a good, efficient irrigation system with an irrigation controller. "Smart" weather-based irrigation controllers take the worry out of programming. If your controller is not weather-   based, it is your responsibility to update watering times monthly. Don't leave it to your gardener.

• Limit your lawn space to the amount needed for pets, small children, and rec-reational games. If you simply need a green carpet, skip the lawn and plant lower water, lower maintenance ground covers. Better yet, plant a meadow of low-water grasses.

• Choose low-water plants and place them according to their need for sun, shade, and soil type. Always place a plant in a spot that will accommodate its ultimate size.

• Most California native plants and most Mediterranean climate plants prefer our native soils.

• Cover your soil and surround your plants with composted organic mulches. Mulch impedes water loss, keeps weeds down, and improves the soil as it decays. You could even say that composted organic mulch is the silver bullet of the garden. Spread it everywhere, leaving no bare soil.

• Practice good maintenance. Keep the garden tidy by mulching, weeding, pruning, fertilizing when needed, and controlling pests.

It is said that if you can practice all seven water-wise steps in creating or retrofitting your landscape (keeping some water-wise features already in the garden and replacing heavy-water-use areas and plants with more water-efficient ones), you can realize as much as 50 percent water savings. That computes to quite a bit of water and money savings over the lifespan of a garden.

While it may be too costly to yank out all the thirsty plants in the landscape and to install a drip irrigation system at the same time, the practice of applying mulch to the landscape is a step that can be done economically and with immediate results. Even if you have a somewhat tropical or "thirsty" landscape, applying a 2- to 3-inch layer of organic mulch to any bare soil surface is going to give you some benefits. First, the protective layer will reduce loss of water through evaporation, thus allowing you to cut back on watering. Second, a layer of mulch provides a weed barrier, slowing down the germination of weed seeds. If some weeds do pop up through the mulch, they slip out more easily, since the mulch helps the soil hold in moisture. Third, mulches help control erosion and runoff.

WATER-WISE WISDOM

By mulching all landscape beds on your property, you can reduce the runoff and accompanying loss of soil to erosion by as much as 80 percent.

MARY IRISH (AZGG) discusses the two types of mulches and their uses:

In the low zones, the great summer heat results in the rapid loss of soil moisture through evaporation. The easiest way to help plants cope with the heat is to provide mulch around the root zones to help slow down evaporation. There are two styles of mulch—organic and inorganic.

Organic mulch—leaves, pine needles, prunings—does two things for plants. Organic mulch cools the soil surface and thus slows down evaporation, thereby making more water available to the plants over a longer time. This can mean the difference between watering a plant every day or two and watering it every three or four days. As an added bonus, organic mulches provide tiny amounts of organic matter as they break down, essentially acting as compost piles right next to a plant. Over the years, this action of decomposition enriches the bed, changes the texture of the soil, and makes it able to hold much more moisture.

Inorganic mulch—rock, stone, granite

It is popular to use inorganic mulch like crushed granite throughout the state, especially in the low zones. Rock mulch also cools the soil and slows down the rate of evaporation. Gravel mulch is hot on its surface and can create a lot of reflected heat if the rock covers more area than the plants. It is not always necessary to have a blanket of rocks to have useful rock mulch. Large rocks can be highly effective as an inorganic mulch. Succulents, in particular, which have shallow root systems, thrive in the shade of a nice rock. Under that rock mulch, the soil is a bit cooler with just a little more moisture, and that may be all that it takes to keep that plant fit through the long desert summer. Many of the desert species used in annual wildflower displays grow best with a rock mulch. Rocks are also a treasured addition to a garden with their strong presence and stunning regional appeal, and rocks that come with the site always look better than the ones that are added to the garden. Rocks also are used in the garden to line a pathway as walls, as well as accents. Use them for seating, to mark boundaries, or as a transition to tie together a highly cultivated area with a more natural one.

SOMETHING YOU SHOULD KNOW

According to one estimate, Southern Californians water their gardens with the equivalent of 84 inches of rainfall each year. That is as much rain as falls in the Amazon jungle, two and a half times the rainfall of Seattle, and four times the rainfall of Honolulu!

In my Utah garden, I alternate between natural mulches such as compost, tree shavings, and chips with sand, gravel, and rock. Some water-wise trees and shrubs favor organic mulches, whereas some perennials such as lavender and penstemon prefer sand or rock as a mulch. Usually when using small river rock, it's best to use a weed barrier cloth underneath to avoid the stone working its way into the soil. Someday I may want to plant some companions in the same bed, and I would rather not have to dig through soil and rock to create a planting hole.

In this plant guide, specific mulches are recommended for plants. Mulching should be considered the final step of the planting process and an essential part of water-wise gardening.

WATER-WISE WISDOM

In the state of California, 20 percent of all the energy used in the state goes to purifying and transporting water. That is one-fifth of all the energy used in the entire state!

Smart Watering

Arid climate gardeners chronically overwater their gardens. We water too long, too often, and at times when the plants simply don't need more water than Mother Nature provides. What value is there to growing water-wise plants, mulching them, and doing all the "right things" if you water plants more than they need? As silly as that sounds, it is often the case.

Where does your water come from? How do you get water to your plants? How do you know when to water? How do you know how long to water? These are the most often asked questions about irrigation.

Where Water Comes From

Why the big deal about water? You just turn the spigot and water comes out, right? Not exactly. In the arid Southwest, demand for water far exceeds the amount naturally available. Few of us have underground aquifers that recharge fully with the seasonal rainfall or snowfall. Instead, water is governed by public and governmental water agencies that typically import it from mountains and lakes that are often hundreds, if not thousands, of miles away. To reach our communities and our homes, the water has to be pumped. Energy conservation is a natural byproduct of water conservation.

As access and availability of water become even more limited, people are becoming more creative about ways to capture and to reuse the water that is available to us. Sometimes, that means going back to tried-and-true methods such as reusing water. Reusing graywater (water from washing dishes, hands, and clothing) was standard practice until recent generations. As our lives became more urbanized, health departments everywhere outlawed this most commonsense practice.

Today, we are finally seeing a reversal of those policies, though not without careful regulation and guidelines as to the sources of water that can be reused, how to store and apply that water, and the kinds of plants it can be used on. Graywater does, after all, contain bacteria and other microorganisms that could make us sick. Graywater is best used on ornamental plants rather than on edibles.

In addition to reusing water, Southwesterners are paying more attention to capturing the rain as it falls onto our homes and gardens. Rain barrels are growing in popularity. They attach to downspouts to capture the rain that falls into rain gutters from the roof. Just an inch of rain falling on 1000 square feet of roof, for example, can generate 550 gallons of water! Rain barrels usually have a spigot near the bottom; attach a hose to the spigot and allow water to run downhill to the plants in your garden. Or, dip a watering can in the top and water plants by hand.

More sophisticated and expensive rainwater collection systems can collect thousands of gallons of rain in a year. At that scale, large cisterns and pumps, aboveground or belowground, store the water, which can then be pumped as needed.

Bioswales are another technique for directing and capturing rainwater. These shallow, human-made depressions create a topography designed to slow water enough for it to percolate down into the ground rather than running off before it can be used.

How to Water the Garden

You can plant the most water-wise plants in the world (literally) but if you water them with water wasting methods, you won't save much. Traditional overhead sprinklers fall into this category. These sprinklers spray water over the top of plants with the intent of simulating rainfall from above. That's not a bad idea but it turns out to have some significant problems, among them:

✖ Overhead sprinklers systems are installed when gardens are first planted, usually with small plants. In a mixed planting of perennials, grasses, shrubs, trees, and so on, plants eventually grow to different heights. Tall plants soon block the spray so those nearest the spray head get too much water, while those farther away get none at all—the spray simply doesn't reach them.

✖ Overhead sprinklers spray water out into the air. In our arid climates in particular, up to half the water evaporates or runs off before it ever reaches a leaf! That is a huge waste.

✖ Overhead sprinklers put water onto leaves, but plants don't need water *on* their leaves, they need water *on* their roots. Sometimes water reaches the roots but often it doesn't. Wet leaves, particularly leaves that are wet overnight, are susceptible to molds, fungi, and other disease-causing organisms.

✖ Overhead sprinklers put out a very broad spray, often covering bare dirt!

Some people like watering their gardens by hand. While standing in the garden with a running hose may be relaxing after a hard day at work, it isn't a very good way to water plants. Few people have the patience to stand long enough to give each plant as much water as it needs, and certainly not with the consistency that inground plants need to grow healthy and strong.

Water container plants by hand (fill each container to the top; let the water drain through; repeat) but for inground plants, newer irrigation technologies are far more water efficient and far better for your plants. Here are two of the best:

New matched precipitation, rotating head sprinklers function much like traditional overhead sprays but put out larger, heavier drops of water that don't evaporate as readily. You can adjust the volume of water as you adjust the distance they spray. Old heads, on the other hand, put out a set amount of water, whether they spray 10 feet or 15 feet. These new heads are easy to install as a retrofit. Simply unscrew the old heads and screw in the new ones. They are especially good for low, even height plantings.

Drip irrigation is the best choice for water conservation. This puts water where it is needed, at plant roots. Whereas traditional overhead sprinklers are only 50 percent efficient (in other words, 50 percent of the water is wasted), drip is about as close to 100 percent efficient as you can get. With drip irrigation, you can customize the amount of water each plant gets. Drip comes in different styles and types, all of which are extremely easy to use—and not very difficult to care for. Read more about drip irrigation on page 226.

Control the water

Once you decide on the best irrigation technology, the next decision is to control when and how long it runs. Again, turning each valve on and off manually is not very reliable. You can set a timer to remind you to turn the system off, but how often and how consistently will you remember to turn it on?

Irrigation clocks are a much better option. These automatic clocks allow you to set the time each irrigation valve goes on, how long it runs, and the days of the week it runs. There are the standard irrigation clocks and "smart" clocks. With the standard irrigation clocks, keep in mind that:

Each clock *has* to be set. The factory sets a default schedule, often 10 minutes for each zone, each day. No matter where you live or what you grow, that setting allows too much water.

Your gardener doesn't necessarily know the best timing for your clock. Some gardeners know, but many don't. When there is a problem in the garden, those who don't know often turn the water up. Talk to your gardener. Either come to an agreement about the watering schedule or take the responsibility yourself and *lock the controller box* so no one else can change the setting.

Adjust your irrigation clock from month to month, as the plants' needs change. In general, the hotter, dryer months are those when your plants need the most water. But, when the sun is low in the sky, or the air is cool, plants simply don't need that much water.

Smart clocks decide on their own when and for how long to water. You have to set them up initially, but once you enter your zip code, soil type, the kind of irrigation system you have, and some additional information, you set each clock for the type of plant (low water, medium water, natives, and so forth) that zone waters. Smart clocks base their decisions either on a small weather station attached to your roof, or a signal from a weather satellite, or historical weather data for your area.

Smart clocks automatically adjust the watering schedule to weather conditions. If it rains, they turn off. If you have hot, drying winds, they cycle extra times. You still need to pay attention, but they pretty much make the critical decisions.

If you decide to use a smart clock, shop around. There are several types on the market, some that are more technical and some that are more user-friendly. A handy do-it-yourselfer can install one. Otherwise, hire a professional to do the installation.

Another way to control watering is by using a soil moisture sensor. This technology is used more for agriculture but home scale products are slowly coming onto the market. Basically, a sensor monitors how wet the soil is. When a standard irrigation clock (not a smart clock) attempts to turn a valve on, the sensor determines whether the soil is dry enough to need watering. If it isn't, the sensor interrupts the signal to the valve and prevents it from turning on. Watering is then delayed until the next cycle.

As soil moisture sensors' reliability and ease of use improve, they show promise. Keep an eye on this technology.

Remember that in that first year or two after planting, all low-water-use plants need regular, deep watering to saturate the entire rootball and beyond. Watering deeply encourages roots to go deep, which is one reason plants can survive on less water later on. Only after they are established can you set your irrigation clock to a low water setting. Don't be surprised, then, if the irrigation goes on only once a month or less, even in summertime—depending on the plants you choose and your garden's growing conditions.

But, what does one do if you are filling a "hole" or replacing a plant in an established bed? Just remember, for any type of automatic system, you will have to hand water any new plantings until they are established.

For more water saving ideas and irrigation resources, visit the water-wise gardening resources information in the Resources.

HOW TO MAKE WATER-WISE PLANT SELECTIONS

This book is designed to assist you in making plant selections to fulfill your garden design criteria. With the assurance that the plants highlighted in this book are water-wise, some of the guesswork involved in planning a drought-tolerant garden is eliminated. Over time as you garden with water-wise plants, you will get to know them and gain an appreciation for just how water efficient and tough these plants are. As the plants grow and flourish, you will be amazed at how well they perform, but mostly of how truly beautiful they are with their various textures, colors, and forms.

Knowing how daunting it can be to start down the design path to create a water-wise garden, this book begins at the foundation of a landscape with the chapter on trees. Trees will frame a garden, give structure to a space, and provide shade for understory plantings. After making tree choices, direct your attention to shrubs that will be used to surround a garden room, provide a privacy screen, or become a focal point in a flower bed. From there follows perennials that give bursts of color from foliage or flower and sustain themselves in the garden for years to come. The remaining chapters are full of other plant types that might fill a small niche, such as succulents or annuals, or cover a path or a wide expanse like water-wise lawns, meadowlike grasses, ground covers, and vines. Start with the sky and work your way down to a water-wise and beautiful garden.

Sun icons share important information on the type of *exposure* each plant needs. A tremendous amount of designated full-sun plants do not mind being planted under the protective branches of a tree where they might have a reprieve from the hot afternoon sun. So some of the plants will list icons for full sun as well as part sun/part shade, making them very versatile and suitable for many areas of the garden. Additional icons are listed below and illustrate other benefits of the plant. You will be surprised at how many additional attributes the plants have—in addition to being water-wise and visually stunning.

Full sun

Part sun/part shade

Full shade

Attracts butterflies and/or moths

Attracts hummingbirds

Some or all parts of this plant are edible

Leaves or flowers are fragrant

Plants have attractive fruits

Flowers, leaves, branches, and/or fruits are suitable for bouquets or cut flower arrangements

Long bloom period

Supports bees

Provides food or shelter for wildlife

Has colorful foliage

Grows well in a container

The **USDA Cold Hardiness Zones** are listed for each plant. The Cold Hardiness Maps begin on page 30. The zones are listed as a guide, and we recommend consideration be made for microclimates, potential for frost protection, and other criteria. For more information on determining cold hardiness, refer to the map in the front section of the book.

While designing any garden space, it is crucial to design to a plant's maximum size at maturity. With water-wise gardening this is critical. The goal is to create the healthiest plant possible so that at maturity it can survive almost entirely on its own. Part of that healthy life comes from giving the plant enough room to grow naturally.

That is how a plant best performs. If a plant has the space it needs, both in height and width, then no pruning is needed. So, know the dimensions of the garden spaces that you have to work with and pay particular attention to the height and width listed for each plant. We have followed the standard of listing mature height of a plant first with the second measurement representing its width. For example: 2 to 4 feet x 1 to 3 feet represents a plant growing to a maximum height of 2 to 4 feet and spreading to 1 to 3 feet in width. Also under **Growth and Mature Size**, we let you know how fast or slow the plant grows so you will know how much space you might want to fill while it matures.

The plant profiles include the **Form** of the plant at maturity to assist in making design decisions on the overall silhouette of the plant. Additional information is given on any special **Soil** that may be required and any known **Pests** to watch for.

Shared Spaces takes some of the research out of determining the companion plants a plant may prefer because of similarities of cultural or cultivation needs. From a design aspect, this section gives tips on what plants look well with others, either by contrasting foliage or coordinating colors, and what job the plant performs either as a background, midground, or foreground position in the garden bed.

Cultivation addresses any special care required, such as protection from frosts while the plant is immature, additional fertilizer needed during the early years, structural pruning, and most important, watering regimes from newly planted to maturity.

Finally, with continual research and development being done by plant breeders on new water-wise plant species, cultivars, and varieties, **Other Species and Cultivars** are added to keep you up-to-date on new plant introductions.

Nature will bear the closest inspection.
She invites us to lay our eye level with her smallest leaf,
and take an insect view of its plain.
HENRY DAVID THOREAU

WHAT MAKES A PLANT WATER-WISE?

In order to understand the steps of gardening with water-wise plants, you need to examine the plants that grow and flourish on natural rainfall and that have the ability to survive periods of drought. "Nature will bear the closest inspection," and will teach you how a plant survives and thrives. Nature teaches how the root system anchors it to the earth to provide the plant with moisture and nutrients. Some low-water-use plants may be deep rooted (oaks), with the roots going deep into the soil to the water source, or shallow rooted (cacti), with the roots growing near the soil surface to take full advantage of the moisture that summer rainstorms provide. "Nature will bear the closest inspection," and is teaching that the smallest leaf (even a blade of grass) is actually a mini-photosynthesis factory, and if it has special characteristics, it also offers the plant protection during periods of drought.

Generally speaking, the larger a leaf, the more water a plant requires. The exception to this rule is if the plant loses its leaves in the winter (deciduous). Many deciduous plants are considered water-wise plants since supplemental watering is provided only once or twice during unusually dry winter months. Some water-thrifty plants take care of their own needs by storing moisture in their leaves, such as the large succulent group of plants. Other special leaf characteristics protect the leaves from burning under the harsh sun, from drying out in winds, and from precious moisture loss from the leaf surfaces.

Come "lay your eye level" for a time, and "take an insect view of its plain." Get down close and look at the shape of the leaf and the tiny veins running through it. While you have your "insect view," look for these special characteristics:

✿ **Needle-like leaves** (rosemary) and **feathery leaves** (artemisia) are very small leaves on plants that require minimal water to thrive.

✿ Plants that have a **serrated leaf edge** (Oregon grape) or are **deeply lobed** (desert marigold) are drought tolerant. Picture water drops hitting the leaf. The tiny serrates and lobes slow down the droplets as they run off the leaf, and some of the moisture actually collects within the crevices, giving the plant just a bit more moisture.

✿ The **coating on a leaf** protects the plant from drying out. Leaves that have **waxy** coatings (privets), **fuzzy** coatings (dusty miller), and **rough** surfaces (silverberry) use those coatings to protect the leaves from water loss (transpiration) and sun and heat burn.

❧ Likewise the **color of the leaf** plays a part in how the sun is absorbed into the plant. Leaves that are **gray** (Texas ranger), **blue-green** (rabbitbush), or **white** (big sage) reflect the sun, thus protecting the plant from its drying affects.

❧ Leaves that contain **oils** (lavender) are generally drought tolerant. The oils protect the plant from the heat and sun, and help the plant conserve moisture.

If you can find just one of these leaf characteristics on a plant, then you probably have a plant that can withstand the harmful effects of drought. It is common to find two or three water-saving characteristics on a single leaf. Now, step out of your "insect view" and just imagine a blending of all these leaf sizes, textures, colors, and coatings in the garden, and you will see how very beautiful and lush your water-wise garden can be.

ARIZONA

Zone 1	35° F to 30° F
Zone 2	30° F to 25° F
Zone 3	25° F to 20° F
Zone 4	20° F to 15° F
Zone 5	15° F to 5° F
Zone 6	5° F or below

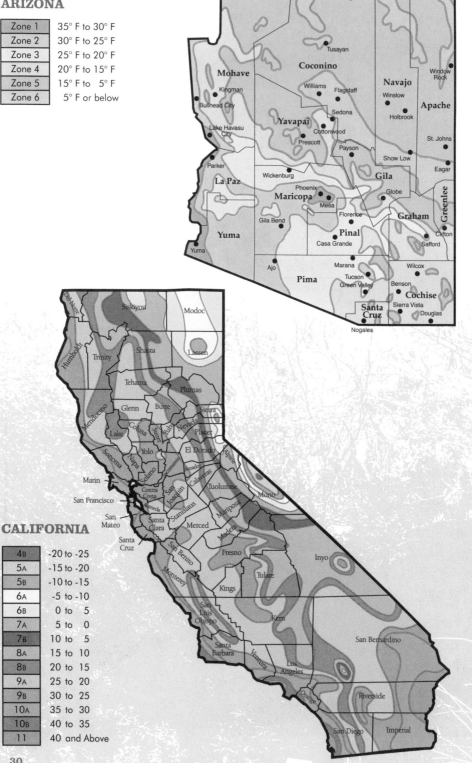

CALIFORNIA

4B	-20 to -25
5A	-15 to -20
5B	-10 to -15
6A	-5 to -10
6B	0 to 5
7A	5 to 0
7B	10 to 5
8A	15 to 10
8B	20 to 15
9A	25 to 20
9B	30 to 25
10A	35 to 30
10B	40 to 35
11	40 and Above

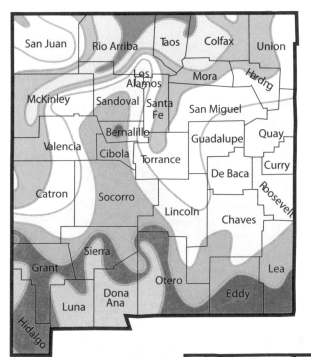

NEW MEXICO

4B	-20 to -25
5A	-15 to -20
5B	-10 to -15
6A	-5 to -10
6B	0 to -5
7A	5 to 0
7B	10 to 5
8A	15 to 10

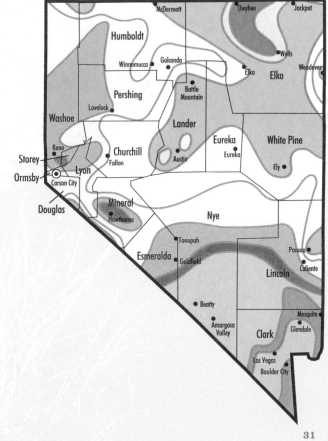

NEVADA

4B	-20 to -25
5A	-15 to -20
5B	-10 to -15
6A	-5 to -10
6B	0 to -5
7A	5 to 0
7B	10 to 5
8A	15 to 10
8B	20 to 15
9A	25 to 20
9B	30 to 25

TEXAS

Zone	Temperature (°F)
6a	-5 to -10
6b	0 to -5
7a	5 to 0
7b	10 to 5
8a	15 to 10
8b	20 to 15
9a	25 to 20
9b	30 to 25

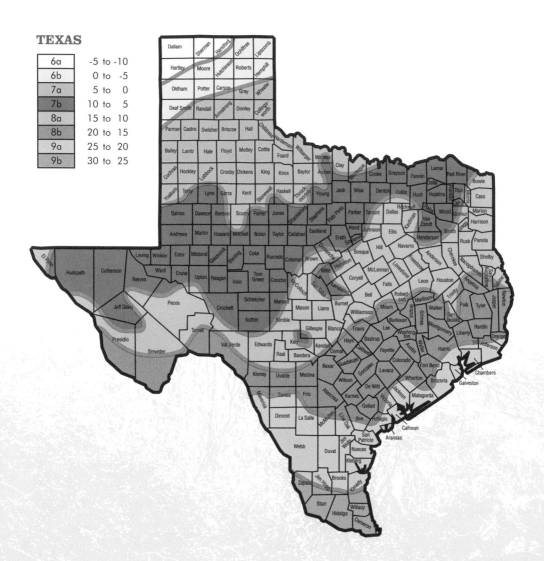

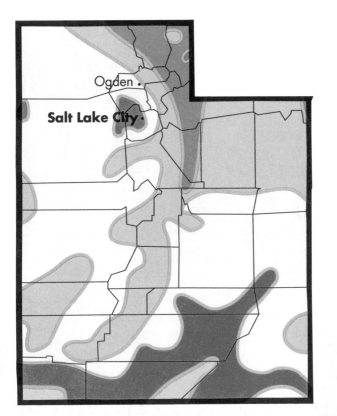

UTAH

ZONE	Average Annual Min. Temperature (°F)
2	-40 to -50
3	-30 to -40
4	-20 to -30
5	-10 to -20
6	0 to -10
7	10 to 0
8	20 to 10
9	30 to 20
10	40 to 30

FEATURED WATER-WISE PLANTS FOR THE SOUTHWEST

TREES
Arbutus
Australian Willow
Cedar
Chaste Tree
Chinese Pistache
Crapemyrtle
Desert Willow
Granite Honey Myrtle
Hackberry
Japanese Scholar Tree
Juniper
Kidneywood
New Mexico Locust
New Mexico Olive
New Zealand
Christmas Tree
Oak
Palo Blanco
Palo Verde
Pine
Smoke Tree
Velvet Mesquite
Western Redbud
Willow Acacia
Windmill Fan Palm

SHRUBS
Apache Plume
Arizona Rosewood

Barberry
Butterfly Bush
California Flannel Bush
California Lilac
Cotoneaster
Damianita
Desert Mallow
Emu Bush
Fairy Duster
Firethorn
Four-wing Saltbush
Lady Banks Rose
Little-leaf Cordia
Mahonia
Manzanita
Mormon Tea
Pink-flowering Currant
Purple Rockrose
Santolina
Shrub Salvia
Shrubby Senna
Sugarbush
Texas Ranger
Toyon

VINES AND GROUNDCOVERS
African Daisy
Arizona Grape Ivy
Bougainvillea

Chinese Wisteria
Climbing Bauhinia
Coral Vine
Creeping Germander
Iceplant
Lilac Vine
Moss Verbena
Prairie Zinnia
Silver Carpet
Silver Lace Vine
Sundrops
Sunrose
Trailing Indigo Bush
Trailing Lantana
Trumpet Vine
Vinca
Yerba Mansa

PERENNIALS
Agastache
Autumn Sage
Bear's Breech
Blanket Flower
Brittlebush
Dianthus
Gaura
Gayfeather
Globemallow
Greek Germander
Hellebore

Jerusalem Sage
Kangaroo Paw
Matilija Poppy
Partridge Feather
Penstemon
Prince's Plume
Russian Sage
South African Geranium
Spurge
Sticky Monkey Flower
Torch Lily
Western Mugwort
Yarrow

GRASSES AND LAWNS

Beargrass
Big Bluestem
Blue Fescue
Blue Grama
Blue Oat Grass
Buffalo Grass
Deer Grass
Dwarf Fountain Grass
'Jose Select' Tall Wheatgrass
New Zealand Flax
Sedge
Silver Grass

BULBS

Baboon Flower
Blazing Star
Blue-eyed Grass

Clivia
Crocus
Daffodil
Daylily
Forest Lily
Freesia
Gladiolus
Grape Hyacinth
Iris
Mariposa Lily
Naked Lady
Ornamental Onion
Rain Lily
Spider Lily
Tulip

SUCCULENTS

Aeonium
Agave
Aloe
Blue Chalk Sticks
Flame Flower
Giant False Agave
Hardy Iceplant
Manfreda
Red Yucca
Sotol
Stonecrop
Yucca

ANNUALS

African Daisy
Annual Coreopsis
California Poppy

Cowpen Daisy
Creeping Zinnia
Desert Bluebell
Gazania
Mexican Hat
Mexican Sunflower
Moss Rose
Mullein
Nolana
Scarlet Flax
Shirley Poppy
Sunflower
Tidy Tips
Toadflax
Verbena
Wallflower 'Bowles Mauve'
Zinnia

EDIBLES

Artichoke
Bay Laurel
Curry Plant
Edible Oregano
Fig
Garden Sage
Garden Thyme
Grape
Jujube
Lavender
Olive
Persimmon
Pomegranate
Rosemary

Trees

Many ancient trees such as this pinyon pine grow in the southern Utah outback.

I f you travel throughout southern Utah, you will be awestruck by the majestic ponderosa pines that seemingly jut out of the terracotta red cliffs. You can camp under ancient junipers, picnic beneath the enormous shade canopies of gnarled and worn cottonwoods, or share a camp space with a 100-foot-tall Douglas fir that could be five centuries old. These native trees live for hundreds of years, each surviving all types of adversity to reproduce and to perpetuate their species.

Many old, beautiful, mature trees also exist in the landscape. While they are large and well established today, they were once just small saplings someone planted with the vision of what they would be for future generations. On a corner in Springdale, Utah, for example, a fully mature deodar cedar is perfect in its conical shape with its classic, slightly bent top, as if it is nodding its head. You can find a shady grove of mature silver maples situated in a park adjoining a golf course in Mt. Carmel in southern Utah that someone planted more than 100 years ago.

Not all trees are as happy in their circumstances. You've probably noticed a scrawny, struggling, and perhaps messy tree and thought, "I wonder who on earth planted that tree there?" It is the classic example of ignoring the adage we've presented in the previous chapter: "Choose the right plant for the right place."

If you are considering trees for a new landscape or replacing an inappropriate selection, do your homework and research the trees before you buy and plant them. Here are some guidelines:

- Choose trees than can live in your USDA Cold Hardiness Zone. If you plant a tree from a zone warmer than the one recommended, it may survive for years through mild winters, but when it's subjected to frigid extremes, it could suffer and die.

- Consider soil needs. Most Southwest soils are alkaline so avoid planting trees that require acid conditions. Even if you plant the tree in pure peat moss, its roots will eventually grow beyond the amended planting hole and into the native alkaline soil. Trees that are known to thrive in lean, alkaline, sandy, or clay soils are the better choices.

- Water is a big issue for gardeners in the Southwest. Our extensive list of low-water-use trees makes it easy to find the perfect tree for your garden. But even water-wise trees need regular water during their establishment years. During that period, they are developing a strong root system by sending roots deep into the soil. A strong root system means a strong, healthy mature tree able to survive on little more than natural rainfall, except perhaps during the longest periods of drought. For this reason, we have a suggested watering regime for newly planted trees and one for mature trees.

Determine whether the tree's maximum height and width fit into the space you have. Don't make the mistake of thinking you can control the growth or size of a tree.

Proper planting is critical to a tree's success. Information on how to properly plant trees can be found on page 233. Young trees need slow, deep, but infrequent watering (allow the soil to dry out a bit between waterings) to develop a deep, wide, strong root system.

For the water-wise trees listed here, there is no need to amend the soil. Recent research shows that overworking soil destroys the soil texture along with the micro-flora/fauna that work synergistically to support plant roots. It is best to work the backfill soil with your hands only, to break up the larger clods and to increase airspaces. Then water, water, water.

Trees can add thousands of dollars to the value of a property. But much more than that, they add beauty, shade, cool the air, anchor the soil, and most important, release oxygen into the air we breathe. Plant a tree. There is at least one, if not several, perfect tree for the perfect place in every garden.

Arbutus
Arbutus species

ZONES: 6 to 9
FORM: Dense canopy
GROWTH AND MATURE SIZE: Slow-growing evergreen tree to 20 to 50 feet x 40 to 50 feet
USES: Standards as a focal point, multi-trunks as a screen, compacts as a container tree
SOIL: Tolerates a wide variety of soils, but it must be well drained
PESTS: Control ants to control aphids and black sooty mold

Arbutus are stunning evergreen trees and shrubs with rusty cinnamon or mahogany-brown bark and a dense canopy of deep green leathery leaves. These small trees look like the big brothers to their shrubby cousins, the manzanita. In fall they are covered in hanging clusters of small, pale pink or white, pitcher-shaped flowers with a sweet scent. Flowers are followed by marble-sized yellow, red, or orange berries much beloved by birds. Often flowers and fruits are present at the same time. 'Compacta' is smaller than the species, to about 6 feet tall, and makes a good container plant.

Shared Spaces

Arbutus are usually available as standards (single trunk) or multi-trunk specimens. Standards look more formal, while the multi-trunks look more informal. Mass multi-trunk trees for an evergreen screen. Mix with other native and Mediterranean climate plants. Underplant with flowers in shades of yellow and orange, especially orange-colored Peruvian lily.

Cultivation

Keep roots moist (not wet) through their first year by deep watering, allowing the soil to dry a bit between waterings. Once plants are established at three years, provide occasional deep summer watering. No fertilizer is needed. No regular pruning is required. Prune minimally to enhance shape, but don't try to make a formal hedge from this tree. Prune to remove dead or diseased wood and discard (do not compost) the wood.

Other Species and Cultivars

Sun-loving *Arbutus* 'Marina' (25 to 50 feet tall and nearly as wide) has pink-blush white flowers in spring and fall, and is very well adapted to garden conditions. Dwarf 'Compacta' is only 6 to 8 feet tall and 5 to 6 feet wide and is hardy to 10 degrees F. Strawberry tree (*Arbutus unedo*) grows 20 to 30 feet tall and 5 to 40 feet wide. Fall flowers are pink or white.

Australian Willow
Geijera parviflora

ZONES: 8 to 11
FORM: Round, weeping canopy
GROWTH AND MATURE SIZE: Quick-growing evergreen tree to 20 to 40 feet x 20 to 25 feet
USES: Light shade tree, airy screen
SOIL: Any well-drained soil
PESTS: Occasional aphids

A weeping willow is too thirsty for a Southwest garden's dry climate, but that doesn't mean that you can't have weeping trees in your garden. Australian willow is the perfect weeping form, especially for today's smaller garden spaces. Despite its common name, this is not a true willow. True willows belong to the genus *Salix*. Australian willow is in the genus *Geijera*, which is a cousin to citrus. Australian willow doesn't produce edible fruits like citrus, but it does produce tiny, creamy white flowers in spring. This medium-sized evergreen desert native grows quickly, forming an oval canopy of long (3- to 6-inch), narrow, deep green leaves hanging from the branches.

Shared Spaces

Australian willow generates minimal litter, so it can be planted near a deck or patio. Deep roots won't damage sidewalks or structures. Grow it a bit back from the salt spray zone at the beach.

Cultivation

Water deeply once a week for the first two to three weeks, and then once a month until winter rains arrive. In subsequent years, start irrigating when soil dries in late spring. Water deeply once a month until winter rains and until trees are mature. Spray periodically to rinse dust off leaves. Since these trees come from areas where soils have even fewer nutrients than ours, they don't need fertilizer. If the leaves turn yellow, sprinkle the soil beneath the branches with iron sulfate or powdered sulfur and iron chelate (follow directions). These are extremely low maintenance trees. If they're planted along a walkway, street, or driveway they may need trimming to keep branches from interfering with traffic.

Other Species and Cultivars

There are no known new cultivars or species at this time.

Cedar
Cedrus species

ZONES: 5 to 8

FORM: Conical shape with distinctive flat or nodding tops at maturity

GROWTH AND MATURE SIZE: Slow-growing evergreen trees to 40 to 60 feet x 25 to 30 feet

USES: Focal point, windbreak

SOIL: Well drained, but not bone dry

PESTS: None

True cedars are elegant behemoths with soft foliage and strong, arching branch patterns distinctive both at a distance and close at hand. Long-lived and adapted to a broad range of rainfall, in Southwestern gardens moderately watered cedars remain a modest size, a mere 50 feet, sweeping half as wide. Blue atlas cedar (*C. atlantica* 'Glauca'), while tall and straight when young, expands to a flat-topped, tiered pyramid as it matures. 'Glauca' is blue needled. Cedar of Lebanon (*C. libani*) grows very wide at the base with stiff, horizontal branches that broaden to a flat-topped crown with age. 'Pendula' is a slow-growing prostrate form.

Shared Spaces
Allow enough space to accommodate the mature size of the tree and showcase its form. For a windbreak, space trees 15 feet apart so that they grow together. Cluster smaller blooming shrubs such as blue mist, sand cherry, 'Gro-low' sumac, or rockspray cotoneaster 10 or more feet from the cedar trunk as mid-ground filler. Creeping germander, yerba mansa, yarrow, giant four o'clocks, and prairie sage are all good ground cover companions.

Cultivation
After five years, cedars become rooted well enough to be drought tolerant and cold hardy. Water established cedar trees to a depth of 2 feet every two weeks when temperatures are above 80 F, and monthly during cooler weather. Layer at least 4 inches of shredded bark, pecan shells, or compost mulch over the root zone. During establishment years, fertilize with a slow-release formula each spring, and water once a week when temperatures exceed 90 F. Apply granular iron-and-sulfur fertilizer in summer if the foliage becomes chlorotic (yellowing occurs between the leaf veins).

Other Species and Cultivars
C. atlantica 'Glauca Pendula' makes an elegant draping form when trained against a wall or fence. 'Fastigiata' maintains a tighter, more columnar shape. 'Compacta' grows more slowly and densely.

Chaste Tree
Vitex agnus-castus

ZONES: 5 to 11
FORM: Wide-spreading tree or large, airy shrub
GROWTH AND MATURE SIZE: Moderate-growing deciduous tree to 10 to 25 feet x 10 to 25 feet
USES: Screening, focal point, small grove planting
SOIL: Well drained; tolerates fertile, lean, or dry soils
PESTS: None

Chaste tree is a moderate-sized tree or large shrub with glorious sprays of deep blue, purple, or pink flowers in early summer. The deciduous, aromatic leaves are made up of five to seven lance-shaped leaflets that are deep green above and silver below. Trunks are dark brown, almost black, and although naturally multi-trunked, trees are often trained to a single trunk. Extremely tough and loved by bees, chaste tree is widely used from the high desert to the coast. The variety *V. latifolia* has larger than average leaflets. The tall spires of flowers are usually blue to purple, but white forms known as 'Alba' and 'Silver Spire' and a pink form, 'Rosea', are sometimes offered by nurseries.

Shared Spaces

Chaste tree complements any perennial planting with its colorful summer bloom, multi-trunked form, and dusky green leaves. Since chaste tree creates little litter during the summer, it is a good choice for a patio or seating area. Plant in groupings of three or more, either alone or with other trees, or to fill barren areas as a screen.

Cultivation

Water thoroughly after planting and then every three to four days for two or three weeks if planting in the summer when temperatures exceed 90 degrees F. The first year, water every seven to ten days if there is no rainfall. Water established trees (at four years) weekly in summer; and every three to four weeks in winter, unless rain or snowfall occurs. Mulch the root zone, but be sure mulch does not touch the trunk. Apply slow-release or organic fertilizer in fall and early spring to young plants. Established plants do not need fertilizer. To train the chaste tree to a single trunk, prune off the three or four lowest branches, suckers, and side shoots each spring until the crown is as high as you want it. Do not prune off more than a quarter of the tree in any single year. Dead wood or damaged limbs are best removed in late spring.

Other Species and Cultivars

Roundleaf vitex (*V. rotundifolia*) is a low-spreading shrub, to 3 feet high x 6 feet wide, with beautiful pale green leaves on arching stems. *V. agnus-castus* 'Montrose Purple' grows at all elevations to Zone 6. Slow-growing to 25 feet x 25 feet, it has large spikes of indigo flowers.

Chinese Pistache
Pistacia chinensis

ZONES: 6 to 8
FORM: Matures to vase shape with spreading canopy
GROWTH AND MATURE SIZE: Moderate-growing deciduous tree to 30 feet x 20 feet
USES: Focal point, shade tree, grove planting
SOIL: Tolerant of most soils
PESTS: None

Chinese pistache is one of the best large shade trees for xeric gardens. The deep root system that makes pistache so water efficient in the garden also makes it harder to produce commercially, but the main reason Chinese pistache has been slow to find commercial success is that it looks like a hat rack when it's young. It more than compensates for an awkward adolescence, however, as its blunt, stiff branches assume an appealing vase shape, and finally, mature trees develop irregular spreading canopies. The glory of pistache is its end-of-season color, a range of brilliant scarlet and orange that looks lit from within in the autumn sun.

Shared Spaces

Pistache's deep root system allows planting near foundations and paving, making it an ideal street tree and shade tree for patios and courtyards. Its roots don't interfere with the growth of other plants sharing its space, but companions need to be shade-tolerant and low-to-moderate water users such as prairie sage, whiplash daisy, or catmint. Pistache is not a good tree to plant in fescue lawns. The water and fertilizer needed to maintain cool-season turfgrass are more than pistache can tolerate.

Cultivation

Water weekly to a depth of 30 inches in summer the first year or two after planting, but cut back to monthly watering in September so it hardens off before the first frost or before cooler winter weather commences. Once it is well-rooted (2 years), water pistache monthly. Water deeply, but infrequently, in clay soils, allowing the soil to dry out between waterings. A slow-release fertilizer applied in spring promotes a strong start, but do not fertilizer after that. Tip prune young pistache whips to push side branching.

If you create a solid branch structure in the trees first few years, you are essentially done with the major pruning.

Other Species and Cultivars

P. chinensis 'Red Push' is a hybrid with a broad spreading crown. New foliage has a red tint with spectacular fall foliage of red, orange, and yellow. Moderate growth rate to 30 to 40 feet x 30 to 40 feet. *P. chinensis* 'Sarah's Radiance' is hardy to Zone 5 and has a deeper, more intense red fall color. Slow growing to 50 feet x 50 feet.

Crapemyrtle
Lagerstroemia indica

ZONES: 5 to 9
FORM: Upright vase-shaped tree or shrub
GROWTH AND MATURE SIZE: Slow-growing deciduous tree or shrub to 25 x 25 feet
USES: Street trees, landscape trees, screening shrubs, containers
SOIL: Adaptable to all soils
PESTS: Watch for aphids, mealy bugs, scale, and powdery mildew

One of the ways to mark the change of seasons is by noting when particular plants bloom, especially crapemyrtle trees. They all seem to bloom at once, right in the heat of summer. Cranberry-colored buds open to magnificent sprays of crinkly-petaled raspberry red, deep lilac, pale pink, fiery red, or bright white flowers. Clusters of green fruits follow the flowers in early fall. By winter, their leathery green leaves turn gold, orange, and copper before they drop. Fall color intensifies at higher altitudes. After fall, the focus shifts to the tree's fantastic mottled and peeling bark in shades of pink, pale green, red, and soft brown.

Shared Spaces

Crapemyrtle works well in the background as part of a screen of evergreens including bay, arbutus, chaste tree, or pineapple guava. In a beachside garden, plant crapemyrtle a bit away from the spray zone. Since its roots don't damage sidewalks or structures, crapemyrtle can be grown near walkways and foundations. Dwarf varieties are wonderful container plants and can be trained as bonsai. Use them as a focal point in a perennial garden surrounded by zonal geraniums with pale pink blooms, gladiolus in mixed lavender and pink hues, and scented geranium trailing in the foreground.

Cultivation

Mulch, and water deeply the first spring through late fall. Starting the second spring, this drought-tolerant tree needs only occasional deep watering, though it tolerates more. Fertilize with all-purpose organic fertilizer in early spring before new growth begins. If you'd like, prune young trees to one or three trunks. After that, allow the tree to develop its natural form with only occasional pruning.

Other Species and Cultivars

Along the coast especially, choose the mildew resistant 'Whit IV' (6 to 12 feet x 5 feet) with its clear white blooms and amazing fall foliage, or try old favorites 'Muskogee' with lavender flowers, or 'Seminole' (6 to 12 feet x 6 to 12 feet) with bright pink flowers. *L. indica* x *faueri* 'Arapaho' is a small tree or large shrub growing to 20 feet x 10 feet in ten years. It has true red blooms in summer with brilliant fall foliage.

43

Desert Willow
Chilopsis linearis

ZONES: 6 to 8
FORM: Small tree with weeping profile, large shrub
GROWTH AND MATURE SIZE: Moderate-growing deciduous tree or shrub to 10 to 20 feet x 10 to 20 feet
USES: Informal border, light shade tree, focal point, grove, containers
SOIL: Tolerates deep, well-drained, fertile soil to rocky, native soil; often fails in poorly drained soils
PESTS: None

Few desert trees can rival the beauty of the summer-flowering desert willow. This wide-ranging species grows as either a moderately sized shrub or a large branching tree. The long, thin, willowlike leaves are light green and deciduous. The bell-shaped flowers have open, flared ends with ruffled edges in a wide range of colors from pure white to lavender. There are also many bicolored flowering forms. Some color forms have been named; others have not, so buy this plant in bloom for your best color choice.

Shared Spaces
Mix with other large shrubs or trees such as Texas sage or palo verdes to form an informal border. Plant where reflected heat is intense. Desert willow mixes well with summer-flowering perennials and shrubs such as red justicia, salvias, and yellowbells.

Cultivation
Mulch the root zone heavily to retain soil moisture, but take care the mulch does not touch the bark. Water thoroughly after planting; continue watering every three to four days for two or three weeks if temperatures are above 90 degrees F. For the first year, water deeply every five to seven days. Water established plants deeply every two weeks in summer, and monthly in winter if no rain or snowfall occurs. Apply slow-release or organic fertilizer annually in spring to young trees. Mature desert willow does not require fertilizer. In spring just as leaves emerge, prune to remove winter damage. For a single trunk shape, prune the two or three lowest limbs off every spring until the tree is as tall as you want it. Although this tree accepts a lot of pruning, it is best to remove no more than a quarter of the tree in any year. Prune lightly through summer to maintain form and keep it tidy.

Other Species and Cultivars
The species can reseed heavily in California. 'Lucretia Hamilton' is a new clone hardy to minus 10 degrees. It is a slow grower to 18 feet x 18 feet, with a weeping appearance and intense burgundy flowers. 'Warren Jones' is a more rapid grower to 25 feet x 30 feet and holds its foliage and large pink flowers longer.

Granite Honey Myrtle
Melaleuca elliptica

ZONES: 9 to 11
FORM: Oval canopy
GROWTH AND MATURE SIZE: Medium evergreen tree to 15 to 20 feet x 15 feet
USES: Focal point, grove planting, meadow setting
SOIL: Well-drained soil
PESTS: None

When a Southern California gardener purchased the ranch house of a long ago subdivided avocado grove, he inherited a hillside stand of elderly avocado trees. As the avocados declined, he replaced them with a lovely sloping meadow of yarrow spiked with harlequin flower, daffodil, and other spring-flowering bulbs. Around this beautiful meadow, he planted a lovely small tree with blue-green leaves the size and shape of a woman's pinky nail. In spring, the tree's canopy includes raspberry-colored, bottlebrush-type flowers along branches covered in papery bark. This is the granite honey myrtle, an evergreen Australian *Melaleuca* that performs spectacularly.

Shared Spaces

Grow these small trees as the center of a Mediterranean theme garden with rockrose, sedge, bugle lilies, blazing star, and bush anemone. You can grow them as patio trees or near walkways since roots do little damage.

Cultivation

Water and mulch well. In year one, water deeply once a week for the first two or three weeks, and then water deeply once a month until winter rains begin. In year two, water deeply each month from the time soil dries in spring until winter rains. After that, water deeply just a few times through summer. Spray periodically to rinse dust off leaves. There is no need to fertilize. If leaves yellow, sprinkle the soil beneath the branches with iron sulfate or powdered sulfur and iron chelate (follow directions on the label). Water well and wait for leaves to green up over several months. Avoid overwatering to prevent root rot and deadly soil fungi. Pruning is not necessary.

Other Species and Cultivars

Totem pole (*Melaleuca decussata*) is a large shrub or small tree (6 to 16 feet x 10 to 20 feet) with branches covered in small gray-green leaves, shreddy bark, and lilac flowers in spring or summer. Dotted melaleuca (*Melaleuca diosmifolia*) has curving branches covered in gray-green, scalelike leaves (5 to 12 feet x12 feet), and has yellow-green, bottlebrush flowers from spring to summer.

Hackberry
Celtis species

ZONES: 4 to 11
FORM: Rounded canopy at maturity
GROWTH AND MATURE SIZE: Slow-growing deciduous tree to 25 feet x 20 feet
USES: Street tree, shade tree, grove, focal point
SOIL: Adapts to alkaline and compacted soils; add no soil amendments at planting and loosen the soil well
PESTS: Nipple galls (caused by psyllid insects) that don't harm the tree

Like their close allies the elms, hackberries have a long history of use as street trees but hackberry has proven to be more resilient than elm. Smaller in stature and deeply rooted, the Southwestern native netleaf hackberry (*Celtis reticulata*) is the most drought tolerant of the *Celtis* species. It spends a few years developing an extensive root system before it expends energy on top growth, experiencing a brief awkward adolescence in the garden. Its 2- to 3-inch dark green oval leaves have finely serrated margins and are sandpaper rough on the top surface, and paler with a network of veining on the lower surface. It produces small orange fruits attractive to songbirds in Zones 5 to 8.

Shared Spaces
If galls (round ball-like formations attached to a stem) are present, avoid planting hackberry in sitting areas or near paths where the psyllids' handiwork is likely to be noticed. Netleaf hackberry is a handsome street tree or shade tree near lawns and patios, and all but the most sun-worshipping perennials and ground covers thrive in its dappled light. Prairie sage and other low-growing artemisias contrast the dark foliage nicely.

Cultivation
Use a four-inch layer of either fibrous or stone mulch at planting to keep the soil uniformly moist and cool. Water trees to a depth of 30 inches twice a month during the growing season until plants approach the desired size, then cut back to deep watering once a month year-round if no rains occur to maintain good leaf density and general tree health. Hackberry needs no fertilizing. Wait until the bark on the trunk becomes woody to begin thinning to develop a strong branch scaffold; one-fourth of the twiggy stems can be removed each year.

Other Species and Cultivars
Eastern hackberry (*Celtis occidentalis*) grows from 40 to 90 feet high during its long lifetime, developing a broad rounded canopy 30 feet wide. Its leaves are light green, rough-textured, and dense. It is cold hardy to 7500 feet in Zone 4 gardens. *C. laevigata* 'All Seasons' is fast growing to 40 to 50 feet x 35 feet with a more uniform crown shape, making it a wonderful shade tree.

Japanese Scholar Tree
Styphnolobium japonicum

ZONES: 5 to 8
FORM: Broad crowned with spreading canopy
GROWTH AND MATURE SIZE: Moderate growth deciduous tree to 30 feet x 20 feet
USES: Focal point, shade tree
SOIL: Not fussy about soil as long as it is not kept wet in poorly drained clay
PESTS: Disease and insect resistant

Young Japanese scholar trees have shiny green bark that becomes striated in shades of brown on mature trees. Fragrant white flowers contrast the spreading canopy of dark, glossy leaves in midsummer, looking cool and fresh in 100-degree heat. Small, flat, and pale green seedpods persist through winter, giving it a vibrant look while dormant, and are a clue to its distant kinship with our native mesquite. During severe dry spells, scholar tree is noticeable because its small compound leaves remain rich green while surrounding plants are dull and scorched looking. Once established, it blooms profusely in places that receive little water, rooting deeply and widely enough to avoid the stress other trees suffer.

Shared Spaces

Space trees 10 to 12 feet from walls and paving and 20 feet apart to create a continuous canopy. Use it to shade patios and other outdoor living spaces. Smooth surfaces such as scored concrete are easier to sweep clear of the flowers, leaves, and seedpods that scholar tree sheds seasonally than are flagstones or other rough paving.

Cultivation

Add a generous topdressing of shredded bark or fine gravel mulch at planting to accelerate root development by keeping the soil moist and cool. In summer, the scholar tree may need weekly watering during its first three years of establishment, especially when temperatures are above 90 F. Once well rooted, water to a depth of 30 inches every two weeks when flowering, and once a month during the rest of the year if no rains occur. Trees are usually 10 years old before they flower; avoid fertilizing and pruning as both delay blooming. Selectively thin young scholar trees to develop a strong branch scaffold. Remove suckers that sprout at the base of the trunk, as well as any crossing or rubbing branches.

Other Species and Cultivars

'Regent' is a cultivar that blooms earlier and has a narrower canopy. It is a little less cold hardy than the species, best in Zone 6 and warmer gardens. 'Pendula' is a beautiful weeping form with leaves that hold on longer in fall before turning a soft yellow. Curved and gnarled branches create great winter interest when blanketed in snow.

Juniper
Juniperus species and cultivars

ZONES: 3 to 11
FORM: Forms vary with species; densely columnar, broadly conical, broad trailing
GROWTH AND MATURE SIZE: Slow-growing evergreens to 15 to 30 feet x 8 to 15 feet
USES: Screening, windbreaks, focal point, ground cover
SOIL: Any soils that are not excessively wet; no amendments
PESTS: Hose off dry dusty foliage a few times a season to prevent spider mites

Junipers are among the evergreens used most extensively in Southwestern gardens. Drought-adapted, they root deeply and widely in search of moisture, and their narrow, resinous foliage limits water loss. Juniper foliage colors range from soft silver to ice-blue, deep green, and frosted gray-green. Pollen from male junipers is a major aero-allergen. By planting only female cultivars, gardeners reduce their allergy potential. Female junipers also produce small, waxy, blue berrylike cones that are relished by birds and gin distillers alike. Native Rocky Mountain juniper (*J. scopulorum*) is the source of many useful female cultivars, including metallic 'Blue Haven'.

Shared Spaces
Use junipers as a backdrop for flowering shrubs and as habitat for songbirds. Bright green cultivars contrast with the silver sages and fernbush. Blue and gray cultivars contrast well with rugosa, wood's roses, and sumacs.

Cultivation
Topdress with 4 inches of organic mulch. Junipers don't show moisture stress by wilting. They fade slowly from green to brown, and once dried out, they seldom recover. Provide deep watering at planting, then water once a week through the first year. Gradually increase the depth the water penetrates to 30 inches as you reduce the frequency of watering to biweekly in summer, and monthly in winter. Slow-release fertilizer may be used each spring for a few years to get plants off to a strong start, but junipers don't need regular fertilizing. These tolerant plants are tortured into all kinds of strange shapes from corkscrews to sombreros. When left unsheared, the American species have soft-tapered profiles; the Chinese species develop interesting tiered silhouettes. Varieties that look controlled without pruning include 'Skyrocket' and 'Welchii' with naturally narrow columns, and the densely leafed 'Spearmint'.

Other Species and Cultivars
Compact 'Hillspire' (*J. virginiana* 'Cupressifolia') is deep green year-round. Chinese junipers include *J. chinensis* 'Keteeleri' that grows quickly to 20 feet in a loose open pyramid, spreading 10 feet at its base. *J. chinensis* 'Spearmint' is a deep green column, 15 feet x 8 feet.

Kidneywood
Eysenhardtia orthocarpa

ZONES: 6 to 11
FORM: Open and airy
GROWTH AND MATURE SIZE: Moderate growing, semi-deciduous tree to 10 to 12 feet x 3 to 10 feet
USES: Groves, small garden focal point, containers
SOIL: Any soil that is well drained
PESTS: None

As yards get smaller, and patios replace entire gardens, small, attractive trees have become especially useful. Heading up the list of underused small trees is kidneywood, the perfect size for small gardens or crowded patios. Kidneywood is an open branched tree with dark gray stems that are lightly covered with small, light green compound leaves. The leaves are fragrant with a sharp citrus aroma. Tiny white flowers occur in loose spikes at the ends of the branches intermittently through summer and have an aroma of vanilla. The flat, tan pods are crammed into clusters that look like miniature pagodas. Site this small tree where all can enjoy its heavenly scent.

Shared Spaces
Kidneywood is a superb small tree for a patio or courtyard. Use it as light shade for tender succulents or perennials or place it near walkways, seating areas, or near a pool where the lovely summer fragrance can be enjoyed. Mix unpruned kidneywood with Texas sage, desert senna, or black dalea to form an informal hedge.

Cultivation
Organic mulches are helpful to maintain soil moisture, but make sure mulch doesn't touch the bark. Water thoroughly every three to four days for two or three weeks if temperatures exceed 90 degrees F, then every five to seven days for the first year if no rain or snowfall occurs. No fertilizer is needed. Established plants (second year) should be deeply watered twice a month in summer; once a month or less in winter when rain or snowfall is experienced. Overwatered plants won't bloom well. Plants are often multi-trunked when young but can be trained to a single trunk by removing suckers and the lowest two or three branches in late spring until the tree grows to the desired height. Do not remove more than a quarter of the tree in any year. Prune deadwood or damaged limbs in late winter and early spring.

Other Species and Cultivars
The closely related Texas kidneywood (*Eysenhardtia texana*) has much darker green leaves, a spicier aroma, and grows more as a shrub than a tree. Mexican kidneywood (*E. polystachya*) is larger, growing to 25 feet.

New Mexican Locust
Robinia neomexicana

ZONES: 5 to 9
FORM: Thorny, open-branching
GROWTH AND MATURE SIZE: Fast-growing deciduous tree to 6 to 30 feet x 6 to 20 feet
USES: Small patio tree, steep slopes, grove
SOIL: Well-drained soil
PESTS: None

New Mexican locust is a multi-trunked deciduous tree that is native to the high elevations of the Arizona mountains and other areas of the West. This locust is easily pruned to a small tree. The compound leaves are made up of large, dark green leaflets that are in handsome contrast to the dark-brown-to-black bark. But the full glory of New Mexican locust is its spring bloom. Dozens of pale pink, pealike flowers are clustered in drooping heads at the ends of the stems each spring. Black locust (*Robinia pseudoacacia*) is a much larger multi-trunked tree, up to 75 feet tall, with inky black trunks and large, deep green compound leaves.

Shared Spaces

New Mexican locust is lovely mixed with other summer-flowering shrubs or small trees in a mixed hedge or border. This species is very drought tolerant when mature, and its suckering habit makes it a good choice for erosion control on steep slopes or for areas of the garden that receive minimal care. When pruned to a single or few-trunked tree, use as a specimen or focal plant for small patios, courtyards, or near a pool.

Cultivation

Mulch the root zone generously, but keep mulch away from the bark. Water thoroughly after planting then water every three to four days for two or three weeks, and every seven to ten days for the first year if no rain or snowfall occurs. New Mexican locust trees need no supplemental fertilizer, even when young. Deeply water established plants every month or two during the growing season; rely on natural rainfall in winter. Prune unwanted stems and root suckers, dead or damaged wood, and crossing branches in spring. To maintain a single trunk or selected trunks, cut out the three or four lowest branches each spring and regularly remove root suckers. Do this yearly until the tree is the height you want. Continue to remove root suckers every spring to keep it in good shape.

Other Species and Cultivars

R. pseudoacacia 'Lace Lady' has year-round interest with its contorted multi-trunk form. A dwarf-sized moderate grower to 15 feet tall and wide, it is hardy in Zones 4 through 9. This tree may be invasive in northern parts of California and some wetter regions of Texas.

New Mexico Olive
Forestiera neomexicana

ZONES: 5 to 8
FORM: Crooked, curving branches with open crown
GROWTH AND MATURE SIZE: Moderate-growing deciduous tree to 18 feet x 15 feet
USES: Small focal point tree, large screening shrub, shady grove
SOIL: Any well-drained soil
PESTS: Leaf cutter bees cause temporary damage, but this rarely has any effect on overall health; no pests otherwise

New Mexico olive is one of the few plants adaptable enough to thrive in colder northern and mountain gardens as well as in low-desert locations. The smooth gray bark of branches that crook and curve in interesting ways, and the small bright green leaves make it a pleasant companion for other plants. It roots deeply, sharing its space with low shrubs or wildflowers, and after a year or two in the garden grows a consistent 12 to 18 inches a year until nearing its mature height. New Mexico olive's clusters of small greenish yellow flowers in early spring aren't showy, but they smell like honey. Apparently bees think so too, because a tree hums with their activity.

Shared Spaces

New Mexico olive makes a sculptural focal point for an entryway, or a lovely small accent specimen or shade tree for a patio or sitting area. It can also be left unpruned as a screen or habitat thicket, or sheared as a Southwestern version of a privet hedge. (Shearing is an insult to the natural character of this fine plant; we mention it only to illustrate how forgiving New Mexico olive is.) Space 8 to 10 feet apart for screening; 12 to 15 feet apart in groves for shade.

Cultivation

Any type of mulch works well. Water newly planted trees deeply once each week in summer. Gradually increase the depth that the water penetrates to 30 inches as you reduce the frequency of watering to biweekly in summer, and monthly in winter if no rain or snowfall occurs. After three years, water to a depth of 30 inches once a month year-round. Plants growing in storm runoff catchments or other low-lying areas with shallow groundwater may not need supplemental water once they are well rooted. Apply slow-release fertilizer each spring for a few years to speed growth. New Mexico olive needs no regular fertilizing once established. To shape small trees, gradually remove all the twiggy growth within several feet of the ground in early summer, exposing more of the shapely trunks as plants grow taller. As olives mature, they require less pruning except to remove basal suckers

Other Species and Cultivars

None at this time.

New Zealand Christmas Tree
Metrosideros excelsa

ZONES: 9 to 11
FORM: Erect free-branching tree; dense shrub
GROWTH AND MATURE SIZE: Slow-growing evergreen tree or shrub to 20 to 40 feet x 10 to 30 feet
USES: Street tree, specimen tree, evergreen hedge, garden background, screen
SOIL: Any well-drained soil
PESTS: None

The most magnificent New Zealand Christmas trees you will ever see grow in a most unexpected location—on a windy hillside of Alcatraz, the former prison island in San Francisco Bay. Planted in the early 1940s, these trees stand at least 40 feet tall and 30 feet wide. In June you can see the trees in full glorious bloom; silvery green buds and crimson red flowers of fringy stamens blanketing the canopy of shiny, deep green, leathery leaves, whose undersides are silvery with fine hairs. Alcatraz's seaside exposure is similar to the trees' native coastal New Zealand. Fortunately, they do nearly as well in milder climate gardens away from the coast.

Shared Spaces
Use as smog-tolerant trees; New Zealand Christmas trees make good street trees (but not under power lines). They tolerate salt and wind for beachside gardens and as windbreaks. Both treelike and dwarf varieties do well in very large containers.

Cultivation
Water deeply and mulch well after planting. Water young trees regularly from spring to early fall. In year two, soak monthly from late spring until temperatures cool in fall. By the third year, water only occasionally in summer. Mature trees need little to no water in milder parts of the Southwest. Water container-grown plants regularly and deeply. Fertilize in early spring with a balanced organic fertilizer. If leaves are pale or yellow, treat with iron sulfate or powdered sulfur and iron chelate (follow label directions). Leaves green up over several months. Young trees are more shrub shaped, single- or multi-trunked, and low branched, but with age they become tree-shaped (more so with judicious pruning). Avoid overwatering, which can cause root rot and encourage fungi.

Other Species and Cultivars
Leaves of 'Midas' (20 feet x 8 feet) are deep green edged in yellow. 'Aurea' has green leaves and golden yellow flowers. *Metrosideros collina* 'Spring Fire' (8 to 12 feet x 4 to 6 feet) blooms orange in spring. Shrubby *Metrosideros excelsa* 'Gala' (6 feet x 6 feet) has variegated leaves, green with creamy yellow centers.

Oak
Quercus species

ZONES: Varies by species
FORM: Tall silhouette; large, upright, or rounded crown
GROWTH AND MATURE SIZE: Slow-growing evergreen or deciduous trees or shrubs to 10 to 50 feet x 15 to 50 feet
USES: Shade and street trees, focal point, shrub screens
SOIL: Well-drained soil
PESTS: Host to gall wasps that may cause leaf dieback or develop globular amber nodules (non-damaging)

Smaller oaks have a solidity that is reassuring, and larger species are nothing short of magnificent. Oaks root deeply and extensively, mining a large area of soil for moisture; their crisp or leathery leaves minimize evaporation. No matter where you garden, easy-growing oaks are available. Adapted deciduous oaks include clump-forming Gambel oak, *Quercus gambelii*; Texas red oak, *Q. texana*; *Q. buckleyi* with red fall foliage, and massively impressive valley oak, *Q. lobata*. Evergreen oaks include escarpment live oak, *Q. fusiformis*; shrub live oak, *Q. turbinella*; Southern live oak; and cork oak, *Q. subera*.

Shared Spaces
Oaks are beautiful street and superb accent specimens. Evergreens are used for screening; their strong resilient wood makes them great wind buffers. To prevent root rot, avoid planting beneath established oak trees. The root disturbance and additional water can kill them.

Cultivation
Provide loosened, unamended soil for planting. Use shredded bark or pecan shells as mulch where acorns will be left for wildlife; fine gravel is the best mulch where acorns will be cleaned up. Establishment takes four or five years; during that time, water twice monthly in the hottest months of the year, allowing the soil to dry out between waterings, and monthly during cooler weather unless rains occur. Water well-rooted trees to a depth of 30 inches once a month year-round if no rains occur. Water sparingly to avoid the greatest threat to oak survival: root rot caused by excess moisture in poorly drained soils. Slow-release fertilizer applied in spring helps plants establish more quickly. Once well rooted, stop fertilizing.

Oaks need little pruning. Leave all the large, shapely branches as the framework; each year in early summer, remove only suckers and small twiggy shoots from the lower stems to expose more trunk.

Other Species and Cultivars
Two larger species are options where there is sufficient water and space. Bur oak (*Q. macrocarpa*) is a rugged Great Plains native that grows best in Zones 3 through 6. Chinkapin oak (*Q. muhlenbergii*) is best adapted in Zones 6 through 8. Both grow at least 40 feet tall.

Palo Blanco
Acacia willardiana

ZONES: 9 through 11

FORM: Upright with loose, open vase-shaped crown

GROWTH AND MATURE SIZE: Moderate-growing evergreen tree to 10 to 20 feet x 5 to 10 feet

USES: Focal point, grove, narrow areas, patio tree

SOIL: Any well-drained soil; does not tolerate heavy or poorly drained soils

PESTS: None

The delicate beauty of palo blanco belies its desert origins. Native to Sonora, Mexico, palo blanco is a striking choice for a small narrow place or a crowded courtyard. Plants have a solitary trunk with few branches, giving it an overall vase shape. Branches are covered with thin, white bark that gracefully peels away to reveal the cream-colored trunk. The odd draping foliage is made up of elongated petioles, called phyllodes, that are up to 12 inches long. These leaf mimics cascade and fall from tall, thin stems that float gracefully in the slightest breeze. The real leaves are tiny, and sprout at the ends of the phyllodes briefly in spring, along with the creamy white flowers.

Shared Spaces

Use palo blanco for light shade in small patios. Their delicate appearance and upright form make palo blanco useful in narrow or crowded patios and courtyards, or between structures. The peeling bark and graceful form make palo blanco a good specimen or focal point. Plant in groups to create groves for barren areas or to fill corners in hot, dry locations. Plant against hot walls, around a pool, or in other areas where reflected heat is intense.

Cultivation

Water thoroughly after planting and continue deep-watering every three to four days for two or three weeks when temperatures exceed 90 degrees F. Water newly planted trees every seven to ten days for the first year or two. Palo blanco does not require supplemental fertilizer, even as a young tree. Water established trees every two to three weeks in summer; every month in winter if no rain or snowfall occurs. Prune lightly to remove dead or damaged branches in early spring or summer. It is tempting to stake young trees because the trunk is so thin, but trees straighten quickly and are stronger if they are not staked.

Other Species and Cultivars

A. farnesiana, sweet acacia, is hardy to Zone 7 and is extremely desert tough, growing to 25 feet x 25 feet. Its thorny branches are adorned with perfumed masses of yellow-orange puffball flowers in spring. Sonoran catclaw, *A. occidentalis*, grows to 25 feet x 25 feet, is ideal for tough, hot sites, and provides a dense shade canopy and highly fragrant creamy yellow flowers.

Palo Verde
Parkinsonia species

ZONES: 8 through 11
FORM: Small stature with spreading, sometimes weeping canopy
GROWTH AND MATURE SIZE: Fast-growing evergreen tree to 25 feet x 25 feet or wider
USES: Shade trees, groves, a focal point, and parking lots
SOIL: Well drained
PESTS: Short-lived, powdery mildew in coastal areas

Among the dazzling mosaic of springtime desert blooms are wispy, green-barked trees covered in brilliant yellow flowers that peak in spring, but bloom sporadically through summer. These are palo verde "green stick" trees, and they are great trees for low-water gardens. Palo verde is very drought tolerant, heat resistant, and tolerant of poor soils. Some palo verde are spiny, and most are fast growing. While most plants photosynthesize with green pigments in their leaves, the leaves of palo verde are so small and short-lived that the tree has green bark that photosynthesizes like a giant leaf. These trees are best suited for hot inland valleys, deserts, and most of Southern California.

Shared Spaces
These small trees are perfect for shading patios, courtyards, and small gardens, especially in hot valleys and desert areas. Site palo verde against a terracotta or deep-purple colored wall for a beautiful silhouette. Plant as an open canopy over a colorful succulent garden, or mix with drought-tolerant flowering perennials and shrubs such as California poppies, Mexican tulip poppies, low-water sages, grevillea, and Texas ranger. If your palo verde is a spiny species, plant it well away from pathways and play areas.

P. aculeatea can be invasive if planted next to natural areas, so confine their seeding capabilities to courtyards if your garden is adjacent to native growth areas or natural landscapes.

Cultivation
Water deeply after planting, and mulch. Palo verde are extremely drought tolerant once established. Water deeply but infrequently through the first summer. Starting in the second year, water deeply once or twice in summer and not at all the rest of the year. When in doubt, don't water. Too much water makes palo verde grow too fast and become too top-heavy. No need to fertilize. Prune regularly to shape, starting when trees are young. Multi-trunked trees can be reduced to a single trunk if you prefer that style.

Other Species and Cultivars
Parkinsonia 'Desert Museum' does well both in hot areas and in milder areas, but not right along the coast. 'Desert Museum' has the largest flowers of all palo verde. It's a good street tree.

Pine
Pinus species

ZONES: Varies by species
FORM: Conical
GROWTH AND MATURE SIZE: Slow-growing evergreen to 25 to 60 feet x 20 to 30 feet
USES: Focal point, screen, windbreak
SOIL: Well drained and unamended
PESTS: In urban trees, pinetip moth is a problem; bark beetles disrupt sap flow in drought-stressed pines; remove infested trees; control needle scale with horticultural oil sprays

All ninety pine species are native to the Northern Hemisphere—from the Arctic to subtropical mountain slopes and from inland plains to coastal cliffs—varying greatly in size, form, needle color and length, and adaptation to cold, heat, and drought. Southwest native pines include (among others) bristlecone pine, *P. aristata* (Zones 2 to 7); limber pine, *P. flexilis* (Zones 2 to 7); pinyon, *P. edulis*, the most heat- and drought-hardy of the native pines (Zones 4 through 8); and Southwestern white pine, *P. strobiformis* (Zones 3 to 7). The non-native fast-growing pines include Aleppo pine, *P. halapensis*; Afghan pine, *P. eldarica* (Zone 6); and Austrian pine, *P. nigra* (Zones 4 through 7).

Shared Spaces

For screens or windbreaks, space Afghan pines 10 to 12 feet apart; pinyon, limber, and Southwestern white pines 12 to 18 feet apart; Austrian pines 18 to 25 feet apart. Slow-growing bristlecone pine is usually used as an accent specimen. Giant four o'clocks, prairie sage, and whiplash daisy are good ground covers around pines. Avoid planting with intermediate-sized shrubs that could act as a fire ladder, allowing wildfire moving through lower vegetation, to climb into the pine canopy.

Cultivation

Large transplants need water twice monthly when the temperature is above 80 degrees F; monthly the rest of the year unless rain or snowfall occurs. Once they are well rooted, water to a depth of 30 inches monthly year-round. Pines rarely need fertilizing. Stake larger specimens loosely until they establish.

Other Species and Cultivars

Aleppo, Afghan, eldarica, and pinyon pines are heat tolerant enough for Zone 8 gardens. *P. flexilis* 'Cesarini Blue' has stunning blue needles and is a slow grower to 12 to 15 feet x 5 to 6 feet, making it an excellent cultivar for small gardens or large containers. Also good for small spaces is *P. leucodermis* 'Gnome' (Zones 4 to 8), growing to 8 to 10 feet x 4 to 5 feet at maturity. Grafted *P. cembra* 'Chalet' (Zones 3 to 8) is a moderate grower to 10 to 12 feet x 4 to 5 feet, and is a good choice for corners and entrances.

Smoke Tree
Cotinus coggygria

ZONES: 5 to 8
FORM: Broad urn-shaped crown
GROWTH AND MATURE SIZE: Slow-growing deciduous tree or shrub to 15 feet x 15 feet
USES: Small shade tree, midground tree
SOIL: Well-drained soil, but adapts to any soil as long as it isn't too wet, especially when soil is cold
PESTS: None

Smoke tree is grown for its handsome foliage and the cloud of seedheads that inspire its common name. The seeds are a little larger than sesame seeds but are rough-surfaced and hard, attached to slender branched filaments that form a silken haze. The smoky seedheads are emphasized by the backdrop of 2-inch oval leaves. The species has dark blue-green foliage, but the purple-leafed cultivar is more readily available. Smoke trees develop a harlequin mix of fall color in gold, scarlet, and burgundy. There is nothing subtle about 'Royal Purple' smoke tree, a cultivar with deep red-purple foliage throughout the growing season.

Shared Spaces
Used as a small specimen tree, surround smoke tree with a sweep of artemisia, garlic chives, Jerusalem sage, or fleabane. It grows tall enough that the canopy is cooling for patios and sitting areas. It is outstanding against a backdrop of fine-textured foliage such as cedar or blue spruce.

Cultivation
Do not amend backfill soil. Use 4 inches of mulch to insulate the roots and keep the soil moist with less frequent watering. Plant purple-leafed cultivars in a protected spot in full sun. Water established plants to a depth of 30 inches every two weeks when temperatures are above 90 degrees F, especially when the plants are flowering, and once a month when the weather is cooler and there is no rain or snowfall. Use a slow-release fertilizer each spring for the first three or four years after planting to give plants a strong start. When you begin shaping smoke tree, reduce or eliminate the fertilizing. Early each summer, remove any suckers as well as the twiggy offshoots from the lower stems, leaving the strongest, most shapely branches as the tree's framework and exposing more of the trunk as the plant matures.

Other Species and Cultivars
Cotinus coggygria 'Purpurea' produces new growth that is tinged with purple, turning green as the leaves mature. Consider the muted purple blush of 'Purpurea' rather than the red-purple of 'Royal Purple,' which is so strident that the variety of plants that complement it is limited to those with pale yellow flowers or silver-green foliage.

Velvet Mesquite
Prosopis velutina

ZONES: 7 to 11
FORM: Open, wide-crowned
GROWTH AND MATURE SIZE: Fast to slow-growing semi-evergreen to deciduous tree to 20 to 30 feet x 25 to 30 feet
USES: Shade tree
SOIL: Any well-drained soil; does not tolerate heavy or poorly drained soils
PESTS: None

Long used by both Native American and later Anglo settlers of the Southwest for construction, food, and medicine, these graceful trees are now a mainstay of gardens in the low desert. Velvet mesquite has dusky, gray-green soft leaves that are deciduous in only the coldest weather. The new leaves emerge in early spring and are bright yellow-green. Velvet mesquite is a low-branched open tree with dark, almost black, shaggy bark. Chilean mesquite (*Prosopis chilensis*) and Argentine mesquite (*P. alba*) both have wide, spreading crowns and narrow, green leaflets. There are countless hybrids between the two offered under both of these names.

Shared Spaces

Velvet mesquite is unrivaled as a large, fast-growing, spreading shade tree. The light shade provides protection for tender succulents such as small cacti and agaves, as well as most perennials, without impeding growth or bloom.

Cultivation

Mulching the root zone helps retain soil moisture, but do not allow mulch to touch the bark. Water thoroughly and continue to water every three to four days for two or three weeks if no rains occur and temperatures exceed 90 degrees F. For the first year or two, water every seven to ten days if no rain or snowfall occurs. Velvet mesquite does not require supplemental fertilizer, even when the trees are young. Established trees should be watered deeply every three to four weeks in summer, once a month or less in winter. In California gardens, supplemental watering can be eliminated after it is established. Mesquites are often overwatered or watered too shallowly, resulting in a huge crown and insufficient roots that cause them to fall in high winds. For best results, water deeply at infrequent intervals. Prune in late summer to thin, shape, or raise the crown. Pruning in winter invites bacterial infections, and pruning in spring and early summer encourages rampant growth. Prune dead wood anytime.

Other Species and Cultivars

P. glandulosa 'Maverick' is deciduous and the most cold tolerant of the mesquites, to 0 degrees (Zone 6). Fast growing to 35 feet x 35 feet, it is thornless with lacy bright green foliage with smooth gray bark.

Western Redbud
Cercis occidentalis

ZONES: 5 to 11
FORM: Multi-trunked, open-branching crown
GROWTH AND MATURE SIZE: Deciduous slow-growing tree, to 15 to 20 feet x 15 to 20 feet
USES: Focal point, screen, grove
SOIL: Well drained
PESTS: None

If you hike through California's Sierra foothills in early spring, you'll notice small trees blooming rosy pink on the hillsides. Those beauties are western redbuds, and the pink spots are tiny pealike flowers that line bare silvery branches in spring. This phenomenon of bloom before leaf is typical of deciduous plants. As redbud flowers fade, they become long, flat seedpods that start out bright green and turn purple. Soon soft, light green, heart-shaped leaves cover the branches and turn leathery blue-green as they age. In cold winter gardens, redbuds flower more prolifically and foliage turns yellow and red before leaves fall in autumn, revealing handsome bare branches.

Shared Spaces

Plant this native in formal or informal gardens, as a single specimen plant or combined with mounding shrubs for a background or screen. Plant with other natives such as California lilac, flannel bush, and fragrant California buckeye, all of which bloom around the same time.

Cultivation

Water well after planting, and mulch. Water deeply and regularly from spring until the weather cools first in fall. After that, water deeply and occasionally in summer. While drought tolerant, redbuds grow faster with some summer water. Avoid overwatering. No fertilizer is needed. These fast growers take well to pruning that reveals their handsome structure. For a tree shape, limit redbud to three upright trunks (for multi-trunk) or one trunk (for a standard).

Other Species and Cultivars

Forest pansy redbud (*Cercis canadensis* 'Forest Pansy'), hardy to minus 20 degrees, has plum-colored leaves that turn greenish then yellow before they drop in fall. It grows to 20 feet x 25 feet. Flowers are rose-pink. 'Hearts of Gold', 15 feet x 18 feet, has fantastic gold-colored leaves and lavender blooms and is hardy to minus 20 degrees F. Mediterranean redbud (*Cercis siliquastrum*) has magenta pink flowers with purplish leaves that mature dark green. It grows to 15 to 25 feet x 15 to 25 feet and is hardy to minus 10 degrees F. Mexican redbud (*Cercis mexicana*) has purple flowers and blue-green leaves, likes full sun, and is hardy to 20 degrees F. It grows to 12 to 15 feet x 7 feet.

Willow Acacia
Acacia salicina

ZONES: 8 to 11
FORM: Open crown with semi-weeping habit
GROWTH AND MATURE SIZE: Fast-growing
evergreen tree to 20 to 40 feet x 10 to 20 feet
USES: Shade tree, screen, focal point, grove
SOIL: Well-drained, no heavy or poorly
drained soils
PESTS: None

Hundreds of acacias thrive around the world. They are generally thorny shrubs or trees except in Australia, but willow acacia is a handsome tree that provides a thornless shade tree for low-elevation gardens. The flat, gray-green foliage falls gracefully from the branches; the tiny leaves emerge briefly in spring. However, this delicate appearance is deceptive; willow acacia is immune to heat, alkaline soils, and drought. Willow acacia blooms in fall, and the small clusters of creamy white, puffball-like flowers are lightly fragrant. Blue-leaf wattle (*Acacia saligna*) is a multi-trunked, rounded tree with blue-gray leaves and bright yellow flowers in spring.

Shared Spaces

The thornless branches make willow acacia a fine choice to use as a shade tree near walkways, patios, or areas of heavy traffic. The minimal litter makes it useful near pools; in fact, it can even overhang a pool successfully. Plant against hot walls, around pools, or other areas where reflected heat is intense. Willow acacia mixes well with other shrubs or trees to form an informal border or visual screen. Its drought and heat tolerance make it a good choice for areas of the garden that receive minimal care.

Cultivation

Mulch the rootzone but do not allow mulch to touch the bark. Water thoroughly. Water every three to four days for two or three weeks if temperatures exceed 90 degrees F, then water every seven to ten days for the first year if no rain or snowfall occurs. Willow acacia does not require fertilizer. Water established trees sparingly—every three to four weeks in summer even in the lowest elevation zones, every other month in winter if no rain or snowfall occurs. Willow acacia has a graceful natural form and does not need pruning for shape. Prune dead wood or damaged limbs in fall or early spring. Willow acacia becomes chlorotic (yellowing between the leaf veins) when grown in poorly drained soils or with frequent, shallow watering. Watering deeply at long intervals prevents this.

Other Species and Cultivars

A. stenophylla, shoestring acacia, is a beautiful, symmetrical tree, growing to 20 to 30 feet x 20 feet. It is considered longer lived than other acacias.

Windmill Palm
Trachycarpus fortunei

ZONES: 7 to 11
FORM: Single trunk with dense crown
GROWTH AND MATURE SIZE: Slow-growing palm to 20 to 30 feet x 10 to 15 feet
USES: Focal point, boundary planting
SOIL: Any well-drained soil
PESTS: None

Out of the mountains of China comes one of the sturdiest palms for both low- and high-zone gardens. The windmill palm is a modest-sized plant. The solitary trunk of the windmill palm is densely covered with persistent, tough leaf bases. Inside all the leaf bases are dense mats of dark brown fiber, giving the plant a shaggy look. Birds are enormously fond of this matting for nesting material and routinely raid old plants. The deep green, fan-shaped fronds are relatively short. They are held on long, thin petioles and are widely spaced, making the head look open and spare, and creating an appearance that accounts for its common name.

Shared Spaces

Windmill palm makes a superb specimen or accent plant in small gardens or courtyards. Use this palm to provide contrast to large perennial plantings or as part of a large, mixed hedge or boundary planting. The spare form and the firm, deep green leaves of this species make it particularly effective in very formal or Oriental style gardens. Windmill palm blends well with succulents, particularly in the intermediate and high zones. Plant it in groups to create a dramatic effect around pools, seating areas, or patios.

Cultivation

Mix a thin layer of compost or mulch with the backfill. Fill the hole, pressing the soil gently around the roots to remove air pockets. Water thoroughly, watering every two to three days for a month and every week for the first summer. Apply slow-release or organic fertilizer annually in spring. Water established plants every week or two during summer in the low desert; every month in summer if temperatures consistently are above 90 degrees F and if there is no rainfall. In other Southwest gardens, you can rely on natural rainfall or supplement watering every other month or so in winter if no rainfall occurs. Prune dead leaves or spent blooming stalks anytime. Do not prune living leaves unless they present a danger or are damaged.

Other Species and Cultivars

Also hardy to 5 degrees F, the Mediterranean fan palm (*Chamaerops humilis*) grows slowly to 10 to 20 feet x 10 to 20 feet. This palm is naturally multi-trunked with curving stems, creating an elegant structure.

Shrubs

O nce we decide on the trees that will create the structure of our gardens, we can turn our attention to the rest of the space. Drought-tolerant shrubs offer seemingly endless options for the background, midground, and foreground of our Southwest gardens. Shrubs come in a wide variety of shapes and sizes. Their forms and structures can fill out a design, and their leaves, bark, and flowers offer contrast, color, and texture. Most water-wise shrubs require little to no care at all.

When it comes to water-wise shrubs, the list is so long that is impossible to list them all here. We have narrowed down the list to some of the best, most versatile, and easiest to maintain.

The plants we highlight are not picky about soils. Indeed, the beauty of water-wise shrubs is that they are used to living in quite harsh conditions that include alkaline, dry, rocky, sandy, and shallow soils. There is no need to add amendments, and in most cases water-wise shrubs don't require fertilizer . . . ever. Add the fact that they are content to grow into beautiful shapes without ever being pruned, and you have perfect plants for the Southwest. All you have to do is make your selections.

In each shrub profile we have listed whether they are suitable for background, midground, or foreground plantings of the garden:

Background: *Large Shrubs—10 to 20 feet x 5 to 15 feet*

Give these shrubs plenty of room to achieve their natural size and beauty. Use them as focal points or as the background for perennials, annuals, and succulents. Plant in a cluster and you'll soon have an informal screen, hedge, or edge to your garden room. Background shrubs make excellent garden room walls, forming a soft dense wall of green and perhaps even filling the room with heavenly scented blooms or foliage. Before you plant—even before you buy— read the plant tag to be sure the space you'd like to plant in is large enough. Some large shrubs are also used as small trees, a real boon for homeowners who want to plant something smaller under a power line that doesn't need continual trimming to control its size. Start training shrubs into tree shapes by beginning the pruning while the shrubs are young. A snip here, a cut there, and a main branch becomes a "trunk." Trim off a few lower branches each season, building up the trunk over a few years' time (visit www.urbantree.org for more information).

Midground: *Medium Shrubs—5 to 10 feet x 3 to 10 feet*

Medium shrubs give gardens character. Use them to frame a vignette, enclose or accent a focal point, or as an understory planting around a statuesque tree. These shrubs make excellent smaller hedges to define an outdoor space or to create privacy in an apartment or condo garden. Remember to plant in odd numbers, in groups of threes, fives, and sevens, to keep the garden comfortably informal and organized. Shrubs of this size can live for several years or more in large pots on a patio or deck.

Foreground: *Small Shrubs—1 to 5 feet x 1 to 5 feet*

There is a huge selection of small evergreen and deciduous shrubs and even some shrublike perennials that fulfill the foreground planting criteria. Small shrubs can be used to enhance the features of other plantings by surrounding a focal plant or enclosing a special grouping. Foreground plantings can provide the contrast and balance that pull a composition together. These shrubs' small size lend themselves to groupings of two or three species in the same area. Allow them to weave together to create a diverse floral texture, or plant them in sweeps to give full impact of their individual beauty. Water-wise shrubs of this size make wonderful ground covers to carpet the garden floor. When planted on slopes, their deep root systems anchor the soil, while providing beautiful texture and color.

What shrubs to choose? Whatever your decision, remember to design to the maximum size of the shrub at maturity. That is the best way to ensure you select healthy and beautiful water-wise shrubs that have no need for a pair of pruners.

Apache Plume
Fallugia paradoxa

ZONES: 4 through 9
FORM: Mounded shrub
GROWTH AND MATURE SIZE: Fairly quick-growing deciduous shrub to 5 to 6 feet x 4 to 6 feet
USES: Focal point, low screen, midground, border for wildflower meadow plantings
SOIL: Well-drained soils, but does poorly in heavy clay
PESTS: None

Apache plume is found throughout the intermediate and high elevation desert zones throughout the Southwest, including the historic homelands of the Apache people. In late summer and fall, the solitary, five-petaled white flowers give way to clusters of tiny fruit, each of which sports a feathery pinkish white appendage that is the plume. The result is arresting; the entire plant looks like a cloud on the ground. To add another spurt of color, the fruit turns from pale green to dark rosy-purple in fall. The leaves are small and green to gray-green. Young twigs are coated with gray hairs but turn a rich, dark brown as they age.

Shared Spaces

Mix Apache plume with shrubs such as sugarbush, barberry, or scrub oak to form an informal hedge or boundary planting. The bloom and subsequent plumed fruit is fascinating enough to use the plant as a specimen or focal plant. Within its native range, use Apache plume in outlying areas of the garden that receive minimal care or as part of a naturalistic garden. It serves as a good background for colorful annual wildflower displays.

Cultivation

Mulch the roots but do not allow mulch to touch the bark. Water thoroughly. Water every three to four days for two or three weeks, then water every seven to ten days for the first year if there is no rainfall. In the low desert zones, water established plants every two to three weeks in summer, every month or two in winter. In temperate and higher elevations, rely on natural rainfall for established plants unless the weather is exceptionally hot or dry. Like most drought-adapted shrubs, Apache plume requires no fertilizer. Prune to remove dead or damaged wood in spring. Apache plume has excellent natural form and rarely needs pruning for shape.

Other Species and Cultivars

No other cultivars or species are known at this time.

Arizona Rosewood
Vauquelinia californica

ZONES: 5 through 11
FORM: Dense rounded shrub
GROWTH AND MATURE SIZE: Fast-growing evergreen shrub to 10 to 25 feet x 5 to 15 feet
USES: Screen, hedge, border, background, small tree
SOIL: Any well-drained soil
PESTS: None

This large, dense shrub, native to Arizona and Mexico, has long, leathery, dark green leaves and a loose, rounded form that is reminiscent of oleander from a distance. The naturally rounded form and wide tolerance of growing conditions make this evergreen shrub useful in the low and intermediate elevation zones. In early summer, the plant is resplendent with its tiny, creamy white flowers held in large, showy clusters. Chihuahuan rosewood (*Vauquelinia corymbosa*) is a more cold-hardy species with thin, drooping leaves and much larger, flowering heads. Leaves of both species often take on a bronze caste in cold weather.

Shared Spaces

Use Arizona rosewood with hopbush, jojoba, or Texas ranger to create an informal hedge, screen, or border planting. The dark green leaves serve as a perfect backdrop for perennial or annual plantings. As a small tree, it makes a fine specimen plant for a small garden, courtyard, or patio. It is useful against hot walls or around pools where reflected heat is intense.

Cultivation

Mulch the roots, but do not allow mulch to touch the bark. Water thoroughly. Water every three to four days for two or three weeks, then water every seven to ten days for the first year. In the low desert, water established plants every two weeks in summer, and every month in winter if there is no rainfall. In temperate and higher elevations, rely on natural rainfall unless the weather is exceptionally hot or dry. Arizona rosewood requires no fertilizer. Arizona rosewood can be trained as a small tree by pruning the lowest two or three branches each year in early spring. Do not remove over a quarter of the plant in any year. When grown as a shrub, it rarely needs pruning for shape. Prune in early spring to remove dead or damaged wood.

Other Species and Cultivars

V. californica v. *pauciflora* has smaller and thicker leaves, smaller flower clusters, and a more limited range to Zone 6. It is also smaller, growing to 14 feet x 8 feet, making it ideal for smaller spaces.

Barberry
Berberis species and cultivars

ZONES: 5 through 11

FORM: Dense and compact or open with arching branches

GROWTH AND MATURE SIZE: Slow-growing evergreen or deciduous shrubs to 2 to 7 feet x 2 to 7 feet

USES: Borders, hedge, screen, midground, foreground

SOIL: Unamended, well-drained soil

PESTS: None

The handsome barberries are prickly shrubs with honey-scented yellow flowers in spring, and red berrylike fruits later in the season. The three species described here are long-lived and easy to grow, and spend at least one, and sometimes two, growing seasons rooting before they grow much aboveground. 'William Penn' (*Berberis* x *gladwynensis*) grows to 4 feet x 6 feet, has leathery, spine-tipped evergreen leaves, and takes heat well (Zones 5 through 8). Mentor barberry (*B. mentorensis*) is 5 to 7 feet tall and wide. 'Crimson Pygmy' barberry (*B.* 'Atropurpurea Nana') is popular for its small rounded purple leaves and compact 2-foot mounded form.

Shared Spaces

Evergreen barberries mix well with deciduous shrubs in borders and screens as barrier and security plantings, and their seasonal fruits make them an excellent songbird habitat. 'Crimson Pigmy' contrasts nicely with artemisia, curry plant, the silver-leafed sages, and 'Moonshine' yarrow.

Cultivation

Barberries used as a hedge should be planted a few feet closer than their mature width. When used as accent plants, space them a few feet farther apart than their mature width to emphasize their silhouettes. Barberries require water to a depth of 2 feet weekly when temperatures are above 90 F, every two weeks when temperatures are 65 to 90 F, and monthly during cooler weather if there is no rain or snowfall. Allow the soil to dry out between waterings. Slow-release fertilizer applied in spring for the first few years after planting gets them off to a faster start. In the long term, no fertilizer is necessary. None of the barberries require much pruning. If the soil is strongly alkaline, they may need an iron-and-sulfur fertilizer to prevent chlorosis.

Other Species and Cultivars

Great for small spaces is 'Crimson Ruby®' Japanese barberry (*C. thunbergii* 'Criruzam'), 2 feet x 2 feet and covered with burgundy red foliage in the warm seasons (Zones 4 through 8). Also the diminutive dwarf coral hedge barberry (*B.* x *stenophylla* 'Coralina Compacta') is hardy in Zones 5 through 10, has prolific yellow-orange flowers, and grows to just 1½ feet x 2 feet.

Butterfly Bush
Buddleja species

ZONES: 5 to 11
FORM: Open, vase-shaped with sprawling branches
GROWTH AND MATURE SIZE: Moderate-growing deciduous shrub to 8 to 10 feet x 15 feet or dwarf to 6 feet x 5 feet
USES: Focal point, screen, midground, background
SOIL: Well drained; add a bit of amendment if desired
PESTS: None

Every garden needs plants with tasty leaves for caterpillars and with sweet nectar for butterflies. These large vigorous shrubs produce 10-inch-long fragrant flower clusters that are butterfly magnets. The most commonly planted butterfly bushes are varieties of *Buddleja* (also spelled *Buddleia*) *davidii*, a deciduous shrub that grows to 10 feet x 15 feet. Long pointed leaves are shiny green or blue-green on top (some are variegated) and silvery-white below. Flowers range from deep to light purple and from rose-pink to white. Other species have yellow or orange flowers. They are beautiful when covered in swallowtail or monarch butterflies.

Shared Spaces
Butterfly bush makes an excellent screen, either pruned or unpruned. Plant several (spaced 10 feet or farther apart) or integrate with other shrubs. If you prefer not to prune on a regular basis, place butterfly bush in the background where its large size can perfume the air without dominating the garden. Alternatively, train butterfly bush to arch over a walkway.

Cultivation
Water well after planting, and mulch. Water regularly from the time soil dries in spring until the winter rains. Starting in year three, butterfly bushes in coastal gardens need only occasional deep watering in summer. In hotter areas, water regularly and deeply during the growing season. Deadhead to prolong bloom. To control size and shape, cut upright stems back to knee high in fall or winter. Or, reveal the plant's vertical arching form by selectively removing all but one, three, or five stems. Then remove the lower branches and all new sprouts as they develop along the stems.

Other Species and Cultivars
B. weyeriana 'Bicolor', is a fast grower to 5 to 6 feet x 4 to 6 feet. Its stunning pink flowers have peachy throats. *B. davidii* 'Monrell', Strawberry lemonade butterfly bush, is hardy in Zones 5 through 9, grows 6 to 8 feet x 4 to 6 feet with variegated creamy yellow and green leaves; its 5- to 10-inch-long blooms are bright pink.

California Flannel Bush

Fremontodendron species

ZONES: 8 through 10

FORM: Large round shrub, mounding ground cover

GROWTH AND MATURE SIZE: Fast-growing evergreen shrub to 4 to 20 feet x 6 to 40 feet

USES: Screen, border, ground cover, background, midground, foreground

SOIL: Well-drained soil

PESTS: None

Evergreen California flannel bushes (*F. californicum*) are some of California's most beautiful native shrubs. Flannel bushes have cupped golden-yellow flowers shaped like a star, 3 to 4 inches across, that take on a coppery tint as they age. The bright colored flowers make a strong contrast against olive-green and deeply lobed leathery leaves that are flocked on the underside with coppery fuzz. There are low-growing and mounding ground cover flannel bushes, large shrub flannel bushes, and almost tree-sized at 20 feet tall and twice as wide. Withhold water through the summer. Flannel bush is extremely vulnerable to fungi that thrive in wet soil during warm summer months.

Shared Spaces

Try the combination of flannel bush and California lilac so the branches interweave. They bloom together in spring, contrasting the flannel bush's golden yellow-orange flowers next to cobalt blue lilac flowers and all against deep green leaves. Plant flannel bush *en masse* as an evergreen screen in an informal garden. In a more formal garden, train as an espalier.

Cultivation

Protect shallow roots from wind. Allow enough room for this plant's ultimate size. Keep it away from paths and walkways (the fuzzy leaf flocking is a skin irritant). Water well at planting and mulch. Deep-water occasionally through the first fall and winter if rains are sparse, but let soil dry several inches down between waterings. Plant flannel bush when the weather cools in early fall. In coastal and inland valleys, water at planting and then never again. Plants are susceptible to fungi that proliferate in warm, wet soils. No fertilizer is needed, nor is pruning.

Other Species and Cultivars

'Ken Taylor' is 6 to 8 feet x 12 feet with 3- to 4-inch flowers. 'Pacific Sunset' grows 12 to 20 feet x 12 to 20 feet with 4-inch orange-yellow flowers. 'San Gabriel' grows upright to 10 to 18 feet x 8 to 12 feet, with bright yellow flowers. 'California Glory' is one of the largest at 20 feet x 20 feet with yellow flowers.

California Lilac
Ceanothus species

ZONES: 7 through 11
FORM: Upright dense mounding shrub to sprawling ground cover
GROWTH AND MATURE SIZE: Fast-growing evergreen shrub to 1 to 30 feet x 8 to 15 feet
USES: Border, screen, ground cover, accent, background, midground
SOIL: Any, but must be well-drained
PESTS: Watch for aphids, mealybugs, scale, and whiteflies

Once winter rains end, start watching for the brilliant blue blooms of California lilac. Grow several California lilacs, ranging from the 3-foot-tall mounding ground cover 'Louis Edmunds' to 18-foot-tall 'Ray Hartman'. 'Dark Star' (6 feet tall) has unbelievably deep blue flowers and green leaves. *Ceanothus thyrsiflorus* 'El Dorado' has bright chartreuse and green variegated leaves. These natives (and their hybrids) vary not only in their sizes and growth forms but also in their flower color, from violet-indigo to pale blue to white. Leaves and flowers are fragrant. Viewed as short lived (10 to 15 years), they live longer with well-drained soil and natural rainfall once established.

Shared Spaces

Low-mounding varieties help stabilize slopes or form a "green carpet" in place of a lawn. Mass plant larger varieties for blooming evergreen screens or hedges. *Ceanothus* species are especially effective lining a long driveway. Large specimens can be shaped as small trees. Combine with other Southwest natives and Mediterranean climate plants.

Cultivation

Water well after planting, and mulch. Provide occasional deep water from the time that soil dries in spring until winter rains begin. Let soil dry several inches down between waterings. Keep water off leaves. After the second summer, many garden cultivars survive on rainfall alone. In a coastal garden, water established California lilacs monthly in summer and not at all the rest of the year. No fertilizer is needed. Prune if desired, just after bloom to remove dead wood and shape plants. Avoid cutting into the hardwood.

Other Species and Cultivars

'Concha' (6 to 9 feet x 6 to 9 feet) has narrow green leaves with serrated edges and magenta buds that open dark blue. Easy to grow, especially in mountain gardens, beach gardens, and in heavy soils. 'Dark Star' (6 feet x 8 to 12 feet) has small, dark green leaves with burgundy buds that open to cobalt blue flowers. Good for coastal gardens with well-drained soils. 'Frosty Blue' is fast growing to mature size (6 to 9 feet x 8 to 10 feet) in 18 months. It is cold tolerant to 0 degrees.

Cotoneaster
Cotoneaster species and cultivars

ZONES: 5 to 11

FORM: Dense mounding, arching vase-shaped, low-spreading

GROWTH AND MATURE SIZE: Slow- to moderate-growing evergreen or deciduous shrub, growing to 2 to 3 feet x 3 to 6 feet

USES: Screen, border, ground cover, foreground

SOIL: Any well-drained soil

PESTS: Susceptible to fireblight; cut back to healthy wood and disinfect shears

The cotoneasters most useful in Southwestern gardens are small-leafed evergreens with clusters of small white flowers that have a light, lacy look against the dark foliage. Bright red fruits add color later in the season. Grayleaf cotoneaster (*C. buxifolius*) grows 2 to 3 feet high x 6 feet wide. This shrub is the most relaxed in form and the most heat and drought tolerant, so it is the species best suited to the low-desert areas. Its ¼-inch evergreen leaves are steel gray during the growing season, turning deep plum during cold weather. Pyrenees cotoneaster (*C. congestus*) grows slowly to 3 feet high and wide with dark evergreen leaves, and is a nice filler for small spaces.

Shared Spaces

Grayleaf cotoneaster is a perfect foil for the silver leaves and bright flowers of woolly butterfly bush, garden sage, and Mexican blue sage. Pyrenees cotoneaster can be used to neatly frame roses or other taller flowering shrubs. Cotoneaster is beautiful cascading over the edge of a retaining wall.

Cultivation

Cotoneaster takes a few years to develop an extensive root system; during this time, cotoneasters do best if fertilized lightly in spring and watered once a week when the temperature is above 85 degrees. A 3- to 4-inch layer of mulch helps suppress weeds until the plants fill in. Water established plants to a depth of 30 inches every two weeks when the tempera-ture is above 70 F and monthly during cooler weather. Most cotoneasters require little pruning.

Other Species and Cultivars

C. apiculatus 'Tom Thumb' is semi-evergreen to deciduous and is cold hardy to Zone 4. It has pink blooms, followed by bright red berries, and encored by brilliant amber and burgundy fall foliage. Small and mounding, with a moderate growth rate to 1 to 2 feet x 2 to 5 feet, it works well in rock gardens or massed as a ground cover. For a medium-sized shrub, try *C. acutifolius*, Peking cotoneaster (Zones 4 through 8), moderately growing to 10 feet x 10 feet or wider. It is deciduous, has red flowers, long-lasting black fruit, and beautiful fall foliage in orange and red hues. Do not plant these invasive species: *Cotoneaster franchetii*, *Cotoneaster lacteus*, and *Cotoneaster pannosus*, in California.

Damianita
Chrysactinia mexicana

ZONES: 7 through 10
FORM: Dense mounded
GROWTH AND MATURE SIZE: Moderate-growing evergreen shrub to 1 to 2 feet x 2 to 3 feet
USES: Shrub border, perennial bed, massed as a ground cover, foreground
SOIL: Well drained
PESTS: None

Damianita is a dense shrub with small, dark green leaves that are evergreen and highly aromatic. The flowers have bright yellow or gold rays and yellow discs and are prolific on the plant from April through September. The flowers are held above the foliage on thin stalks and seem to coat the plant when it is in full bloom. This charming Chihuahuan shrub looks remarkably like the Arizona native turpentine bush (*Ericameria laricifolia*), which is a larger plant with similar flowers that bloom only in fall. Low desert gardeners find that damianita blooms less vigorously in the hottest part of summer, but in other zones, it blooms all summer.

Shared Spaces

Use damianita in hot, rocky locations and for erosion control on steep slopes. Plant generously to form informal hedges or borders. It is an excellent choice for areas with strong reflected heat—around pools, near driveways, walkways, or streets. Damianita mixes well both with summer-flowering perennials or succulents. In hot summer areas, it is advisable to provide afternoon shade in the summer for best results.

Cultivation

No soil amendments are needed. Mulch the root zones but do not allow mulch to touch the bark. Water thoroughly, every three to four days for two or three weeks, then every seven to ten days for the first year in desert gardens. Damianita needs no supplemental fertilizer. In low desert locations, water established plants weekly in summer; water monthly or less in winter. In other zones, water established plants every three weeks in summer, relying on natural rainfall in winter. In all zones, avoid extensive overhead watering. Prune to shape; remove dead wood or damaged stems in fall or early spring. Go easy with the pruners as it does not like to be cut too short and may retaliate by dying. Avoid hot weather pruning; it can cause sunburn of the stems. Remove spent flowering heads anytime to continue the bloom.

Other Species and Cultivars

There are no new species or cultivars known at this time.

Desert Mallow
Sphaeralcea ambigua

ZONES: 5 through 11
FORM: Mounding or open vase-shaped,
GROWTH AND MATURE SIZE: Evergreen or semi-deciduous shrubs grow quickly to 1 to 2 feet x 2 to 3 feet.
USES: Desert wildflower garden, mass color, perennial garden, midground, foreground
SOIL: Well-drained soils with little organic matter
PESTS: None

During springtime trips through the desert, it is a delight to see the desert mallow blooming orange or red along the roadside. The petite shrubs erupt in wands of miniature hibiscus-shaped flowers that bloom in shades of raspberry, watermelon, pink, orange, and coral, on and off throughout the year and peaking in spring and summer. Their small silvery green leaves are covered with fine hairs—typical adaptations for plants native to hot, dry, sunny environments. Globe mallow grow wild throughout the West. In colder regions, they die back in the cold winter months, then pop back up in early spring, sending out tufts of gray-green leaves and coral blooms.

Shared Spaces

For a spectacular spring display in a dry garden, plant desert mallow with purple-flowered foothill penstemon, white-flowered Matilija poppy, and golden orange California poppies. The gray-green leaves complement deep green foliage plants such as Mexican grass tree and California bush anemone. Because desert mallow is fairly open and lanky, you get a better show from three or five plants grouped together. In a Mediterranean garden, plant desert mallow beneath a sculptural dragon tree or next to a succulent shrub aloe.

Cultivation

Water well after planting, and mulch. In the first year or two, apply occasional deep water from the time soil dries in spring until winter rains. After that, water deeply and only occasionally during spring and fall, and a bit more in summer, especially in hot inland and desert gardens. Let soil dry several inches down between waterings. No fertilizer is needed. Prune back branches by a third or so after flowering and if plants become too leggy. Avoid cutting into harder wood. Prune out the occasional dead branches.

Other Species and Cultivars

'Louis Hamilton' has watermelon-colored flowers and gray-green leaves. 'Papago Pink' blooms light pink. Fendler's globemallow (*Sphaeralcea fendleri*) is a mounding shrub with pale orange to bright orange and even purple flowers (3 feet x 3 feet). Munro's globemallow (*Sphaeralcea munroana*) has apricot flowers, silver foliage, and upright branches (2 to 4 feet x 2 to 4 feet). It tolerates clay soil if you water sparingly.

Emu Bush
Eremophila maculata

ZONES: 8 through 11
FORM: Sprawling branches form loose mounds
GROWTH AND MATURE SIZE: Slow-growing evergreen shrub to 5 to 10 feet x 5 to 10 feet
USES: Low hedge, screen, midground
SOIL: Any well-drained soil, but does poorly and is short-lived in heavy clay or consistently moist soils
PESTS: None

Emu bush, a member of an Australian genus of shrubs, is an effortless evergreen shrub that is virtually immune to heat, alkaline soils, and drought. As an added benefit, the emu bush blooms from fall through late spring with thickly clustered tubular flowers in shades of deep red, rose-pink, magenta, and yellow rising up and down the stem from each leaf base. The blooms turn down, making it hard to see their spotted interiors. 'Pink Beauty' is a large shrub with pink or mauve blooms that is variously described as a cultivar or hybrid of this species. Some unnamed forms bloom yellow. The selection 'Valentine' is compact with deep magenta blooms and dusky purple-tinged foliage.

Shared Spaces

The evergreen leaves of the emu bush make it an excellent background plant for perennial or annual plantings. Mix with other shrubs such as jojoba, Arizona rosewood, and Texas ranger to create an informal hedge, visual screen, or boundary planting. Emu bush is drought tolerant enough to grow in areas that receive minimal care. Plant emu bush to protect a hot wall, or for added color around pools, patios, or other areas where reflected heat is intense.

Cultivation

Mulch the roots but do not allow mulch to touch the bark. Water thoroughly, then water every three to four days for two or three weeks, and weekly through the first winter. Water established plants every two to three weeks in winter while they are growing and blooming, and every month in summer. Emu bush requires no supplemental fertilizer, but annual applications of mulch help provide needed nutrients. Prune in late summer to shape, reduce size, or remove dead or damaged wood. The emu bush has a complicated branching habit, making it difficult to prune well. Remove shoots that grow horizontally or toward the ground and cut the branch to a junction well inside the bush.

Other Species and Cultivars

E. hygrophana Blue Bells™ is a petite evergreen growing at a moderate rate to 2 to 3 feet x 3 feet. *E. glabra* 'Kalgoorlie' has gray-green leaves with gold and orange tubular flowers.

Fairy Duster
Calliandra eriophylla

ZONES: 6 to 8
FORM: Open vase-shaped with slender arching stems
GROWTH AND MATURE SIZE: Slow-growing semi-deciduous shrub to 3 feet x 4 feet
USES: Accent shrub, dry stream beds, desert landscapes, foreground
SOIL: Prefers gritty, sandy, well-drained, infertile soil
PESTS: None

Fairy duster is a Chihuahuan Desert native with an open, twiggy form and finely divided leaves. It epitomizes the paradox of resilience and fragility characteristic of the most drought- and heat-loving plants. Fairy duster is fancifully named for its pink powder-puff flowers and 1-inch bundles of stamens that look like a soft pink haze from a distance. It blooms most heavily in spring, providing a welcome home for returning hummingbirds. Throughout the summer, flowering recurs sporadically. The tiny leaves drop in the winter or in response to drought. Baja fairy duster (*Calliandra californica*) is semi-deciduous in harsh climates, evergreen in milder ones.

Shared Spaces

Use as an accent along dry streambed pathways and between the boulders that stabilize slopes in xeric gardens. The best complements to fairy duster's featherlight appearance are offered by architectural plants such as prickly pear, yuccas, and century plants.

Cultivation

The taproot of nursery-grown desert plants is interrupted by confinement in a container, which causes roots to branch. So, despite its preference for unimproved conditions, loosen the soil well so that the lateral roots have an easy time breaking through the ground. Even when it's first transplanted, water sparingly, never more than once a week. To keep plants leafy and encourage flowering, water established plants once a month, especially from March through August, to a depth of 3 feet. Fairy duster needs no fertilizer. Protect new plants from rabbits with repellents or wire mesh fencing until fairy duster is well established and able to outgrow the feeding. No pruning is needed.

Other Species and Cultivars

There is a newer hybrid of fairy duster and Baja fairy duster, *Calliandra* 'Sierra Starr'™, that grows more dense and has large red flower puffs on and off throughout the growing season. It may be more cold hardy than its Baja parent, and if so, would be a gorgeous addition to the xeric palette in the hottest low desert gardens in the Southwest.

Firethorn
Pyracantha species and cultivars

ZONES: 5 to 8
FORM: Dense rounded shrub with arching branches
GROWTH AND MATURE SIZE: Slow- to moderate-growing evergreen shrub to 4 to 8 feet x 4 to 8 feet
USES: Screen, barrier, espalier, foreground, ground cover
SOIL: Any well-drained soil
PESTS: None; if you must prune, do so in summer to prevent the spread of fireblight

Pyracantha has been used extensively in the Southwest because it is adaptable, lush looking, and reliably evergreen with narrow, dark green leaves densely cloaking the stiff thorny stems. In spring, clusters of small white flowers foretell its true glory, the brilliant autumn display of red-orange berries. The desire to conserve water makes the smaller selections more attractive. 'Gnome', a cultivar of *P. angustifolia*, is the most cold hardy (to Zone 4). It grows 4 feet high x 6 feet wide with orange berries. 'Fiery Cascade', a cultivar of *P. coccinea*, is cold hardy in Zones 6 to 8. 'Fiery Cascade' features red berries and grows 4 feet high x 6 feet wide.

Shared Spaces

The thorns create an excellent security barrier. The strong leafy branches espalier nicely against walls and fences in tall, narrow spaces. The low-spreading cultivars are a colorful foreground for blue and silver evergreens such as blue Atlas cedar and blue spruce.

Cultivation

Cultivars grown in Zone 6 may freeze to the ground in colder areas, but they regrow rapidly in spring. Four inches of mulch keeps the soil cooler and more uniformly moist. During establishment (2 to 3 years),

water once a week when the temperature is above 85 F. Water established plants every two weeks when the temperature is above 70 F, and monthly during cooler weather if there is no rain or snowfall. Fertilizer is not needed, but plants growing in strongly alkaline soils need an iron-and-sulfur fertilizer to prevent or reverse summer yellowing. Rather than prune, choose the cultivar that fits the space available. If pruning is needed, cut vigorous new stems back to short lateral branches after plants have flowered and daytime

temperatures begin to soar. Do not shear.

Other Species and Cultivars

Compact varieties include 'Low Boy', 2 to 3 feet x 6 to 8 feet with orange berries, and fireblight-resistant hybrid 'Red Elf ', growing to 2 feet high and wide with red berries. *P. x cadaver*, 'Silver Lining™', (Zones 7 through 10) a fast-growing round shrub with silver-white variegated foliage that turns bronze-pink in the fall. The species *angustifolia*, *crenulata*, and *coccinea* may become invasive.

Four-wing Saltbush
Atriplex canescens

ZONES: 5 through 9

FORM: Dense, rounded

GROWTH AND MATURE SIZE: Quick-growing evergreen or semievergeen shrub to 4 to 8 feet x 5 to 8 feet

USES: Screen, border, focal point, midground

SOIL: Any well-drained soil, including ones that are salty, very alkaline, or rocky

PESTS: None

The four-wing saltbush is a semievergreen shrub with dense, grey-green leaves that grows best in the intermediate mountain and deserts of the Southwest. Its large, tan, winged pods stay on the plant a long time and are excellent for dried arrangements. The related quail bush (*Atriplex lentiformis*) is much larger, growing to 3 to 9 feet x 6 to 12 feet, and while nearly as cold hardy, it is a better choice in the heat of the low elevation zones. The amazingly xeric desert holly (*A. hymenelytra*) is a small shrub from the lower Colorado River area of Arizona with holly-shaped ghostly white leaves.

Shared Spaces

Four-wing saltbush is effective as a screen or boundary planting where supplemental irrigation is difficult. It mixes well with other shrubs such as Texas ranger, sugarbush, or hopbush to create an informal hedge or background for more colorful perennial or annual plantings. Four-wing saltbush is resistant to fire and is useful in areas where fires are common.

Cultivation

Mulch the roots, not allowing mulch to touch the bark, and water thoroughly. Water every three to four days for two or three weeks, then water every seven to ten days for the first year if no rainfall occurs. Four-wing saltbush needs no fertilizer as all saltbushes become very large with generous watering. Plan watering schedules to achieve the size of plant that is desired. Water established plants monthly in summer and rely on natural rainfall in winter. Prune to remove unwanted branches; clear out dead, damaged stems in late winter. Plants have excellent natural form and rarely need pruning for shape.

Other Species and Cultivars

A. nummularia, old man saltbush (Zone 8), is a slow grower to 6 to 9 feet x 10 feet. It is extremely tough and has been introduced as a pioneer plant for extreme desert locations. *A. polycarpa*, desert saltbush, is a Southwestern native shrub that grows to 3 feet x 6 feet and is capable of growing on minimal rainfall as well as in wet conditions. Do not plant *A. semibaccata* in California where it is invasive.

Lady Banks' Rose
Rosa banksiae

ZONES: 5 to 11
FORM: Large fountain-like mounding shrub or trained as a vine
GROWTH AND MATURE SIZE: Evergreen moderate-growing shrub to 10 to 20 feet x 12 to 20 feet
USES: Screen, background, focal point, bank cover, arbor or trellis
SOIL: Well drained, amendments at planting are fine
PESTS: None

This old rose variety was introduced in 1807. It sends out long, virtually thornless shoots with dark green leaves. Lady Banks' rose is much more tolerant of the hot and dry conditions of the low desert than are most hybrid roses. Left alone, this rose grows naturally into a large, fountainlike shrub, but it is more often grown up a trellis or support. Small, yellow flowers occur in dense clusters.

Shared Spaces

Plant against a trellis, wall, or on an arbor for the dramatic spring flowering. This large, heat-tolerant rose is also useful to cool hot walls or areas where reflected heat is intense. Plant as a hedge or screen where space permits, or use as a focal or specimen plant. It's excellent for erosion control where there is sufficient space.

Cultivation

Mulch the root zones heavily but do not allow mulch to touch the bark. Water thoroughly. Water every two to three days for three weeks after planting.

In summer, water deeply every four to seven days; in winter, every ten to fourteen days if no rainfall occurs. Lady Banks' generally don't require fertilizing. Prune carefully; this rose blooms on old wood. In spring remove canes that are too long or are growing in the wrong direction by cutting them as close to the base of the plant as possible. Prune secondary branches each spring to train them along the arbor or trellis.

Other Species and Cultivars

'Lutea' is a scentless double-yellow, and 'White Banksia' is a double-white that smells like violets. In 1885, the white Lady Banks' rose was reportedly brought to the mining camp in Tombstone, Arizona, by a young bride from Scotland. The rose flourishes to this day, covering an arbor that estimated to cover 8000 square feet.

Little-leaf Cordia
Cordia parvifolia

ZONES: 8 to 11
FORM: Dense and wide spreading
GROWTH AND MATURE SIZE: Moderate-growing evergreen shrub to 4 to 8 feet x 4 to 10 feet
USES: Hedge, screen, focal point, midground
SOIL: Tolerates any well-drained soil from fertile, garden soil to rocky, native ones, but not heavy clay
PESTS: None

White is so delightful in the summer; just looking at it makes you feel cooler. A favorite white-flowered, summer-blooming shrub is little-leaf cordia. The shrub is well named, as the leaves are small, crinkled, and smoky gray-green. The dark branches make fanciful turns and twists to give the plant a complicated, dense appearance. The small, paper-thin white flowers form in clusters at the ends of branches and are prolific from early spring to late fall. The delicate beauty of the flowers entirely belies the rugged heat and drought tolerance of this shrub. In areas with summer monsoons, the little-leaf cordia can still take the humidity.

Shared Spaces

Little-leaf cordia makes an impressive hedge or screen when planted *en masse*. It can be mixed with other shrubs such as jojoba, sugarbush, Texas ranger, or Arizona rosewood to create an informal hedge or boundary planting. The relentless bloom through the summer makes it a splendid specimen or accent plant, particularly around small patios, courtyards, or seating areas. Use it against hot walls, near a pool, or in other areas where reflected heat is intense.

Cultivation

Maintain mulch around the roots in summer (without touching the bark) to keep soil from drying out too quickly and provide any needed nutrients. Water thoroughly after planting. Water every three to four days for two or three weeks, then water every seven to ten days for the first summer if no rainfall occurs. Water established plants every two to three weeks in summer, once a month or less in winter if there is no rainfall. Water much less frequently in temperate climates, allowing the soil to dry between waterings. Little-leaf cordia has a beautiful natural form; it is rarely necessary to prune for shape. Prune dead or damaged wood in spring. Little-leaf cordia drops its leaves in response to severe drought, stress, or exceptionally cold weather, but recovers quickly.

Other Species and Cultivars

Texas olive (*Cordia boissieri*) is a taller shrub with large, olive green leaves and large clusters of white flowers with yellow throats. Much less tolerant of salty soil or water than little-leaf cordia, Texas olive blooms in spring and fall.

Mahonia
Mahonia species

ZONES: 5 through 11
FORM: Dense thicket or sprawling
GROWTH AND MATURE SIZE: Slow- to moderate-growing evergreen shrub to 1 to 6 feet x 4 to 5 feet
USES: Midground, screen, informal hedge, focal point, ground cover, understory
SOIL: Prefers rich, well-drained garden soil; adapts to heavy clay if not kept too wet
PESTS: None

All three of the mahonias described here have leathery, evergreen holly-shaped leaves and fragrant yellow flowers in spring. Leaf color changes through the year: the new growth in spring is copper-colored, summer leaves are a deep blue-green, and foliage turns a rich plum purple after frost. Oregon grape holly (*M. aquifolium*) grows 6 feet tall and 5 feet wide, root sprouting at the base to form a dense thicket. Compact mahonia (*M. aquifolium* 'Compacta') is the most versatile and smaller in form, growing 2 feet high and spreading 4 feet wide. Creeping mahonia (*M. repens*) is slower to establish and less heat tolerant than the others, perfect in small shady spaces.

Shared Spaces

Use as an informal hedge or screen plant; compact mahonia works as filler between flowering shrubs, and as a tall ground cover under redbuds, golden raintree, or Japanese scholar tree. The plum-colored winter foliage blends well with 'Powis Castle' *Artemisia*. Creeping mahonia combined with blue oat grass or blue fescue makes a handsome ground cover in the shade.

Cultivation

Backfill soil requires no amendment. Set plants out 1 to 2 feet apart. Water 30 inches deep once a week when the temperature is above 85 F for three to four years, then every two weeks when temperatures are above 70 F, and monthly during cooler weather. Adjust watering to allow for natural rainfall. A spring application of slow-release fertilizer for the first few years gives plants a faster start. Four inches of composted mulch mulch helps suppress weeds and keeps the soil cool and moist.

Other Species and Cultivars

Newer introductions include evergreen *M. aquifolium* 'Orange Flame' with awesome foliage color and moderately growing to 2 feet x 3 feet. *M. japonica* 'Bealei', leatherleaf mahonia, is a good barrier plant with its spiny leathery leaves, a moderate grower to 6 to 10 feet x 4 to 5 feet. Both like part shade and are hardy in Zones 5 through 8.

Manzanita
Arctostaphylos species

ZONES: 5 to 11
FORM: Low growing, dense upright
GROWTH AND MATURE SIZE: Slow-growing evergreen shrub to 3 to 10 feet x 3 to 10 feet
USES: Ground cover, slope stabilizer, focal point, screen, hedge, background, midground
SOIL: Unamended but well-draining soil
PESTS: None except occasional branch dieback (see below)

Among the western native manzanita species and cultivars are several hundred wonderful evergreen manzanitas, all with leathery, deep green leaves. Some leaves are the size of peas, others the size of silver dollars, and some are covered in silvery hairs. In summer, manzanitas produce clusters of sweetly fragrant, upside-down, pitcher-shaped flowers, white to pale pink, that turn to reddish berries that draw birds. Upright manzanitas have gnarled and twisted mahogany-colored branches; some are smooth and sculptured. Once a year, the bark sheds, revealing patches of cinnamon-colored wood. Low-growing manzanitas make terrific ground covers.

Shared Spaces

Use low-growing manzanita to create a drought tolerant "green carpet" instead of lawn or to help stabilize a slope. Shrub-sized manzanitas make great screens, hedges, and foundation plants. Tree-sized manzanitas make fabulous specimens, especially when pruned to reveal their gorgeous branching structure and beautiful bark.

Cultivation

In humid coastal gardens, space plants to prevent leaf spot and keep water off leaves. Water deeply and mulch. Provide deep periodic water through the first year to establish. After that, manzanita will survive on rainfall alone or with occasional deep summer water. Let soil dry several inches down between waterings. No fertilizer is needed. Prune to shape just after bloom or fruiting. Occasional dead branches result from fungal "manzanita branch dieback." Prune the dead branches off in summer, cutting a few inches into healthy-looking live wood. Sterilize pruning shears between cuts and after you finish to avoid spreading the fungus.

Other Species and Cultivars

For more temperate climates, try 'Emerald Carpet' (1 to 2 feet x 3 to 6 feet) with small leaves and pale pink flowers; *A. hookeri* 'Sunset' (5 feet x 5 feet) has pink flowers, as well as *A. densiflora* 'Howard McMinn' (4 to 6 feet x 4 to 6 feet). Hardier manzanitas include New Mexico native *A. pungens*, growing to 3 feet x 12 feet; *A. patula* growing 5 feet x 10 feet; and common manzanita, *A. manzanita*, growing 10 or more feet tall.

Mormon Tea
Ephedra species

ZONES: 5 to 8
FORM: Sprawling mound
GROWTH AND MATURE SIZE: Moderate-growing evergreen shrub to 3 to 6 feet x 4 to 8 feet
USES: Evergreen accent, dry stream beds, boulder accent, midground
SOIL: Well-drained rocky or sandy soil
PESTS: None, except gall formation; remove infected stems

Ephedra is a genus related to conifers and native to arid regions across the globe. They are all heat and drought tolerant, and rarely have leaves; instead, they photosynthesize through chlorophyll in their slender stems. Their frilly flowers are small, yellow, and eye-catching in spring; Southwest natives have papery cones that glisten in bright sunlight. Cultivated species include *Ephedra nevadensis* with pale green stems growing 3 to 5 feet tall and wide; *E. viridis* and *E. trifurca*, both have bright green stems 4 to 6 feet x 6 to 8 feet; and *E. torryana* has gray-green stems 1 foot x 2 feet.

Shared Spaces

Joint fir (*Ephedra*) is an interesting evergreen accent mixed with fernbush, globemallow, and prince's plume. Ephedra's broomy texture makes it a natural companion for grasses large and small. Deergrass, green ephedra, thread-grass or blue oat grass, blue ephedrine, and 'Powis Castle' artemisia are pleasing mixes.

Cultivation

Always water sparingly, even when plants are first set out; no more than once a week to a depth of 3 inches the first summer. Water established plants once a month to a depth of 3 feet late spring through early fall, and only once or twice during warm spells in winter. No fertilizer is needed. After several years in the garden, the oldest gray stems can be thinned out to renew the plants' color. Ephedras are generally disease free; they're only susceptible to root rot if they are watered too often, especially when the soil is cold.

Other Species and Cultivars

Asian species include blue joint fir (*E. equisetina*), with elegant blue stems growing 4 feet x 6 to 8 feet, and miniature joint fir (*E. minuta*) with fine green stems hardly 10 inches tall with rootsprouts that form a mat 18 inches across. Unlike Southwest natives, they have red berrylike fruits. Blue joint fir is similar to the natives in water and sun preferences, but the mini ephedra forms prefer partial shade and watering once a week in summer.

Pink-flowering Currant
Ribes sanguineum var. *glutinosum*

ZONES: 4 through 8
FORM: Open branching to dense and narrow
GROWTH AND MATURE SIZE: Evergreen or deciduous shrubs grow moderately to 5 to 12 feet x 3 to 6 feet
USES: Shrub border, focal point, ground cover, natural hedge, midground, background
SOIL: Well-draining soils are best; tolerates heavy soils
PESTS: Thrips and spider mites

Currants grow naturally under oak trees and in other dry, shady spots. Their slightly toothed, fuzzy, miniature, maple-leaf shaped leaves line upright branches. Hanging tassels of pale pink, rose, or white flowers turn to bluish black fruits. Pink-flowering currants are one of many shade-loving evergreen and deciduous currants native to scrub, chaparral, and woodland areas from Baja to Oregon and from mountains to the coast. These tall, narrow shrubs grow in all but desert and high mountain gardens. Pink-flowering currant's show runs in the "off" season from winter through early spring, making it especially valuable for extending garden interest through the year.

Shared Spaces
Plant at the same time as new oaks or sycamores. Combine with redbud, toyon, and hummingbird sage. Currant's tall, narrow profile fits into narrow planting strips, as well.

Cultivation
Water deeply and regularly through the first year to establish. Currants in the wild survive on rainfall; however, once a plant is established, a bit of supplemental garden water through the growing season makes for a more vibrant currant. In milder gardens, currants need little to no water when they're dormant in summer. In hot inland gardens, water occasionally in summer. Mulch with composted organic matter. No fertilizer is needed. Prune if desired after flowering (or after berries are gone) to shape and encourage additional bloom the following year. Pruning for good air circulation prevents rust, as does keeping water off leaves and not watering too much in summer.

Other Species and Cultivars
'Inverness White' and 'White Icicle' (both 8 feet x 6 feet) have white flowers. 'Claremont' (8 feet tall), with pale pink to rose-pink flowers, and 'Tranquillon Ridge' (10 feet), with deep pink flowers, tolerate more arid and temperate conditions. Catalina perfume (*Ribes viburnifolium*) is an evergreen ground cover with tiny deep green fragrant leaves. Small burgundy flowers appear in winter to early spring. *R. odoratum* 'Crandall' is deciduous and prefers the cooler Zones 4 through 8. It has clove-scented yellow spring flowers, is fast growing to 4 to 6 feet tall and wide, and has beautiful mahogany-red fall foliage.

Purple Rockrose
Cistus x purpureus

ZONES: 6 through 11
FORM: Upright bushy to branching and trailing
GROWTH AND MATURE SIZE: Evergreen moderate-growing shrub to 3 to 4 feet x 4 to 5 feet
USES: Firescapes, focal point, borders, small gardens, midground
SOIL: Prefers well-drained calcareous soil
PESTS: None

We have a soft spot for Mediterranean natives because of the wealth of garden plants that originate there, and the way they fill out our native palettes with water-wise evergreens, culinary gems, and gorgeous color. There's also an aroma—a slightly biting, resinous, fresh scent—that transports one to the countryside in Spain or beyond. Purple rockrose, a modest-sized hybrid, has wiry stems densely covered with narrow, coarse-textured, dark green leaves that are blushed deep purple in winter. In late spring, the flower show is brief, but memorable. The 3-inch, bright, crepe-like pink blooms have a wine-red dot in the center surrounding a frill of golden stamens.

Shared Spaces

This is an ideal plant for courtyards, patios, and entryways. The dark foliage contrasts with silver artemisia, compact Texas ranger, and Greek germander. 'Moonshine' yarrow, the white forms of lavender, garden sage, creeping baby's breath, and gaura are complementary companions.

Cultivation

The roots are brittle, so unpot gently, disturbing the roots as little as possible. Fine gravel or shredded bark as mulch keeps the soil moist and more moderate in temperature, which also helps root development and suppresses weeds. Water every two weeks to a depth of 30 inches when the temperature is above 80 F; water monthly the rest of the year if there is no rainfall. After deep soaking in late summer, withhold water until after a few hard freezes to avoid new growth late in the season. Rockrose needs no fertilizer and very little pruning if plants are watered sparingly and not fertilized.

Other Species and Cultivars

Purple rockrose is one of the most cold-hardy *Cistus* species, reliable in Zone 6 and warmer gardens, or to 5000 feet in elevation. White-leafed rockrose (*C. albidus*) grows 4 feet tall and twice as wide with rose-pink flowers contrasting with its fuzzy white foliage. Avoid planting *C. ladanifer* in California as it has become invasive.

Santolina
Santolina species

ZONES: 5 through 11
FORM: Mounding
GROWTH AND MATURE SIZE: Fairly fast-growing evergreen to 2 feet x 2 feet
USES: Texture, filler, border, foreground
SOIL: Any well-drained infertile soil
PESTS: None

Santolina is quite at home in cold and warm desert regions. The soft, finely divided leaves on stiff stems grow into a dense mound. Yellow, button-shaped, ¾-inch flowers appear in June on short, wiry stems a few inches above the foliage. Gray santolina (*S. chamaecyparissus*, sometimes labeled *S. incana*) is the most heat and drought tolerant and robust of the species. Its foliage is pale silver; flowers are a contrasting bright yellow. The leaves have a pleasant aroma, but some people find the scent of the flowers to be unpleasant, especially as they mature. Since santolina is grown primarily for its form and foliage, shear off the blooms if their scent is offensive.

Shared Spaces

Santolina is used as filler and as a color foil for pineleaf, Rocky Mountain, and desert penstemons; gaillardia; valerian; and salvias in low-water perennial beds and borders. Santolina's well-defined cushion shape is an interesting counterpoint to the fountain forms of ornamental grasses.

Cultivation

Mulch with 3 inches of fine stone, shredded bark, or pecan shells to moderates soil temperatures and helps suppress weeds. Space plants three feet apart to create a gentle undulating effect. Santolina needs full sun at elevations above 6000 feet, but grows well in dappled shade in the low desert. Water to a depth of 2 feet every two weeks when temperatures are above 90 F; water monthly the rest of the year if there is no rainfall. Excess water in winter heavy soil kills santolina even after it is well established. Plants have the best form when they're grown in lean soils without fertilizer. In early spring, trim santolina back one foot from the ground so that new growth can replace the winter-weathered stems. Tidy up plants in summer by trimming the flower stems down into the foliage.

Other Species and Cultivars

S. chamaecyparissus, gray santolina, is cold hardy to Zone 5. It has silver-gray foliage and bright yellow button flowers. Also cold hardy is *S. rosmarinfolia* 'Morning Mist' (2 feet tall and wide), which has showy blue evergreen foliage with the classic yellow blooms in summer.

Shrub Salvia
Salvia species

ZONES: 5 to 11
FORM: Vase-shaped and bushy
GROWTH AND MATURE SIZE: Moderately-growing evergreens, 2 to 6 feet x 2 to 4 feet
USES: Perennial borders, lining paths, mass xeric color planting, midground
SOIL: Any well-drained soil
PESTS: Insect pests and diseases are rarely a problem (unless plants are watered excessively)

Plants sometimes don't fit easily into the neat categories we'd like to assign them. These salvia differ from the herbaceous types by having a woody crown similar to lavender or santolina. In temperate climates, salvias abound year-round. In colder zones, shrub salvia bloom during warm spring and hot summer months, are slow to fade away in winter, and pop back up in early spring. Heat-loving and xeric, cherry sage (*S. greggii*) grows brittle branches 2 feet high and to 3 feet wide, and flowers heavily in spring and fall, and lightly all summer; Mexican blue sage (*S. chamaedryoides*) has small, silver evergreen leaves and gentian-blue flowers.

Shared Spaces

The evergreen forms are used in dry borders for winter interest among herbaceous plants. Group them along paths, dry streambeds, and patios, or cluster them in the light shade of desert willow, acacia, or mesquite. Mexican blue sage mixes nicely with cliffrose, pineleaf penstemon, desert penstemon, and Greek germander.

Cultivation

Mulch with composted mulch, fine gravel, pecan shells, or shredded bark to insulate the roots and help suppress weeds. Water to a depth of 2 feet every two weeks when temperatures are above 80 F; water monthly the rest of the year if there are no rains. Applying a slow-release fertilizer in spring keeps plants long-blooming and vigorous. To stimulate new growth, cut back faster-growing cherry sage to 8 to 12 inches aboveground each spring just as it begins growing new leaves. The smaller, slower-growing types need rejuvenating only every three to five years.

Other Species and Cultivars

So many new crosses and cultivars come out each year it's hard to choose. For the low desert regions, *S.* x Trident™ offers a strong pungent aroma, compact moderate growth to 3 feet tall and wide, and whorled flower spikes in cobalt blue. For cold-hardy introductions, *S. greggi* 'Wild Thing' is a vigorous fast grower to 3 feet tall and wide with glorious coral pink blooms. *S. greggi* 'Raspberry Delight' is newly registered and offers foliage that has a sweet herbal fragrance, fast growing to 3 feet x 3 feet, and topped with deeply colored raspberry red blooms.

Shrubby Senna
Cassia wislizeni (Senna wislizeni)

ZONES: 6 through 11
FORM: Dense, vase-shaped
GROWTH AND MATURE SIZE: Slow to moderate deciduous shrub to 5 to 8 feet x 5 to 10 feet
USES: Border, succulent garden, informal hedge, drifts, midground, background
SOIL: Tolerates a wide variety of soils, including well-drained, fertile, rocky, and native
PESTS: None

Deciduous, shrubby senna is one of the last garden plants to emerge from its winter rest. This habit makes it look pathetic in nurseries because it has just a few gray stems and only a leaf or two. However, buy it with confidence; shrubby senna is a spectacular shrub once planted. The leaves are a dark, brooding green, growing thick on the plant. Coupled with the complex branching, shrubby senna grows into a shrub that seems to be impenetrable. The round flower buds fly open like popped corn to display the flat, five-petaled, bright yellow flowers, profuse on the plant and lasting throughout summer.

Shared Spaces

Mix shrubby senna with other desert shrubs such as Texas ranger, jojoba, or sugarbush to form an informal hedge or border planting. Shrubby senna has terrific heat tolerance and can be used to protect hot walls, buildings, areas around a pool or patio, or anywhere that reflected heat is intense. Use shrubby senna in areas of the garden that receive minimal care to add bright summer color. This large shrub blends well with succulents such as purple prickly pear, ocotillo, and various agaves.

Cultivation

After planting, mulch the roots but do not allow mulch to touch the bark. Water thoroughly. Water every three to four days for two or three weeks, then water weekly for the first summer. Shrubby senna does not require supplemental fertilizer, and established plants need watering only every three to four weeks in summer. In winter, supplemental water is necessary only during extended dry spells. Plants are extremely drought tolerant; general appearance and bloom are best with minimal summer irrigation. Prune in late winter while the plant is still dormant to remove dead or damaged wood. It does not require consistent pruning for shape.

Other Species and Cultivars

C. leptophylla is treelike with a broad canopy growing to 20 to 25 feet x 30 feet. *C. phyllodinea (Senna phyllodinea)*, silver senna, has silvery gray, leaflike phylloides on 5-foot-tall by 3-foot-wide shrubs. This prolific bloomer is covered in bright yellow flowers, fall through spring in milder climate regions.

Sugarbush
Rhus ovata

ZONES: 5 through 11
FORM: Loosely branched and rounded
GROWTH AND MATURE SIZE: Moderate-growing evergreen and deciduous shrub to 3 to 15 feet x 5 to 15 feet
USES: Borders, natural hedges, background
SOIL: Any well-drained soil from fertile, garden soil to rocky, native ones; does poorly in heavy clay
PESTS: None

As soon as you travel outside most Southwest cities, you'll notice large, dark green, round shrubs lining the roadsides; they are sugarbush. The large, waxy green leaves are attached to the stems by reddish petioles, and the small white flowers of spring have dark pink bracts. The fruit of sugarbush is a bright red berry. The smaller, glossy-leaved evergreen sumac (*Rhus virens*) is equally at home in Southwestern gardens. Lemonade bush (*R. trilobata*) is a deciduous shrub with fuzzy three-part leaves turning orange and yellow in autumn. The fruit tastes of lemon. Desert sumac (*R. microphylla*) is also deciduous with small, compound leaves, and sticky red fruit.

Shared Spaces

Mix with shrubs such as Arizona rosewood, jojoba, or saltbush to create an informal hedge or border planting. The smooth green leaves make an excellent background for colorful perennial or annual plantings. Plant against a hot wall, around a pool or patio, or in other areas where reflected heat is intense. Sugarbush is an outstanding shrub for areas of the garden that receive minimal care.

Cultivation

After planting, mulch the roots but do not allow mulch to touch the bark, and water thoroughly. Water every three to four days for two or three weeks, then water every seven to ten days for the first summer. No fertilizer is needed. Water established plants every two weeks in summer in low desert zones, and every three or four weeks in other areas. In temperate climates, rely on natural rainfall in winter. Overwatering or poor drainage is the most common cause of disease or death for sugarbush. Prune only to remove dead wood or damaged limbs in spring.

Other Species and Cultivars

R. aromatica 'Gro-Low' makes a wonderful ground cover for flat or sloping areas. A fast grower to 3 feet x 8 feet, it has tiny yellow blooms in spring and vibrant fall foliage in orange, red, and burgundy. Pink flowering sumac, *Rhus lentii*, from Baja and Cedros Island has round, gray-green leaves and pink flowers in spring.

Texas Ranger
Leucophyllum species

ZONES: 6 to 11
FORM: Vase-shaped, bushy
GROWTH AND MATURE SIZE: Slow-growing evergreen shrub to 3 to 8 feet x 4 to 8 feet
USES: Hedge, border, mass, midground
SOIL: Extremely intolerant of heavy, poorly drained soils; prefers well-drained, fertile, rocky, native soils
PESTS: Palo verde beetles feed on roots and kill older plants

Its durability, easy care, and beautiful blooms have made Texas ranger one of the most common evergreen shrubs in the Southwest. They are immune to heat, extremely drought tolerant, and thrive in highly alkaline soils. *Leucophyllum frutescens* is a large shrub with gray-green leaves and fragrant pink flowers. Most widely grown selections come from this species; they include 'Green Cloud'™ with dark green leaves and magenta flowers, 'White Cloud'™ with gray leaves and white flowers, and 'Thundercloud' with whitish leaves and deep purple flowers. 'Silver Cloud'™, a selection of *L. candidum*, has bright white foliage and dark royal-purple flowers.

Shared Spaces
Mix Texas ranger with other shrubs such as sugarbush, jojoba, Arizona rosewood, yellowbells, or Texas mountain laurel to form an informal hedge or border planting. The tremendous heat tolerance and light-colored foliage make Texas ranger particularly effective against hot walls or buildings, around pools or patios, and in other areas where reflected heat is intense.

Cultivation
Mulch the roots but do not allow mulch to touch the bark. Water thoroughly. Water every three to four days for two or three weeks, then water every seven to ten days for the first summer if there is no rainfall. No fertilizer is needed. Water sparingly in summer, even in low desert zones. Water established plants every two to three weeks in summer; once every month or two in winter if there is no rain. In temperate climates, rely on natural rainfall unless the weather is exceptionally hot or dry. All Texas ranger plants have excellent natural form and rarely need pruning for shape. Prune to remove dead or damaged wood in spring.

Other Species and Cultivars
L. langmaniae 'Lynn's Legacy' is a clone and known for its profuse and frequent floral displays. A moderate grower to 5 feet tall and wide, it has a dense rounded form that is covered with lavender flowers in summer. It is hardy to 10 degrees. *L. frutescens* 'Compacta' is a dense grower to 4 to 5 feet tall and wide with silver leaves and pink flowers.

Toyon
Heteromeles arbutifolia

ZONES: 7 through 9
FORM: Bushy, full rounded
GROWTH AND MATURE SIZE: Slow-growing evergreen shrub to 6 to 15 feet x 6 to 10 feet
USES: Screen, background, hedge, focal point
SOIL: Prefers well-draining soils, but tolerates clay
PESTS: Susceptible to aphids, mealybugs, thrips, and fire blight; prune infected branches and discard

We think of Hollywood as the birthplace of the movie industry, but long before the silver screen, Hollywood was known for toyons. When Easterners first arrived, Hollywood's hillsides were covered in thickets of evergreen shrubs with leathery, deep green, toothed leaves and bright red fall berries. Not surprisingly, they referred to the shrubs as hollies and named the area for the shrubs. Toyon (the native American name) is common in chaparral and oak woodlands throughout California. Garden-grown toyons are big, beautiful shrubs that fill open spaces in a short time. They are suitable for all gardens except those in the deserts and highest mountains.

Shared Spaces

Toyons are a fantastic background for flowering plants and quickly stabilize slopes, screen out neighbors, and hide unsightly fences. A favorite fall display is a toyon in full red berry alongside blue fall-blooming California lilac and the bright gold fall flowers of perennial marigold. Add yellow-blooming daylilies, tufts of teal blue fescue, and a purple leaf New Zealand flax for contrast.

Cultivation

In a beach garden, keep toyons out of the spray zone. Water deeply and maintain a thick layer of organic mulch. Water regularly and deeply through the first year or two to help roots go deep. Once established, toyon can survive on rainfall in most gardens, but grows faster and looks lusher with deep monthly summer watering. But, too frequent water can lead to root rot. No fertilizer is needed. These shrubs flower (and make berries) on the previous year's growth. If your toyon needs pruning but you want berries, selectively remove branches rather than pruning it back. Cut all branches at the base.

Other Species and Cultivars

Toyon 'Davis Gold' grows just like the species but with narrower leaves and gorgeous golden yellow berries in fall. *H. arbutifolia macrocarpa* is native to the Channel Islands in southern California and has larger berries.

Vines & Ground Covers

Since so many plants do double-duty, we combined water-wise vines and ground covers into one chapter. Some vines, for example, are just as happy to creep along the ground as they are to climb up a fence. Some climb and wind their way over posts, pillars, or porches. Others need a bit of support and coaxing, but once they're mature, their trunks are strong enough to support the vine on their own. There are vines that thrive in the hot blaring sun, but appreciate some afternoon shade when temperatures soar to 100 degrees. Most offer beautiful flowers, while some release a sweet scent when tromped upon.

"But why would you want to grow that? It's so invasive!" Sometimes the answer to that question is simply, "Isn't that its job—to cover the ground?" When living in California, it is natural to view ground covers like vinca or ivy as more of a nuisance than a beauty, where their boisterous ways try to crowd out other plants, their creeping lush foliage smothers anything that gets in the way, and their clinging tendrils attach themselves to tree trunks, home siding and eaves, or anything else that they encounter.

Perspectives change, though, when gardening in a climate like Utah's. One gains a new respect for any plant that thrives in hot summer temperatures, relentless glaring sun, and whipping winds, yet demands very little water or fertilizer in return. You can truly appreciate plants that hold onto their foliage through below freezing nights, snowy days, and in the icy winds of winter. And what a delight at the first signs of spring thaw, when the seemingly crispy barren stems that you thought for sure were dead and gone start sending forth the greenest-of-green small leaves with new buds already forming for the early spring flowers. "Invasive," you say. "No way!"

On a cold winter February morning, some scraggly branches growing in a brambled clump next to the house may seem to be some sort of weedy thing to be addressed when spring thaw comes. Fast-forward to early spring. Greeting you are those same scraggly vines, but now they are fully leafed out and sending out new green growth all along their stems. In one growing season, the trumpet vine climbs up the house, along the porch, and scrambles over and down the arbor, sending out its tubular blooms all along the way, giving both you and the hummingbirds enjoyment.

The Virginia creeper vine is another surprising beauty. With obvious vigor and persistence, it not only covers the fence, but when it's given room, it provides a lush sea of green ground cover, cooling the soil down. It blankets the fence through the spring, summer, and even showcases red, orange, and yellow foliage in late fall.

And who can forget wisteria? It is smart to start with one-gallon sized containers, allowing yourself some seasons of training before they start to flower. To provide needed shade, consider building a natural framework out of branches to provide support for the young plants, which will form a lovely shade canopy in the summer, yet allow the warm sun to shine through their smooth leafless branches in winter. In three or four years, heavenly scented beautiful purple or white blooms will hang down through the canopy roof in the spring.

Some ground covers, by their very nature, can be drought-tolerant plants. Their low-growing and spreading growth habit shades their roots, cools the soil, and protects the soil from drying out.

The list for low-water-use and fertilizer-efficient ground covers and vines is a long one. Your decision should be based upon what you want to achieve. Do you want to provide a soft green blanket under the canopy of a juniper grove to smother out weeds? Or maybe you want to accent boulders and soften the edges of a dry streambed. And there's that slope surrounding your home—you will want a ground cover that will anchor into the slope and protect it from erosion.

The water-wise vines and ground covers listed here are all pretty forgiving in their needs. Soil and water are not a problem. Once established, they can go it on their own. All you need to do is give them the space they need and they will reward you year after year.

African Daisy
Arctotis hybrids

ZONES: 9 through 11; Grown as an annual in colder areas
FORM: Mounding, spreading clumps
GROWTH AND MATURE SIZE: Fast-growing evergreen ground cover to 6 to 15 inches x 12 to 36 inches
USES: Massed ground cover, color sweeps, foreground
SOIL: Any well-drained soil, but will tolerate heavier soils; avoid areas that are constantly moist
PESTS: None

You might mistake African daisy for gazania, the freeway daisy. Both are low-water, evergreen ground covers with gray-green leaves and daisy-shaped flowers. From a gardener's perspective, the biggest difference between the two is aesthetic. African daisies bloom in shades of bright yellow, brick red, coppery-orange, magenta-pink, and tangerine, often with a contrasting dark ring of color at the center of each flower. Flowers open with morning and close at sunset. Broad silvery evergreen leaves creating handsome expanses of foliage, even in the hottest months.

Shared Spaces

Brightly colored and profusely flowering, the African daisy is perfect for "filling in the spaces" large or small. Be careful to contain the plant if you garden next to natural or open fields; it can invade those areas. African daisy looks beautiful cascading from a container or edging a flower bed. Plant several African daisies around a large specimen plant such as agave, pink-flowering Hong Kong orchid tree, or purple-leaved smoke tree. Plants soon knit together, forming a tapestry of texture.

Cultivation

Water well and mulch after planting. Deep water to keep the root zone moist through the first summer. After that, allow the soil to dry several inches deep between waterings. Apply all-purpose organic fertilizer in spring and fall if desired. Remove spent flowers. Cut plants back to just a few inches in winter if they develop woody stems. If plants begin to look ratty after a few years, simply replace them with newer varieties on the market, take cuttings off healthy growing tips, or anchor down a healthy stem into the soil to propagate a new plant by air-layering.

Other Species and Cultivars

Some of the prettiest African daisies include the deep red, more compact (to 14 inches x 14 inches) Ravers series 'Arc of Fire'; 'Cherry Frost' has brilliant red blooms surrounded by silver foliage; pink with orange 'Pink Sugar'; and bright orange 'Sun Spot'.

Arizona Grape Ivy
Cissus trifoliata

ZONES: 9 through 11
FORM: Trailing, climbing
GROWTH AND MATURE SIZE: Fast-growing semi-deciduous to deciduous vine to 20 to 30 feet x 10 to 20 feet
USES: Ground cover, climbing vine
SOIL: Any well-drained fertile to rocky, native soil
PESTS: None

Vines as a group are sun-loving plants; after all, their rapidly growing stems are an adaptation for reaching up to the sun. But Arizona grape ivy is a vine that grows best in the shade. This Arizona native vine is best suited for low and intermediate desert gardens. Throughout summer, it is densely covered with glossy, dark green, three-lobed leaves, and the tiny tendrils attach easily to limbs, trellises, or walls. The small white flowers are practically invisible, and the minute grapes are not edible, except to birds.

Shared Spaces

Use Arizona grape ivy to cover bare walls or bare tree limbs in shady locations. Provide the plant with a trellis or arbor. Arizona grape ivy is effective as ground cover in dry shade and will quickly cover bare ground. It grows well in containers either as a hanging plant or as a vine in a small or confined space.

Cultivation

Water thoroughly and mulch the roots to keep them from drying out and for winter protection. Water every two to three days for the first three or four weeks, then every five to seven days until established. Apply slow-release or organic fertilizer to young plants in spring. Water established plants every three or four weeks in summer; rely on natural rainfall in winter. Arizona grape ivy is semi-deciduous in most winters but loses all its leaves in a hard freeze. Prune back frost-damaged or dead stems only after all danger of frost is past. Plants can be pruned to within a few inches of the ground in early spring to reduce their size or reinvigorate them.

Other Species and Cultivars

Boston ivy and Virginia creeper are more cold-tolerant deciduous vines (Zones 4 through 9) growing longer (45 to 50 feet). *Parthenocissus tricuspidata* 'Green Shower' grows quickly (to 45 feet) and attaches by tendrils. It has beautiful burgundy fall foliage. *P. quinquefolia* 'Monham' Star Showers® looks as if it's been splattered with paint, white on green foliage that takes on a pink hue in cooler weather. All of these vines do well along the coast and in inland valleys as well.

Bougainvillea
Bougainvillea species

ZONES: 9 through 11
FORM: Varied, from upright with arching branches to mounding or trailing
GROWTH AND MATURE SIZE: Slow- to moderate-growing evergreen vine to 1½ to 3 feet x 5 to 8 feet (mounds) and 20 to 30 feet x up to 8 feet (vines)
USES: Background, screen, ground cover
SOIL: Well-drained soil
PESTS: Watch for whitefly

Bougainvillea are the jewels of low-frost gardens. Though native to Brazil, these woody vines are ubiquitous throughout coastal, valley, and low desert landscapes. From summer through fall, they are covered in cascades of flowers that are not truly flowers at all but rather colorful, papery bracts that frame tiny, cream-colored, tube-shaped flowers. Hybridizers have gone wild creating bougainvillea in every shade from vibrant red to palest pink, raspberry, golden-orange, white, and apricot. Most have heart-shaped green leaves, but some have variegated leaves, yellow and green or cream and green. Bougainvillea are extremely tough plants that, once established, thrive on neglect.

Shared Spaces

They are very thorny and quite messy, so place them well away from play areas, walkways, and swimming pools. While bougainvillea brightens tropical theme gardens, it is also a mainstay of Mediterranean style gardens. Train bougainvillea over an arbor. Use them to cover a slope, to climb a tree, or to be espaliered against a wall. Dwarf varieties are perfect for containers, for hanging baskets, for spilling over low walls, and as ground covers.

Cultivation

If growing as a vine, provide a strong structure before planting. Tie or wire branches into place. Disturb the rootball as little as possible during planting. Water deeply through the first summer. After that, allow soil to dry several inches down between waterings (this applies to bougainvillea in pots as well). Fertilizer isn't necessary, but to encourage growth apply organic fertilizer once in early spring. Prune to shape and control overly exuberant growth.

Other Species and Cultivars

Look for almost thornless 'Silhouette', a slow-growing compact form to 3 feet tall and wide that has giant pink bracts. Dwarf 'Raspberry Ice' (2 to 3 feet x 5 to 6 feet) has raspberry pink bracts, green and cream variegated leaves. 'Purple Queen' (1½ feet x 6 to 8 feet) has deep purple bracts. 'La Jolla' (4 to 5 feet tall) has bright red bracts. For long, vining varieties, try 'California Gold' (20 to 30 feet) with gold bracts or 'San Diego Red' (15 to 25 feet) with deep red bracts.

Chinese Wisteria
Wisteria sinensis

ZONES: 5 through 7
FORM: Full, twining
GROWTH AND MATURE SIZE: Slow- to moderate-growing deciduous vine to 25 to 40 feet x 25 to 40 feet
USES: Arbors, porch frames, pillars, canopy, pergola
SOIL: Adapts to all but very alkaline clay soils
PESTS: None

Imagine wisteria on a cold winter morning, with its smooth, ropy stems and bare branches coiled along the overhang of a front porch. In spring, the pendulous purple flowers will cascade along the porch like an elegant valance. Perfect for covering arbors, its light green compound leaves unfold early in spring, still soft and translucent when the flowers appear, hanging in 12-inch clusters from the stems. Then, leaves expand to a dense canopy offering cool shade in the heat of summer. Blooms are sometimes thwarted if the early spring weather is unsettled. But, if Mother Nature is kind, wisteria provides one of the finest displays of color in the spring garden.

Shared Spaces

Massive wisteria vines needs the sturdy support of an arbor or ramada. Or, train them to drape a high garden wall. To create a graceful curtain effect, twine vines up the post of a porch or portal and across a support attached to the edge of the roof, letting the ends of the stems drape down.

Cultivation

Water summer transplants every few days initially, then weekly until fall or plant in cooler months and water weekly until fall. It takes hold and grows faster on a cooler north- or east-facing exposure. Loosen the soil well and top with 4 to 6 inches of organic mulch. For several years, water weekly to 24 inches when temperatures are 85 degrees Fahrenheit or higher, every two weeks when temperatures are between 70 and 85 F, and monthly during cooler weather if there is no rain or snowfall. Water established wisteria to a depth of 30 inches every two weeks when plants are leafy, and monthly during cooler weather if there is no rain or snowfall. Use slow-release fertilizer for the first few years. Work an iron-and-sulfur fertilizer into the soil every spring to prevent summer chlorosis. If given enough room, wisteria requires little pruning, but the slender stems need to be tied to the support structure firmly. For smaller places, trim back yearly. Trim tree forms twice a year. Note: Wisteria takes four or five years to establish.

Other Species and Cultivars

A hardier cultivar is *W. macrostachya* 'Aunt Dee'. It is also a bit more restrained. Smaller, growing to just 8 to 10 feet, is *W. frutescens* 'Amethyst Falls'.

Climbing Bauhinia
Bauhinia corymbosa

ZONES: 9 through 11
FORM: Full, vining
GROWTH AND MATURE SIZE: Moderate-growing evergreen vine to 25 feet
USES: Fence, wall covering, ground cover on slopes, screen
SOIL: Amended well-draining soil
PESTS: None

A deep green background can bring a garden to life. When that background also has delicate pink, orchid-like flowers, it becomes an even stronger element in the garden. Such is the effect of *Bauhinia corymbosa*. Like its cousin, the Hong Kong orchid tree, climbing bauhinia has deep green, almost blue-green, leaves split down the middle into two oval lobes. Petite grape-sized leaves attach to vigorous vines that have curling tendrils and narrow stems. Spring through fall, the vine is adorned with pale pink flowers, 2 to 3 inches across, with five petals, three of which are veined in bright fuchsia with a long curling pink stamen and pistil.

Shared Spaces

Climbing bauhinia planted on a fence behind a rose garden fills in the visual spaces between the roses and gives the garden a year-round green that roses simply can't provide. It also makes a terrific green screen—whether covering a fence or trellis to make a vertical wall; or trailing over a pergola, arbor, or patio covering to make a ceiling.

Cultivation

Water deeply and mulch after planting. Have a strong support in place first. Water regularly through the first summer and early fall. Once rains arrive, let Mother Nature take over unless there is a long dry period. Once established, climbing bauhinia can get by on occasional deep summer water. With more frequent watering, vines are more vigorous and lush. Climbing bauhinia fixes its own nitrogen. Therefore, fertilize with low nitrogen fertilizer in very early spring, or mulch with good compost and don't bother with fertilizer. Established vining bauhinia is fairly frost tolerant though leaves sometimes drop in the cold of winter. If frost damage occurs, wait until spring to prune; outer leaves will protect the inner leaves from the cold. Train new vines as they develop.

Other Species and Cultivars

Red orchid bush (*B. galpinii*) grows 10 feet x 10 to 15 feet. Flowers bloom in colors of intense coral-red to deep orange with a touch of yellow right in the center. Climbing bauhinia can be trained on a fence, over a wall, or up a pergola; it is hardy to 20 degrees F.

Coral Vine
Antigonon leptopus

ZONES: 9 through 11
FORM: Trailing, climbing
GROWTH AND MATURE SIZE: Quick-growing spring vine to 20 to 40 feet
USES: Screen, wall, fence cover, ground cover, arbor
SOIL: Tolerates poor soils, rocky soils, and sand, as well as well-amended garden soils
PESTS: None

Coral vine is a graceful, ethereal vine with long dense sprays of petite coral-pink or rose-pink (sometimes white) flowers that make a beautiful contrast against frilly, green, heart-shaped leaves. This perennial vine comes from forested areas, from Baja down into Central America, where it climbs trees and shrubs. In our gardens, coral vine's curling tendrils need a strong support structure, be it a fence, wall, sturdy trellis, or tree. Grow coral vine up a south- or west-facing wall or over a patio arbor so its shade can cool your home in summer. With the first frost, coral vine dies to the ground; the next spring, coral vine resprouts from underground tubers.

Shared Spaces

Coral vine is the perfect choice for a fast screen and quick summer shade or to hide an unattractive chain-link fence. Left unsupported, coral vine makes a good summertime ground cover. Or grow it cascading over a wall or down a slope. In a dry garden or Mediterranean theme garden, combine with purple-flowering penstemon and gold-flowered Mexican tarragon. Or, mix with deep green-leaved California lilac and yellow-flowered Mexican tulip poppy.

Cultivation

Have a sturdy support in place before planting. Water well after planting, and mulch. To cover a large expanse, space plants 3 to 5 feet apart. Water deeply and regularly through the first summer to establish. After that, water deeply but only occasionally in summer. One deep watering a week in desert areas keeps the vine going. Apply a half-dose of organic fertilizer with new spring growth. When coral vine starts its rapid summer growth, train branches where you want them to go. Each year, tuberous underground roots send up more stems than it did the previous year. If stems become too dense, prune selectively to open the vine and increase air circulation. In frost-free areas where the vine does not die back, prune to the ground in winter.

Other Species and Cultivars

Flowers of coral vine 'Baja Red' have the deepest rose color; 'Album' (also sold as 'Alba') has white flowers but it is not as cold hardy as the pink varieties.

Creeping Germander
Teucrium chamaedrys 'Prostrata'

ZONES: 5 through 11

FORM: Low, bushy, and spreading with spikes of blooms in summer

GROWTH AND MATURE SIZE: Quickly growing evergreen or deciduous ground cover to 6 inches x 24 inches

USES: Slopes, rock garden filler, understory, mass

SOIL: Any well-drained soil

PESTS: None

Creeping germander is a low-spreading, root-sprouting ground cover that tolerates heat. The glossy dark green leaves are about one-half inch long with notched margins. They grow closely spaced on short, upright stems. The rose-pink flowers are crowded in spikes 2 to 4 inches above the foliage, producing a sheet of color that lasts for several weeks in summer. The species, *Teucrium chamaedrys*, is deciduous and grows taller than 'Prostrata', to at least a foot tall. Bush germander, *Teucrium fruticans*, grows to 4 feet high and spreads twice as wide. It has small, silver leaves and soft lavender flowers on slender, arching stems. It is cold hardy to Zones 7 through 8.

Shared Spaces

This plant makes good filler in large rock gardens and works well as a ground cover under both deciduous and evergreen trees. Plant it along paths and patios with 'Bowles Mauve' wallflower, lavender, curry plant, Texas sage, and other silver-leafed plants.

Cultivation

Transplant from containers anytime; in winter, set out only those plants that are acclimated to the cold. Plants can be easily divided in spring and late summer or early fall. Backfill soil requires no amendment. Pecan shells or fine gravel mulch keeps the soil more uniformly moist and cooler in summer. Water germander to a depth of 2 feet every two weeks when temperatures are above 80 degrees F. Water monthly the rest of the year unless there is rain or snowfall. Slow-release fertilizer will make plants growing in very sandy soil more robust, but plants growing in decomposed granite or clay loam don't need fertilizer. Shear off the spent flower stems in late summer, and pull those few weeds that manage to muscle their way into an established stand.

Other Species and Cultivars

Teucrium chamaedrys 'Nanum' is evergreen with dark green leaves, magenta summer blooms, and grows to a diminutive 4 to 6 inches tall, spreading to almost 36 inches wide. It likes full sun and is hardy to 10 degrees F. *Teucrium laciniatum* grows 6 to 8 inches tall and spreads at least 18 inches wide with dark green leaves and fragrant white flowers in late spring and summer.

Ice Plant
Drosanthemum species

ZONES: 8 through 11
FORM: Clumping, trailing
GROWTH AND MATURE SIZE: Slow-growing ground cover to 1 to 4 feet x 3 to 6 feet
USES: Succulent garden midground, ground cover on slopes or large areas
SOIL: Any well-drained soil
PESTS: None

While ice plants suitable for the low zones are selected for their tolerance to the blazing summers, there is a group of ice plants that is more frost-hardy and better suited to the cooler summers of the intermediate and high zones. The trailing pink-flowered form is *Drosanthemum floribundum*. The deep purple forms are generally *D. hispidum* but are often sold as *D. speciosum*. Plants of this type grow over rock walls and raised beds in the intermediate zones. They bloom for a long time through late winter and early spring, many lasting through summer. All are at least semidormant during the hottest part of summer.

Shared Spaces

Ice plants mix well with other succulents either as a filler in containers or as a ground cover around succulent beds. Use as a ground cover among spring- and winter-flowering bulbs. Ice plants are excellent planted in containers or planters providing a brilliant splash of color to patios, seating areas, or around a pool. Use to fill in barren spots in a dry garden or in areas that receive minimal care.

Cultivation

Use rock mulches; avoid organic mulch as it can encourage root rot. Water every two or three days for two weeks, then every week or two through the first winter if no rainfall occurs. Allow soil to dry out between waterings. Apply balanced, but low-nitrogen, slow-release or organic fertilizer to container-grown plants once in spring. Plants in the ground need no supplemental fertilizer. Water established plants every week or two while they are growing and blooming if rainfall is scarce; most survive well on natural rainfall once established. Plants are semidormant in hot weather and will rot quickly if overwatered at that time. Prune in early spring to remove damaged stems or to cut back the size of the plant.

Other Species and Cultivars

D. micans is a South African native that is low growing to 10 to 12 inches and mounding to 24 inches. Extremely drought tolerant, it has bright yellow blooms with edges that look as though they have been dipped in red paint.

Lilac Vine
Hardenbergia violaceae

ZONES: 9 through 11
FORM: Dense, vining with support
GROWTH AND MATURE SIZE: Evergreen vine moderately growing to 10 to 15 feet x 6 to 15 feet
USES: Trellis, fence, screen, focal point
SOIL: Tolerates a wide range of soils from well-drained, fertile soil to rocky, native soil; does not perform well in heavy or poorly drained soils
PESTS: None

This evergreen Australian native is virtually immune to the heat and dry conditions of the low elevation zones. Lilac vine has long, thin leaves with a dash of purple on the edges. The leaves are so profuse you cannot see through the plant. This dense foliage provides ample cover for patios and porches in the heat of summer. There is both a vine and a shrub form of this species. Lilac vine has small, deep purple flowers that hang off the plant in gentle cascades. This charming vine blooms a long season, from fall through the following spring. In milder summer areas, it blooms in summer. There are white-flowered and pink-flowered forms.

Shared Spaces

Lilac vine is an outstanding choice to cover a sunny fence or provide a privacy screen for courtyards or small seating areas. The dense evergreen foliage makes a splendid living ceiling for a patio or ramada. Plant lilac vine on an arbor or trellis for a burst of cool-season color. A dwarf selection makes a good specimen or focal plant as well as a colorful container plant.

Cultivation

Water thoroughly after planting. Water every two to three days for two weeks, then every five to seven days until established. Apply slow-release or organic fertilizer in fall and spring until plants are a mature size. Fertilize established plants only every year or two in spring or fall. Too much fertilizer grows abundant leaves at the expense of bloom. Water established plants every two weeks in summer, even in the lowest elevation zones. Water monthly in winter. Provide sturdy support for the vines. Prune in spring after bloom is complete to remove dead or damaged wood or to clear out tangled stems. Do not prune in summer; exposed stems are easily sunburned and do not recover quickly.

Other Species and Cultivars

H. comptoniana, the Western Australian coral pea, has blue to purple blooms, growing 8 to 9 feet tall and wide. Provide shelter in frost areas. 'Happy Wanderer' has mauve blooms. 'Mini-Ha-Ha' is a dwarf form growing to 3 feet tall and wide.

Moss Verbena
Verbena pulchella

ZONES: 9 through 11
FORM: Long trailing stems form loose open mounds
GROWTH AND MATURE SIZE: Rapid-growing summer dormant vine to 4 to 8 inches x 2 to 5 feet
USES: Ground cover, border, foreground
SOIL: Tolerant of well-drained fertile soil or rocky, native soil; does not thrive in wet or heavy clay soil
PESTS: None

Moss verbena grows where most plants fear to set down their roots—among rocks, in compacted desert soils, or in neglected parts of the garden. Spreading from a semi-woody base, the long stems create a lacy carpet of the finely cut, dark green leaves. The flowers are tiny and held in tight, round heads, but blooming is prolific throughout winter and spring. Most plants either die or go dormant in summer in the low zones, although those in the shade or near water bloom intermittently through summer. Moss verbena is frequently grown as a summer annual in cold winter areas. Sandpaper verbena (*Verbena rigida*) has larger, rough leaves and purple flowers.

Shared Spaces

Moss verbena is an effortless ground cover for areas of the garden that receive intermittent or irregular watering. Plant generously to create an informal border, line a drive or walkway, or fill in gaps or barren spots in a newly planted garden. This species is useful for erosion control on rocky banks, although in low zones it is generally dormant and unsightly in the summer.

Cultivation

Water immediately, and then water every two to four days for the first month. Water established plants every ten days to two weeks when the plants are actively growing and blooming. No fertilizer is needed. Moss verbena is a vigorous reseeder in the garden, but plants do not transplant well, so keep the ones that come up where you like them and pull out the rest. Prune to reduce size or reinvigorate any time plants are actively growing. In low deserts, clean out dead plants and cut back rank growth in early fall.

Other Species and Cultivars

V. tenuisecta 'Edith' is a low (to 6 inches), spreading (4 to 5 feet) mound of fine-textured bright green foliage with bright lavender flower clusters covering the plant in spring. Short-lived in the hot low deserts. *Verbena* Summer Beauty™ is also short-lived, with velvety dark purple flowers year-round.

Prairie Zinnia
Zinnia grandiflora

ZONES: 7 through 11
FORM: Light, airy, open mounds
GROWTH AND MATURE SIZE: Evergreen ground cover, moderate to fast growing to 6 to 12 inches x 12 inches
USES: Mass ground cover, foreground, succulent gardens
SOIL: Extremely well-drained soil; tolerant of well-drained fertile soil if watering is minimal
PESTS: Root rot develops in poorly drained or too wet soils

Native from the Rocky Mountains south into Mexico, prairie zinnia is a low-growing, slightly mounded perennial that is a reliable, low-care choice for the intermediate and high desert zones. Fine, needlelike leaves give the short plants a light, airy appearance. Flowers have four or five yellow rays and raised golden disc flowers that are long-lived and prolific from spring through fall. Prairie zinnia can be difficult to grow and maintain as a perennial in the low desert with its intense summer heat, and hot, moist soils. It does better getting some afternoon shade in these regions. It is the perfect water-wise plant for borders and cottage, meadow, and prairie gardens.

Shared Spaces

In intermediate and high zones, this is a colorful but sturdy choice for erosion control. Plant close together to form a ground cover or plant in front of a large bed of ornamental grasses, native perennials, or shrubs. For a prairie garden, add dalea, blue grama grass, and asclepias. Prairie zinnia mixes well with succulents such as agaves, sedums, or yuccas. Prairie zinnia also does well in containers or planters as long as it is not overwatered.

Cultivation

Soil amendments are not necessary. It needs partial shade in low desert regions, full sun in other non-desert zones. It is slow to grow until summer sun and heat kick in, so be patient. Water immediately upon planting, then water every two to four days for the first month. Apply slow-release or organic fertilizer annually in spring. Water established plants sparingly. In all but the low desert zones, established plants need irrigation only during extended hot or dry spells. In low desert zones, water every two weeks in summer but be sure that the soil is very well drained. Overhead watering can cause mildew and rotting. In all zones, rely on natural rainfall in winter. Prune severely in early spring to remove dead leaves and debris.

Other Species and Cultivars

Desert zinnia (*Zinnia acerosa*) has light green foliage and white flowers that fade to a parchment-tan color as they age. It grows only one foot tall and a bit wider, and is hardy to Zone 6.

Silver Carpet
Dymondia margaretae

ZONES: 8 through 11
FORM: Dense, low-matting
GROWTH AND MATURE SIZE: Quick-growing evergreen ground cover to 1 to 3 inches x 18 to 24 inches
USES: Filler between pavers, walkable ground cover
SOIL: Well-drained soil
PESTS: None

Tough situations call for tough plants, and silver carpet is one of the toughest. This low-growing ground cover is an evergreen perennial member of the sunflower family and hails from South Africa. It grows flat against the ground in mats with 1- to 3-inch long leaves that look variegated. The leaves are actually deep green on top with curled-up edges that reveal silvery white and slightly fuzzy undersides. In summer, silver carpet produces yellow dandelion-like flowers, but this is not the gardener's main focus. Instead, it is silver carpet's ability to make a dense, drought-tolerant, walkable ground cover that takes the heat.

Shared Spaces

Silver carpet makes a dense mat between pavers, spills over boulders, and finishes the edges of dry gardens and informal pathways. It can also make a beautiful thick variegated lawn. Use silver carpet as living mulch instead of leaving bare ground.

Cultivation

Plants in a nursery flat may look to be all connected but they separate as you pull them out. Space 8 to 10 inches apart (closer for quicker fill). To plant between pavers, look for the largest joints. Soak well after planting. Water these shallow-rooted plants to keep roots moist through the first summer. Once established, let the soil dry out between waterings. Watch the plants to determine how often to water. Leaves on well-watered plants are nearly flat; leaves on severely water-stressed plants curl to the point of looking nearly white. Your goal is to be somewhere in-between. No fertilizer is needed. Silver carpet spreads quickly with regular water but does fine with very little water at all. No pruning is needed.

Other Species and Cultivars

For another very low-growing, very low-water ground cover, try woolly thyme (*Thymus pseudolanuginosus*); it's hardy to Zone 5. This dense creeping thyme has tiny green leaves covered in fine hairs that give the foliage a silvery sheen. Dense, 3-inch-tall mats occasionally sport pink flowers. *Chamaemelum nobile*, German chamomile, forms a dense mat 3 to 12 inches tall and releases an apple scent when walked upon. It takes full sun in coastal areas or part shade in inland and desert climates.

Silver Lace Vine
Fallopia baldschuanica

ZONES: 4 to 8
FORM: Rambling, climbing vine
GROWTH AND MATURE SIZE: Deciduous fast-growing vine to 25 to 40 feet x 20 feet or more
USES: Fences, screening, arbors, shade structures
SOIL: Well-drained soil
PESTS: None

Silver lace vine is a fast-growing, drought-tolerant perennial vine with stems cloaked in small, medium green leaves that are frosted with lacy, lightly scented flowers for most of the growing season. Silver lace vine is tolerant of a wide range of moisture, and its spread is controlled somewhat by limiting water. Even with minimal watering and severe pruning, 20 to 25 feet is probably the least amount of space the plant will cover. Most vines that are as twiggy as silver lace vine look rather ragged in winter, but the previous year's growth of silver lace vine turns golden-brown after frost, creating a finely wrought filigree draping the vine's supporting framework.

Shared Spaces

Its wiry stems twine around fencing or posts, scrambling to the tops of arbors and rambling across ramadas, fast cover for screening and shade. Since it reaches out and entwines anything within its path, it's best to keep other plants well away from its grasp; if it is growing on a fence, set foreground plants 5 or 6 feet away; on arbors or ramadas, let it fly solo.

Cultivation

Plant in loosened, unamended soil. Water vines set out in the heat of summer every few days initially, then once a week until fall. Water established plants every two weeks during the growing season. To keep plants more contained but vigorous, water to a depth of 30 inches once a month year-round if there is no rain or snowfall. This plant grows from the coast up to 9000 foot elevation where, at the limit of its range, grow it in the warmest, driest position available; once established, it needs no supplemental watering. No fertilizer is needed. Rejuvenate a mature plant by cutting it back nearly to the ground in early spring. Extreme pruning is required every few years or once in a decade.

Other Species and Cultivars

Knotweed, *Persicaria affinis*, is a ground cover kin of silver lace vine for gardens above 6000 feet and for Zones 3 through 8. Its wiry, 1-foot-tall stems are topped with 3-inch spikes of lacy rose-red flowers from midsummer to frost, and its foliage turns bronze with cold. *P. affinis* 'Dimity' is a dwarf cultivar growing to 6 to 8 inches x 12 to 24 inches.

Sundrops
Calylophus hartwegii

ZONES: 7 through 11
FORM: Low mounding
GROWTH AND MATURE SIZE: Fast-growing perennial ground cover to 1 foot x 3 feet
USES: Ground cover, understory, rock garden, succulent, dry perennial garden, foreground border
SOIL: Well-drained soil; poor soils are fine
PESTS: None

Sundrops are woody perennials with yellow flowers and fine-textured, dark green foliage that form dense mounds. The plant is native to the Southwest and northern Mexico. Like its more aggressive relative, the evening primrose, sundrops have four crinkled petals that form a slightly cupped flower with an interesting life cycle. Each flower opens as a lemon yellow color. By afternoon, the petals turn apricot pink. By evening, the flower is spent and fades away. Plants flower in spring and again in fall, often taking a break in the heat of summer. This is a tough plant that takes the heat with little water. In colder climates, foliage dies back in winter but sprouts again in spring.

Shared Spaces

Plant beneath Mediterranean climate shrubs such as rockrose and blue hibiscus or under trees such as granite bottlebrush (*Melaleuca elliptica*). Lavender and penstemon make good partners as well. Add to a rock garden to cascade over and between rocks. Plant sundrops in a container as a foil to colorful and sculptural succulents such as flapjack plant, shrubby candelabra aloe, or tall tree aloe. Plant yellow-flowered sundrops beneath red-flowering red yucca and blue-flowering, gray-leaved germander sage.

Cultivation

Water well after planting and mulch. For container planting, use a well-draining potting mix and mulch the surface. Water deeply to keep soil moist 6 inches deep through the first summer so plants become established. In subsequent years, sundrops do fine on a low-water diet, though occasional deep irrigation promotes more flowers. Unless winter rains are sparse, Mother Nature takes care of these plants. Fertilizer is not necessary but can be applied to hasten growth in early spring. Sundrops spread by underground roots and need no pruning, but branches can be trimmed back in early spring if plants get too large, too woody, or suffer frost damage.

Other Species and Cultivars

If you prefer gray-green foliage to deep green, plant lavender leaf primrose (*Calylophus lavandulifolius*). Texas primrose (*Calylophus drummondianus*) is another *Calylophus* offered by nurseries. This native Texan species lies flat to the ground and spreads 2 feet across. Leaves are narrower than sundrops' and are bright green.

Sunrose
Helianthemum nummularium

ZONES: 4 through 11
FORM: Low profile mounds
GROWTH AND MATURE SIZE: Fairly quick-growing evergreen ground cover to 6 to 8 inches x 24 to 36 inches
USES: Borders, rock gardens, slopes, low ground cover, foreground
SOIL: Well-drained soil; will rot in poorly draining soils
PESTS: None

Sunrose is a tiny evergreen shrub related to rockrose but it grows no more than 8 inches high. These Mediterranean natives make round patches, 2 to 3 feet across, with small gray, green, or gray-green leaves. In spring and sometimes again in fall, dozens of tiny rose-shaped flowers float just inches above the foliage. Flowers are singles or doubles and come in shades of red to burgundy, apricot to copper, pink to rose, yellow, and even white. Each flower lasts just a day or so, but there are so many and they open over such a long time that the bloom period lasts three months or longer.

Shared Spaces
Grow sunrose next to their cousin blue chalk sticks, Jerusalem sage, ornamental grasses like blue fescue, and kangaroo paw. Combine with taller plants including shoestring acacia (it casts only light shade) and grevillea. Tiny rockrose flowers are best viewed at eye level, cascading over the edge of a pot or rock wall or on a slope.

Cultivation
Space sunrose 2 feet apart. Water deeply after planting and mulch. To grow in containers, use a well-draining planting mix and mulch with gravel. Water to keep the root zone moist through the first summer so plants can become established. After that, cut back so the soil dries several inches down between waterings. It will take some experimentation to find the right watering frequency. Take care not to overwater, or plants will rot. Fertilizer is not necessary if plants are well mulched. Deadhead as flowers fade. After spring bloom, shear lightly to encourage a repeat bloom.

Other Species and Cultivars
Sunrose flowers come in an amazing color range. 'Wisley Pink' grows quickly to 2 feet x 3 feet, with 1-inch pink flowers with gold centers; 'Rose Glory' is a small mound growing to 6 inches tall and 18 inches wide, with rose-pink blooms; 'Ben More' is diminutive at 4 inches x 15 inches with deep orange blooms; 'Single Yellow' grows 6 to 9 inches x 18 inches, hardy in Zones 4 through 9. It has bright yellow blooms.

Trailing Indigo Bush
Dalea greggii

ZONES: 8 through 11
FORM: Low growing
GROWTH AND MATURE SIZE: Moderate-growing perennial ground cover to 1 to 2 feet x 2 to 4 feet
USES: Slope stabilizer, ground cover, border
SOIL: Tolerant of a wide range of soils including well-drained, fertile soil, and rocky, native soil
PESTS: None

Trailing indigo bush is an attractive, low-growing perennial with tiny, soft, gray leaves. Although solitary plants provide soft color contrast to bright perennial plantings, this species is most often called upon to serve as a ground cover. Numerous fine stems on each plant cascade from the center and root along the ground as they grow. Over a short time, these rooted stems create a dense cover, and if the plants are spaced closely enough, they completely cover the surface of the soil. Lustrous, deep purple flowers cover the plant in spring. *Dalea capitata* has minute, deep green leaves and yellow flowers through spring and summer.

Shared Spaces

Trailing indigo bush is an excellent choice to stabilize slopes or control erosion. Plant closely together to form a continuous ground cover for large, hot areas. This species also works well as an informal hedge or border, along drives or walkways, or against walls or buildings where reflected heat is intense. The soft silvery foliage provides a backdrop or serves as a contrast plant in beds of colorful perennials or succulent gardens.

Cultivation

To use as a ground cover, space plants about 3 feet apart. Soil amendments are not necessary. Water immediately following planting, then water every two to four days for the first month. Water established plants every two to three weeks in summer, and less in winter if there is no rain or snowfall. It may take up to two years for plants to become fully established. Apply slow-release or organic fertilizer annually in fall to young plants; established plants need no fertilizer. Prune in early spring to maintain form and to remove dead or damaged stems. Do not shear. Remove rooted stem sections to reduce size. Old plants frequently die out in the middle, especially when they have been overwatered or were grown in the shade.

Other Species and Cultivars

D. purpureum, purple prairie clover, spreads to 18 inches x 18 inches and is a heavy bloomer covered with intensely red-violet flowers on stiff upright stems. Hardy in Zones 3 through 9.

Trailing Lantana
Lantana montevidensis

ZONES: 9 through 11

FORM: Wide spreading, trailing, and mounding

GROWTH AND MATURE SIZE: Moderate-growing evergreen ground cover to 1 to 2 feet x 2 to 6 feet

USES: Slopes, ground cover, borders, focal point, color beds, drifts

SOIL: Tolerant of almost any soil from well-drained, fertile soil to rocky, native soil and even heavy clay

PESTS: Whiteflies in late summer; spray with insecticidal soap

This reliable South American native is immune to heat, tolerates almost any soil condition, and is remarkably drought-tolerant once established. Trailing lantana has a delicacy that is completely at odds with its toughness, and it is one of the most effective ground covers for softening a hot location. It has small, lance-shaped, dark green leaves and small heads of purple or white flowers. 'Lavender Swirl' has both purple and white flowers on one plant. The numerous hybrids between this species and the shrubby *Lantana camara* come in a bewildering array of colors and sizes. Hybrids 'New Gold' and 'Gold Trailing' are widely used.

Shared Spaces

Plant closely to provide a continuous ground cover. Plant trailing lantana under large shrubs such as red bird of paradise (*Caesalpinia*), or yellowbells (*Tecoma*). Create an informal border around patios, pools, or areas where reflected heat is intense. Trailing lantana is also useful to stabilize a slope or as erosion control. This lantana grows well in containers or hanging baskets, either alone or mixed with other winter-flowering perennials.

Cultivation

Water immediately following planting, then water every two to four days for the first month. Water established plants weekly in summer, monthly in winter if no rainfall. Monitor watering carefully in late summer; plants usually need less water when the humidity is higher. Apply slow-release or organic fertilizer in spring and once during the growing season. Leaves may yellow between the veins when plants are overwatered. Plants are less vigorous in winter, although they rarely lose all their leaves. Prune in early spring to remove frost-damaged stems, or to reinvigorate the plant. Trailing lantana may be lightly pruned through summer to maintain a desired size.

Other Species and Cultivars

These cultivars spread to 2 to 3 feet x 6 to 8 feet and offer continuous bloom in frost-free areas: 'Sunset'™ with red-orange blooms; 'Sunshine' with bright yellow blooms; 'Tangerine' with tangerine blooms. 'White Lightnin' grows to 8 to 12 inches and spreads up to 6 feet. It has clear white blooms.

Trumpet Vine
Campsis radicans

ZONES: 5 through 8
FORM: Full-trailing and climbing
GROWTH AND MATURE SIZE: Moderate- to fast-growing deciduous vines to 25 to 40 feet x 25 to 40 feet
USES: Screen, pergola, arbor, archway, slopes
SOIL: Any well-drained soil
PESTS: Ants will travel to harvest nectar from the flowers, so site the plant away from spots where people gather

Large clusters of brilliant orange tubular flowers cascade from a lush green foliage backdrop. During the growing season, hummingbirds and orioles sip its nectar daily. But this vine becomes a force to contend with, especially in enriched, well-watered garden soil, because it rootsprouts and self-sows unless efforts are made to control it. Poor soils, heat, and aridity are an asset in managing its rampant growth. Even when treated carelessly, trumpet vine becomes a very large plant in need of sturdy support and ample space as it matures. It adheres to posts, fences, and walls by aerial roots. Give it plenty of room and it will reward you with almost continuous blooms all season long.

Shared Spaces

The most handsomely displayed plants are those growing on huge roughhewn timber posts, on crossbeam driveway-entrance archways, and on telephone poles—all of which make adequate stakes. Trumpet vine quickly covers fencing and shade arbors. Used for erosion control on slopes, especially above retaining walls where it can cascade over the edge of the wall. The orange flowers are a striking contrast for *Buddleja* or chaste tree in summer. A heavily mulched companion grouping one of gray-leaved *Artemisia* species for contrast provides interest when the vine is dormant.

Cultivation

Plant in fall in frost-free areas, early spring elsewhere. Add no amendments, but loosen the soil well. Mulch with 4 to 6 inches of shredded bark or compost. Landscape fabric, when used under deep mulch, suppresses most rootsprouting. To promote growth, water plants to a depth of 30 inches twice a month when leafy, and monthly while dormant. To limit growth and maintain vigor, water monthly year-round if there is no rain or snowfall. In alkaline soils, apply a granular iron-and-sulfur fertilizer each spring to prevent yellowing foliage in summer. While dormant, prune to several main stems, and elminate many of the smaller lateral branches.

Other Species and Cultivars

Balboa Sunset® has dark red blooms. *C. x tagliabuana* 'Madame Galen' has salmon-red blooms. 'Flava' is a selection with bright yellow flowers.

Vinca
Vinca minor

ZONES: 4 through 11

FORM: Full-trailing

GROWTH AND MATURE SIZE: Evergreen ground cover growing moderately to 6 inches x 12 inches

USES: Shade ground cover, slopes, understory planting

SOIL: Adapts to most soils, but establishes faster and requires less water over the long term if compost is added to the soil before planting

PESTS: Water conservatively, rarely mow, and mulch to discourage slugs

As a low-maintenance, evergreen ground cover for shade, vinca occupies a niche in the garden palette shared by few other plants. Small, dark green leaves on slender stems form a dense evergreen carpet punctuated with clear blue flowers in early spring. In the Desert Southwest, vinca is best used in wind-protected areas where year-round appearance is important. *Vinca minor* 'Bowles' has larger flowers. *Vinca major* is a coarse, sprawling, sometimes deciduous kin of vinca. It requires close cropping every winter to keep it from building up a mass of dead growth under the current season's greenery. Some have white leaf margins, but variegated foliage takes a beating in the desert, even when the plant is grown in wind-protected shade.

Shared Spaces

Its best use is as a ground cover under shade trees in walled courtyards. Underplanting with dwarf daffodils or weaving a ribbon of woolly lamb's ears through a bed of vinca makes it more seasonally interesting.

Cultivation

Till 1 cubic yard of compost per 80 square feet of bed area into the planting space. To cover an area quickly, space plants 12 to 18 inches apart. Mulch with compost, shredded bark, or pecan hulls to keep the soil cooler and uniformly moist, to prevent frost-heaving in cold weather, and to suppress weeds until the vinca is thick enough to resist invasion. Once well established, water weekly when temperatures are above 90 degrees F, every two weeks in spring and fall, and monthly in winter. Let water soak in slowly to a depth of 18 inches. Mow vinca every three or four years in late winter to rejuvenate a mature planting. Mulch can be renewed and slow-release fertilizer added at the same time.

Other Species and Cultivars

Vinca may be considered invasive in California. Blue is a cooling color, welcome in our hot climate, and the larger flowers of 'Bowles' periwinkle show up well even in deep shade. *V. minor* 'Atropurpurea' grows 6 inches x 2 to 3 feet and has rich burgundy blooms. 'Green Carpet' vinca is just inches high, spreading to 3 feet. It has glossy dense foliage with smaller light blue blooms.

Yerba Mansa
Anemopsis californica

ZONES: 4 through 8
FORM: Thick, lush foliage forming dense mats
GROWTH AND MATURE SIZE: Moderate- to fast-growing deciduous ground cover to 6 to 12 inches x 4 feet
USES: Shade ground cover, understory, slopes, drainage swales
SOIL: Clay or silty soils require no amendment; add compost to sandy soils.
PESTS: In deep shade, rust sometimes develops; infections are superficial and don't weaken plants

Yerba mansa leaves are rubbery green, 2 inches wide and 6 inches long, in rosettes that lie flat in bright sunlight or upright when in shade. Plants become so densely clustered above the mat of rhizomes and pencil-thick deep roots that even the formidable bindweed cedes ground to yerba. Still, it won't extend relentlessly beyond its desired limits; it doesn't self-sow aggressively, and dry soil controls its spread. The flowers are pure white flowers borne on slender, nearly leafless, 12-inch stems. The petals droop like a scalloped skirt from the elongated central cone. The foliage turns red in autumn and dries to deep rust. The leaves produce a fresh astringent aroma when stepped on.

Shared Spaces
Yerba mansa is native to low-lying areas, roadside swales, and under cottonwoods along major rivers from New Mexico to California. It absorbs excess water, suppresses weeds, and prevents erosion when grown as ground cover in runoff basins below canales and roof gutters. As a ground cover under deciduous trees, it grows thick and lush without depleting the nutrients from the soil, nor competing aggressively for available water.

Cultivation
Space plants 2 to 4 feet apart for coverage in one or two seasons. When planting in areas that flood periodically, use coarse gravel as a mulch. In other areas, use organic mulch until the plants fill in. Plants growing in full sun need watering more frequently than those growing in shade. Until plants start sending out stolons, water weekly to 18 inches deep; then water to 2 feet once or twice a month. Plants established in water catchments may not need supplemental watering. No fertilizer is needed, but broadcasting granular fertilizer to supplement companion trees has no adverse effect. Mow with a mulching mower or string trimmer in winter, leaving the shredded stems and leaves as mulch. Or leave the plant alone and rake the brittle leaves and stems at winter's end.

Other Species and Cultivars
It's hard to beat the species. Because it adapts both to intense sun and deep shade, it can be planted when trees are young and thrives as their canopies expand.

Perennials

If you are paying attention, plants will tell you when spring is on the rise. Perennials in particular are good forecasters, letting you know that winter will indeed end, and soon you will be digging in the soil once more. It is always a pleasant surprise to find those first tufts of green sprouting out from the bases of the plants, the sign that the perennials are waking up from their long winter sleep.

Perennials are plants that live year after year Some are short lived in plant years, living three years at the least, while some are as long-lived as any shrub. Water-wise perennials are generally undemanding. They don't require much in the way of care or attention. Pests don't generally bother them. They grow through the year, slowing down a bit in summer if they come from California or other regions where summers are hot and dry. Come fall, they come back to life, often with new growth and new bloom. In colder climates, perennials tend to go through a dormant period, leaf out, flower, then slowly drop their foliage or hold onto the last blooms until the first frost puts them back asleep until spring.

In colder areas of the Southwest, springtime brings us early garden greeters such as prince's plume (*Stanleya*), with its lush foliage and brilliant yellow flowers; western mugwort (*Artemisia*), a big sage-like plant with silvery gray-green foliage; drifts of apricot flowered globemallow (*Sphaeralcea*), and the blue-gray foliage of penstemons. California natives such as yarrow (*Achillea*) serve as a ground covers, covering beds of springtime bulbs. This is when firewheel (*Gaillardia*) can be planted into pockets in rock walls while all sorts of geraniums (*Pelargonium*) emerge from their winter greenhouse vacations to fill entryway beds in spring.

Designing with perennials is a true delight. Use perennials to accent a border, to serve as a backdrop for annuals, to highlight succulents, or as temporary fillers among young shrubs and trees.

Plant smaller perennials in drifts that weave in and out among meadow and native grasses. The larger perennials can serve as a focal point in a color garden with smaller perennials, bulbs, grasses, and annuals all around. Plant native species amid rocks that line a dry streambed.

Always plant perennials in odd number groupings, threes, fives, and so on. Repeat species and combinations throughout the garden for continuity and flow. As you grow to love perennials in your garden beds, experiment with them in containers as well. Grow them as individual plants, or in combination with taller shrubs, spiky grasses, and cascading succulents.

While many perennials are tough enough to withstand the hot, hot sun, some prefer the dappled shade of redbuds or other trees, especially in our hottest desert areas. If you plant a perennial in the wrong spot, don't hesitate to dig it up and move it to a more fitting spot.

As you read about water-wise perennials, realize that what we present is a small sample of what is available. There are seemingly endless colors, textures, sizes, and forms to choose from. Try a few, plant a lot, and then grow some more. There's always room in the garden for another perennial!

Agastache
Agastache species

ZONES: 4 through 11

FORM: Full sprawling mounds with arching long stems

GROWTH AND MATURE SIZE: Moderate-growing perennial to 2 to 3 feet x 2 to 3 feet

USES: Scent garden, border, focal point, foreground, drift

SOIL: Prefers well-drained, unamended soil; also grows well in amended soils

PESTS: Root rot in wet, heavy soil

Agastache species are unlike most mints both in their self-contained growth habit and in their heat and drought tolerance. They don't rootsprout to swallow up great gulps of garden space, yet a single perennial clump can cover four to six square feet in one long growing season. Licorice mint (*A. rupestris*) is the most drought and heat loving. Its narrow, silky, anise-scented, silver-green leaves are topped with arching wands of soft coral flowers. Giant hyssop, *Agastache cana,* has whorls of vivid rose-pink flowers with the unexpected scent of bubblegum! Agastache blooms from midsummer to frost; the color and fragrance are among the best wildflower shows.

Shared Spaces

Agastache flower wands often fall over so plant them midborder, behind a structural plant that will support the leaning branches. Combine with Russian sage, pitcher sage, 'Moonshine' yarrow, dwarf butterfly bush, lavender, Texas sage, and Apache plume. Place them out of the traffic flow, but where their scent perfumes the surroundings including children's play spaces, patios, and benches.

Cultivation

Handle plants carefully, as stems are brittle and break easily. Space 2 to 3 feet apart. Apply mulch with three inches of compost or fine gravel. Water regularly in well-draining soils. Water once a week to 2 feet deep when plants are flowering or temperatures are 85 F or above, every two weeks when temperatures are 65 to 85 F, and monthly or less during cooler weather or if rainfall occurs. In temperate zones, water when soil dries out. In spring, apply a small amount of slow-release fertilizer to support heavy blooming. Use a granular iron-and-sulfur fertilizer if leaves yellow in summer's heat. Deadhead frosted plants down to new growth in spring.

Other Species and Cultivars

'Desert Sunrise' is a hybrid hummingbird mint growing to 4 to 5 feet x 2 feet. Large, scented flower spikes in bright pink fading to orange rise above the minty foliage. 'Acapulco Orange' is compact, growing to 16 inches x 18 inches. A. 'Blue Fortune' grows to 36 inches x 18 inches with large green leaves having silver undersides, and 5-inch-long powder blue blooms.

Autumn Sage
Salvia greggii

ZONES: All zones
FORM: Vase-shaped shrub with open branching and tall upright flower stalks late spring through summer
GROWTH AND MATURE SIZE: Fairly fast-growing perennial to 2 to 3 feet x 3 to 4 feet
USES: Perennial beds, borders, midground with annuals, mass, focal point
SOIL: Well-drained, fertile soil
PESTS: None

Popular in gardens throughout the Southwest, autumn sage is poorly named as it actually blooms from late spring through summer. The short, semiwoody brittle stems are thinly covered with smooth, deep green leaves. Flowers are tubular, with a prominent lower lip, and are incredibly variable in size and color. The most common colors are rose, magenta, and red. 'Furman's Red' has profuse, dark red flowers with a hint of purple. 'Purple Haze' has small, deep violet flowers, and 'Cherry Red' is a bright clear red. 'Desert Red', with its oversized, velvet red flowers, is one of the most striking hybrids. 'Sierra de San Antonio' and 'Hot Lips' are very popular varieties in California.

Shared Spaces

Mix autumn sage with other perennials such as lantana, justicia, Russian sage, and dwarf plumbago. Use autumn sage as the background for low annuals. Plant generously to create informal borders, or to create a mass planting. Use near patios, seating areas, and pools, or in large containers and planters. Because branches are brittle, keep the plants well away from edges and walkways. Hummingbirds adore autumn sage; site plants where you can enjoy these visitors.

Cultivation

Water thoroughly at planting, then every two to four days for two to three weeks. Water every four to seven days until established. Mulch roots during the growing season to keep the soil from drying out. In low desert, water every four to six days in summer, every seven o ten days in winter. In cooler climes, water weekly in summer, every three to four weeks in winter. Prune severely in early spring to remove damaged stems and reinvigorate the plant. Keep spent flowering stalks cut—it encourages continued flowering.

Other Species and Cultivars

S. greggii 'Rachel' is a unique, white-flowering cultivar with variegated gold on green foliage. Growing to a modest 2 feet tall and wide, it was named after a friend of Texas plantsman Greg Grant, who, he says, is also blond, odd, and gorgeous. *S. greggii* Sierra Linda™ is a clone that is more heat tolerant. It forms a 3-foot-round mound and blooms profusely with small hot pink flowers.

Bear's Breech
Acanthus mollis

ZONES: 7 through 11
FORM: Arching large leaves in a rosette with tall stems (to 6 feet) and spring blooms
GROWTH AND MATURE SIZE: Fast-growing summer dormant perennial to 4 to 5 feet x 4 to 5 feet
USES: Focal point, border, understory
SOIL: Prefers moist, well-amended, well-draining soil; adapts to most soils
PESTS: Protect from snails and slugs

Bear's breech is a classic Mediterranean perennial with deep green arching leaves 2 to 3 feet long and 1 foot or more wide, arranged in a rosette. The leaves are deeply sculpted and tipped in soft spines. In spring, bear's breech sends up columnar flower stems 5 to 6 feet tall and lined with blooms. Each flower has olive-gold stamens sandwiched between a canopy-like dusty purple bract above and a white petal below. Plants go dormant briefly if they're not irrigated. Bear's breech leaf is the classic leaf design motif used since ancient times. Greek artisans, Renaissance weavers, and Victorians incorporated the design into their fine and decorative arts.

Shared Spaces
Use bear's breech as a specimen plant or mass plant them in a wide border. For a rich green look, combine with bay laurel, iris, hellebore, shrub fuchsia, and camellia. Plant bear's breech at the base of a tall crapemyrtle or grow masses of them beneath an oak grove. Bear's breech makes a bold statement when planted in a white garden.

Cultivation
Allow enough space for the plant's ultimate expanse. Water well and mulch with a thick layer of organic compost after planting. Bear's breech can be container grown as well. A large pot will accommodate its size. If it's grown on a low-water diet, bear's breech leaves die back in the heat of summer and then return when the weather cools. For year-round greenery, irrigate through summer, but be aware that in a well-irrigated garden, beer's breech multiplies. Use a balanced organic fertilizer monthly through the growing season. Groom to remove spent flower stalks and leaves.

Other Species and Cultivars
A. 'Summer Beauty' has nearly white blooms. 'Tasmanian Angel' (3 feet x 3 feet), variegated bear's breech, has deep green leaves mottled with white and with white margins. Pink and cream flowers line a 3-foot stalk. 'Oak Leaf ' (4 feet x 4 feet) has large oak leaf-shaped leaves. *Acanthus spinosus* is somewhat smaller with more deeply lobed and spinier leaves.

Blanket Flower
Gaillardia aristata

ZONES: All zones
FORM: Low mound with blooms above the foliage year-round
GROWTH AND MATURE SIZE: Fast-growing perennial to 1 to 2 feet x 1 to 2 feet
USES: Border, sweep, mass,
SOIL: Well-drained fertile soil
PESTS: None

This low-growing perennial is almost never out of bloom. Even when one of these short-lived plants dies out, there is always a seedling ready to take its place. The flowers are stunning, up to 4 inches across with petal-like rays that range from pure yellow to yellow banded with reddish brown and all blends in between. Flower centers are dark and can be flat or gently rounded. Plants are low and sprawling and if left to spread would form a ground cover. *Gaillardia* x *grandiflora* is a hybrid between this species and the annual *G. pulchella* and has produced many cultivars including the compact 'Goblin' group.

Shared Spaces

Mix blanket flower with summer-flowering perennials and shrubs such as salvias, lantana, yellowbells, or flame anisacanthus. Set plants closely together to create a big show or for an informal ground cover. Plant to fill in barren spots in newly planted beds, or to fill a difficult corner. Blanket flower blends well in annual or wildflower plantings and grows well in a large container or planter.

Cultivation

Start seeds in fall in mildest climates, early spring in colder climates. To seed a bed, broadcast seed evenly and rake to cover lightly. Keep soil moist until seedlings appear. Water seedlings gently every three to five days until they have five leaves. With spring transplants, mulch lightly and water thoroughly after planting. Water when soil is dry an inch down until plants are established. Add slow-release or organic fertilizer annually in spring. Water established plants every one to two weeks in summer. In winter, water every ten to fourteen days in deserts, and when rains are sparse elsewhere. Prune plants back to the basal leaves in early spring. Divide in spring every two or three years. Remove spent flowers.

Other Species and Cultivars

Gaillardia 'Tizzy' is fuller, with striking scarlet blooms in early spring that turn orange in fall. 'Georgia Sunset' has pink blooms tipped in gold and orange; 'Georgia Yellow' is a long bloomer in sunny yellow. *G. grandiflora* 'Arizona Sun' has 3-inch blooms in mahogany-red with bright yellow edges. Another common name of blanket flower is firewheel.

Brittlebush
Encelia farinosa

ZONES: 7 through 11
FORM: Rounded, compact covered with blooms above the foliage from November to May
GROWTH AND MATURE SIZE: Fast-growing evergreen perennial to 3 to 4 feet x 3 to 4 feet
USES: Native, succulent gardens, mass, border
SOIL: Grows especially well in rocky, native soil
PESTS: None

On rocky slopes in the Southwest, entire hillsides erupt in spring with the bright yellow flowers of brittlebush. The 3-foot-tall plants have gray-green leaves that form in clusters up the stems. They are coated with a thick mat of tiny, soft white hairs. As plants become water-stressed, the leaves become whiter. Flowers are yellow discs with bright yellow rays, which are held on branched stalks high above the foliage. Brittlebush is an outstanding addition to all Southwest gardens regardless of their style. Plants need only minimal care to look their best and grow beautifully on rainfall or with minimal irrigation during extended dry spells.

Shared Spaces

Brittlebush mixes well with other desert perennials such as ruellia, globemallow, and penstemons. Bright yellow flowers and crisp, white foliage are particularly effective with the green leaves and blue to purple flowers of dalea and Texas ranger. Plant in groups or in mass to fill barren spots or use in areas of the garden that receive minimal care. Mix with succulents such as ocotillo, desert spoon, and agaves for a naturalistic look. Plant anywhere that reflected heat is intense.

Cultivation

Water thoroughly after planting. Water every two to four days for two to three weeks, then every four to seven days for the first summer. Water weekly in fall and spring if there are no rains, but reduce watering to once a month in the following summer. Water sparingly in winter, and monthly if the weather is particularly hot or dry. No soil amendments are needed. Prune plants severely in fall to remove summer-damaged stems and to reinvigorate. Remove spent, blooming stalks anytime during the growing season. Although many desert bees and insects use the plants as a gathering spot, they rarely cause harm.

Other Species and Cultivars

E. actoni, mountain bush sunflower, grows 3 to 4 feet x 3 to 4 feet and has larger yellow daisylike flowers. *E. californica* grows 3 to 4 feet tall and wide, has 2-inch yellow daisylike blooms, and tolerates clay soil but is not frost tolerant.

Dianthus
Dianthus species

ZONES: 4 through 8
FORM: Small spawling mounds with blooms above the foliage
GROWTH AND MATURE SIZE: Fast-growing perennial to 6 inches x 18 inches
USES: Border, drifts, rock gardens, mass
SOIL: Well-drained soil
PESTS: None

Dianthus species belong to the "color-per-square-foot" school of plant breeding; sheets of flowers obscure the foliage. In colder climates, they die back in winter, but are among the first perennials to bloom in spring. *Dianthus gratianopolitanus* 'Tiny Rubies' and 'Firewitch' form 12- to 18-inch cushions of pale blue-gray leaves and clove-scented, double rose-pink flowers on 4- to 8-inch stems. *Dianthus deltoides* cultivars may be short-lived at lower elevations, but they are worth replacing every three or four years. Dense mounds of narrow green, blue, or gray leaves set the stage for the mass of dark rose to purple flowers.

Shared Spaces
Used as edging for perennial borders, walkways, patios, and in rock gardens, *D. deltoides* cultivars are so intensely colorful that even when planted in the background, they still draw attention. Artemisia or woolly thyme make good companions for the brazen *D. deltoides*. *Dianthus* x *gratianopolitanus* is more subtle and begs a place in the foreground where its fine flowers and foliage, as well as its clovelike fragrance, can be appreciated.

Cultivation
Before transplanting dianthus, add 1 cubic yard of compost per 100 square feet of bed area. Space plants 12 to 18 inches apart. Topdress with organic mulch or fine gravel. Water dianthus to a depth of 18 inches once a week when temperatures are 85 F or above; water every two weeks when temperatures are 65 to 85 F, and monthly during cooler weather, but not at all if the plants are dormant. Fertilizing is usually not necessary if the soil is organically amended. Apply an iron-and-sulfur fertilizer if foliage yellows in summer. Trim off spent flowers to stimulate continuous blooming. Trim the cushion of foliage down a few inches from the soil in spring.

Other Species and Cultivars
Pineleaf garden pink, *D. pinifolius*, has clusters of deep red flowers drifting nearly 2 feet above the ground on slender stems. It grows quite happily in relatively dry soil in full sun in gardens up to 7000 feet in elevation. 'WP Passion' has dark-red blooms. Hardy in Zones 6 through 11.

Gaura
Gaura lindheimeri

ZONES: 5 through 11
FORM: Open, airy with delicate stems covered with blooms in late spring
GROWTH AND MATURE SIZE: Slow-growing perennial to 2 to 4 feet x 2 to 3 feet
USES: Border, mass, drifts
SOIL: Well-drained, fertile, or rocky native soil
PESTS: None; short-lived if grown in too rich soils or in full sun in low desert

Gaura have deep green basal leaves tinged with maroon or red. In late spring, long, branched blooming stalks rise from the center. Small, starlike white flowers emerge from pink buds and bloom through summer. The stalks are so airy and the flowers so delicate that the effect is of a cloud floating over the garden. As flowers fade, they return to a pale, ethereal pink. 'Siskiyou Pink' has dark pink buds with flowers that open white but quickly change to pink for the rest of the season. The flowers of 'Whirling Butterflies' are white throughout the blooming season.

Shared Spaces
Plant in groups for best effect; solitary plants often fail to show up in mixed plantings. Plant to form a low border, line walkways or drives, or as a filler for barren spots in a newly planted garden. Gaura combines well with spring-flowering bulbs and perennials such as Angelita daisy and verbena, or against a dark green hedge to highlight its delicate flowers.

Cultivation
Plant in fall in mild climate gardens, in spring in colder areas. Water thoroughly after planting. Water every two to four days for two to three weeks, then every four to seven days until established in desert areas. Mulch roots well in summer. In the low desert, water weekly in summer, more often if temperatures are extreme. Water every month or two in winter if plants are dormant. In other areas, water every ten to fourteen days in summer and rely on natural rainfall in winter. Fertilize with restraint; too much feeding fertilizer shortens the plant's life. Prune in spring to remove winter damage, reduce size, and reinvigorate. Prune spent flowering stalks anytime.

Other Species and Cultivars
'Cloud of Butterflies' grows 24 to 30 inches tall and wide and has a summer-long cloud of tiny white flowers. Gaura 'Pink Cloud' grows narrower and is covered with hundreds of deep pink blooms on 4-foot-long willowy stems. 'Crimson Butterflies' is a compact form reaching 2 feet tall. Young leaves and stems are burgundy red in beautiful contrast with the dark pink flowers.

Gayfeather
Liatris punctata

ZONES: 3 to 11

FORM: Clumping and sprawling with maturity with tall flower spikes in midsummer

GROWTH AND MATURE SIZE: Slow-growing perennial to 24 inches x 30 inches

USES: Border, prairie and meadows, sweeps, mass

SOIL: Well-drained, lean soils

PESTS: Pocket gophers decimate a planting; plant in wire gopher exclusion baskets or trap gophers

Native gayfeather starts the season looking very much like a clump of coarse green grass. Leafy flower stems emerge from the basal foliage in midsummer. After three or four growing seasons, a single plant will have perhaps two dozen flower spikes; in six years, twice that many. Bloom time is short, typically three weeks in late summer. Neighbors will ring your doorbell, asking about this glorious plant. *L. spicata* 'Kobold' grows 2 to 3 feet tall with rose-purple flower spikes. 'Floristan' is either violet or white. *Liatris pycnostachya* has 3- to 4-foot stems with rose-purple flowers. All three of the these selections bloom in midsummer, requiring more water than the native species.

Shared Spaces

Fine-textured leaves and stunning blooms give this plant a controlled look in manicured water-wise perennial borders with artemisias, Jerusalem sage, and turpentine bush. It is equally at home among the prairie grasses, adding color to a sweep of grama and little bluestem, or woven like a ribbon through plantings of sand lovegrass or blue oat grass.

Cultivation

Gayfeather has the best form when it is grown in with modest water. While it survives to Zone 11, it is most vigorous in Zones 7 and cooler. It is cold hardy to at least 8000 feet in elevation if the soil is well drained. Space several plants 2 to 4 feet apart. Loosen the soil deeply. Water to a depth of at least 2 feet every two or three weeks when temperatures are 85 F and above and if the soil is well drained; water monthly or less in winter if there are no rains. Fertilizing causes flower stems to grow too tall and soft. Unlike most flowers, it's best to cut back the water when the flower stems begin to lengthen so that stems don't sprawl. Trim off the seedheads when they start to look weathered, before seed scatters to limit self-sowing, or after birds have harvested the seeds if the garden is also a habitat.

Other Species and Cultivars

The native species, *Liatris punctata*, is the best gayfeather for New Mexico gardens.

Globemallow
Sphaeralcea species

ZONES: 5 through 11
FORM: Mounding with thin flower stems covered in blooms in spring and late summer
GROWTH AND MATURE SIZE: Fast-growing woody to 30 inches x 30 inches
USES: Borders, perennial garden, understory, sweeps
SOIL: Well-drained sandy or gravelly soil
PESTS: Susceptible to rust if grown in wetter conditions

More than a dozen species of globemallow brighten the Southwest in spring and late summer. The species that make good garden plants are those with the longest and most intense bloom times, the most refined foliage, and most compact forms. Desert globemallow (*Sphaeralcea ambigua*) starts to bloom in January at the coast, in February in the low desert, March at 6000 feet, and so on. It forms a 24- by 30-inch mound; has small, pale green leaves; and spikes of watermelon or cantaloupe-colored flowers for several months. Gooseberry leaf globemallow (*S. grossulariaefolia*), has 30-inch stems covered in orange-sherbet flowers that resemble hollyhocks.

Shared Spaces

Globemallows blend well with catmint, Mexican blue sage, Rocky Mountain penstemon, and torch lily in spring or Russian sage, turpentine bush, and pitcher sage in autumn. Grouped between Mexican elder or fragrant ash, their color adds dash to the more subtle tones of their companions. They can compete with grasses planted as low-maintenance ground covers. Globemallows give focus to vast sweeps of prairie grasses.

Cultivation

Plant in late summer or autumn, taking care not to overwater plants when the weather turns cold and rainy. Water to a depth of 2 feet every week or two when temperatures are above 85 F, every two or three weeks when temperatures are 65 to 85 F, and monthly or less during cooler weather or if there is rain or snowfall. No fertilizer is needed. To prolong bloom time, trim off the spent flower stems. Plants may self-sow some if seeds are left to ripen.

Other Species and Cultivars

S. ambigua Papago Pink™ grows 3 feet x 3 to 4 feet with extremely large pink blossoms. Munro's globemallow, *S. munroana*, grows 3 feet x 2 feet in Zones 4 through 10. It has deep orange to tangerine flowers. Scarlet globemallow, *S. coccinea*, has flowers in a soft creamsickle orange, is smaller at only 8 inches tall, but can rootsprout and form colonies 30 inches across. The flowers are only part of the value, as the soft green lacy foliage makes a lovely filler in all but the coldest winter months. *S.* 'Louis Hamilton' has amazing grenadine-coral flowers.

Greek Germander
Teucrium aroanium

ZONES: 5 to 10
FORM: Dense low mat covered with close-lying blooms in early spring, repeating through frost
GROWTH AND MATURE SIZE: Moderately-growing evergreen perennial to 4 to 6 inches x 24 inches
USES: Rock garden, ground cover, filler between pavers, low borders
SOIL: Well-drained soil, prefers gritty, unamended soil
PESTS: None

This Mediterranean native forms a dense mat of silver foliage on slender, prostrate stems. The soft, ever-gray leaves have the scent of sweet thyme. In May or June the first flush of dime-sized clusters of brilliant rose-pink flowers nearly hide the foliage. If deadheaded, Greek germander blooms repeatedly until frost. It could be considered a ground cover, but it isn't aggressive enough to overwhelm less vigorous companions. Greek germander grows best in Zones 5 through 11 in the gritty, calcium-rich soils similar to the rocky hillsides of its origins. It adapts to Southwestern sandy loams and decomposed granite, but sulks when it's planted in heavy clay.

Shared Spaces

Tuck it into rock gardens and between paving stones, or plant it in borders along walkways and patios. It is cold-, heat-, and drought-tolerant enough to drape the edges of retaining walls. Colder climates are tough on evergreens so its soft silver foliage in winter is particularly welcome at entryways. Rosemary, shrubby and herbaceous salvias, and yellow pineleaf penstemon are good companions.

Cultivation

Loosen the soil well and space plants 12 to 15 inches apart. Provide a 2-inch-deep mulch of fine gravel. Once plants have rooted deeply, usually after a full growing season, water to a depth of 2 feet every two weeks when temperatures are above 80 F, and monthly during cooler weather if there is no rain and soil is well drained. No fertilizer is needed. Shear off flower heads as they dry to stimulate another flush of blooms, a rather tedious task because there are so many little flower heads. The scent of the foliage is pleasant. Limited watering prevents weed invasion; otherwise, weed newly planted germander monthly to keep invaders at bay until plants fill in. Established plants form such a dense network of roots that weeding becomes only an occasional chore. Transplant rooted sprigs in spring or fall.

Other Species and Cultivars

T. chamaedrys 'Prostratum' grows 12 inches x 24 to 36 inches. Native to the Mediterranean, it is a dense mounding perennial with small dark-green leathery leaves. Short spikes of lavender flowers adorn the plant in spring and summer.

Hellebore
Helleborus species

ZONES: 6 through 9
FORM: Mounds with short stems of cup-shaped blooms from early spring or late fall
GROWTH AND MATURE SIZE: Slow-growing perennial to 18 inches x 24 to 36 inches
USES: Dry shade garden, filler, sweeps, drifts, border, understory (*Note:* this plant is poisonous if eaten.)
SOIL: Well-amended and well-draining soil
PESTS: Snails, slugs, whitefly, and sooty mold

Finding flowering plants for dry shade gardens can be quite a challenge. Hellebore is an exception. This mounding perennial has fascinating foliage and unusual flowers. Hellebore leaves are divided into 3- to 9-inch-long pointed leaflets, some with serrated edges. Leaflets can be wide or narrow and feathery, in dark green, blue-green, or variegated. Some leaves have silvery veins, and others are burgundy or purple on leaf undersides and stems. Clusters of cup-shaped flowers form on those short stems. Each bloom's petal-like sepals are the subtle, calm colors of winter—pale green, ivory, dusky purple, velvety plum, creamy peach, and soft chartreuse.

Shared Spaces
The foliage of hybrid and Mediterranean native hellebores complement woodland gardens, Asian gardens, and traditional perennial gardens. Hellebores 2 feet tall or more are large enough to use as small shrubs in a shady garden and make a statement planted in drifts under the shady canopy of evergreen trees.

Cultivation
Water deeply after planting, and mulch. Continue watering deeply and regularly through the first summer into fall. Once established, water sun-grown hellebore from spring through fall, and water shade-grown hellebore only in the hottest months. Keep plants mulched. Apply balanced organic fertilizer once a year, if desired, according to label directions. Feed container-grown hellebore regularly with diluted liquid fertilizer. Groom to remove spent flowers and leaves that turn brown.

Other Species and Cultivars
Corsican hellebore (*Helleborus argutifolius*) is 2 to 3 feet x 2 to 3 feet with chartreuse flowers. Leaves are blue-green above and blush pink below and along stems. Bear's-foot hellebore (*Helleborus foetidus*) is 18 to 30 inches x 24 to 36 inches. Its mounds of feathery, swirling, curved leaves are deep green or gray-green. Pale green flowers are edged in burgundy. Livid hellebore (*Helleborus lividus*) makes an 18 inch x 18 inch mound of green leaves with silver or purplish veins and undersides. Pale green flowers are blushed purple.

Jerusalem Sage
Phlomis fruticosa

ZONES: 6 through 11
FORM: Tall mounds with blooms in spring and summer
GROWTH AND MATURE SIZE: Fairly quick-growing evergreen perennial to 3 to 4 feet x 4 feet
USES: Focal point, drifts, perennial beds
SOIL: Most soils, poor or rich, but prefers well-drained soils
PESTS: None

Jerusalem sage is a tough, low-water perennial from the dry rocky cliffs in hot inland areas around the Mediterranean. This shrubby evergreen has tall tiers of golden yellow flowers and 2- to 3-inch-long leaves that are soft, felty gray-green on top, fuzzy white or gold underneath. Upright branches form tall, rounded mounds. Jerusalem sage flowers look like snapdragon flowers but smaller, and arranged in golf-ball-sized whorls along flower stalks. Plants produce only a seedling or two each year—making them easy to dig and move or share with friends. Purple Jerusalem sage (*Phlomis purpurea*) leaves are soft green above and silver below.

Shared Spaces

Create a yellow, low-water garden by combining Jerusalem sages with yellow and green striped variegated century plant (*Agave americana variegata*), the succulent leaves of yellow and green variegated aloe, yellow blooming stonecrop, and the sunny yellow flowers of ground cover African daisy 'Big Gold'. For color contrast, mix Jerusalem sage with a 'Rosenka' bougainvillea (pale pink and soft orange bracts) and burgundy-leaved 'Shirazz' or 'Platt's Black' New Zealand flax.

Cultivation

In hotter inland or desert areas, choose a site with part shade, everywhere else plant in full sun. Water well after planting and mulch thickly with composted organic mulch. Apply regular water through the first summer and early fall to establish the plants. After that, occasional summer irrigation is all that is necessary. In hot desert or inland areas, water regularly through summer and minimally the rest of the year. No fertilizer is necessary, especially if you mulch well with composted organic matter. Groom to remove spent flowers and to promote ongoing bloom. After major bloom is over, cut plants back by a third to maintain their shape and promote flowering.

Other Species and Cultivars

Kashmir sage, *P. cashmeriana*, grows to a stately 4 feet x 2 feet. It has spikes of lavender-pink whorled flower clusters and is suitable for sun and shade. Hardy Jerusalem sage, *P. russeliana* (Zones 4 through 11), has wide, olive green leaves, and whorls of yellow flowers on stalks 3 feet tall.

Kangaroo Paw
Anigozanthos species

ZONES: 7 through 11
FORM: Long strappy leaves with tall flower spikes spring through fall
GROWTH AND MATURE SIZE: Evergreen perennials 3 to 6 feet tall and wide multiply at a moderate rate from fleshy rhizomes
USES: Border, mass, drifts, accent, midground, background
SOIL: Well-drained soil
PESTS: Snails and slugs; blackspot fungal disease from close spacing, lack of air circulation, too much shade

Kangaroo paw form fans of tall, strappy green leaves. In spring and fall, slender stems arise from the center of the fans, each topped with a cluster of fuzzy tubular flowers that resemble miniature kangaroo paws. Kangaroo paw hails from western Australia. Hybridizers have had a heyday with kangaroo paws, creating varieties in colors ranging from red to burgundy, saffron, pink, iridescent yellow, soft yellow, bright green, and almost fluorescent green. Often stems are one color and flowers are a contrasting color. Plants also come in different heights, from dwarfs (2 feet tall in bloom) to standards (6 feet tall in bloom).

Shared Spaces

Plant *en masse* for a really impressive show (purchase plants all at once and in bloom to be sure of their color). In addition to their wonderful flowers, kangaroo paw leaf fans make an excellent background for shorter plants. Combine with California natives or other Australian plants such as emu bush, grevillea, and cone bush.

Cultivation

Space plants to accommodate their eventual width and to provide good air circulation. Water deeply after planting and mulch well. Water deeply with drip irrigation once a week or so in spring and summer (more often in hot valley and desert gardens), and occasionally in dry winters. Plants do fine with no fertilizer but grow lush with a light application of balanced organic fertilizer in early spring. At the end of the bloom, cut spent flower stalks to their base. The fuzzy outer parts of the flowers irritate skin, so wear long sleeves and gloves. Remove dead leaves. Divide clumps after several years, as flowers fade, or when tiny new fans appear in spring.

Other Species and Cultivars

'Big Red' has bright red flowers and 'Harmony' has iridescent yellow flowers on bright red stems. Both reach 6 feet tall; 'Bush Pearl' has pink flowers; 'Bush Garnet' has burgundy-red blooms; 'Bush Games' and 'Christmas' have flowers that are red and green; 'Bush Tango' has orange flowers. For small spaces consider *A. viridis* 'Phar Lap', whose green blooms form on 1-foot-tall stalks.

Matilija Poppy
Romneya coulteri

ZONES: 8 through 10
FORM: Upright or sprawling with large blooms at the tips in late spring
GROWTH AND MATURE SIZE: Quick-growing perennial to 8 feet x 6 feet or more and spreading
USES: Background, slopes, focal point
SOIL: Well-draining soil; plants tolerate and spread slower in clay soils
PESTS: None

Matilija poppies are the giants of the poppy family. Each plant sends up multiple stalks, 8 feet tall and thicker than a finger, clothed in fringy blue-green leaves. Come late spring, the tip of every stalk develops marble- to walnut-sized buds that erupt into crepe-paper flowers as large as salad plates. The combination of white petals and the bright yellow center earns this plant the nickname "fried egg plant." Flowers start to open around the end of May and keep going into the summer—depending on your location and the weather. Matilija poppy is native to chaparral and coastal sage scrub habitats of the West Coast, primarily from Santa Barbara County south into Baja.

Shared Spaces

These beautiful plants spread by orange-colored rhizomes that expand seemingly forever in well-draining soil, especially when well watered. This is not a plant for small spaces, but don't let its exuberant growth scare you away. Matilija poppies make a beautiful background for gold-flowered perennial marigolds, coral-flowering desert mallow, and the tiny blue blooms of ground cover germander sage. Add a succulent agave for leaf contrast.

Cultivation

Place root barriers at least 6 feet out from the rootball so plants can spread wide enough for a good flower show. Do not disturb the rootball during planting. Water deeply every week or so through the first summer to establish. Then withhold irrigation to limit growth. No fertilizer is needed. Winter dormancy may turn tops brown, but the roots are fine. Cut stalks down to 3- to 4-inch stubs in fall. Wear protective clothing. This plant can be aggressive. If you are an energetic gardener (and didn't install a root barrier at planting), cut the roots around the base of each plant yearly. Watch for sprouts a surprising distance from the mother plant.

Other Species and Cultivars

Coast matilija poppy (*Romneya trichocalyx*) has a fuzzy calyx beneath the petals, slightly smaller leaves, and may be a bit less aggressive. *Argemone corymbosa*, prickly poppy, has flowers similar to Matilija but smaller and on much, much smaller plants that are not nearly as aggressive. Its name comes from fine spines that line its stems.

Partridge Feather
Tanacetum densum amani

ZONES: 4 through 9
FORM: Low mat with small flower clusters in summer
GROWTH AND MATURE SIZE: Slow-growing perennial to 6 inches x 15 inches
USES: Rock gardens, foreground, entryways, ground cover, understory
SOIL: Well-drained soil; prefers lean, gritty soils, not heavily amended clay soils
PESTS: None

Partridge feather is grown for its finely sculpted silver foliage rather than for its flowers. The leaves are ½ inch wide and 3 inches long, covered with silky silver hairs and closely set on woolly stems that form mats 15 inches in diameter. Clusters of yellow button flowers appear in summer, nicely contrasting against the pale leaves, but it is the leaves that look both velvety soft and etched from stone that win a gardener's heart. If you try to grow it anyplace but in afternoon shade in well-drained soil, you'll think it's difficult, but satisfy those two conditions and it will slowly fill its space, as immutable as stone, demanding little for years to come.

Shared Spaces

Partridge feather is at home in rock gardens where companion boulders collect extra water by recycling condensation, and the root zone of the plants is well aerated. Because the detail of the leaves is so remarkable year-round, use plants where they can be seen close up, such as at entryways and in the light shade of trees around patios or other sitting areas. The pale silver foliage blends well with Turkish speedwell, the spiky veronicas, salvias, penstemon, and rosemary. It complements dark-leafed, bold- or fine-textured foliage, as well as brightly colored xeric plants.

Cultivation

Use fine gravel as mulch to keep the soil moist without staying too wet around the crown. Plants grown in the low desert need afternoon shade. In the north and at higher elevations, plants can be grown in full sun. Water to a depth of 24 inches every two weeks when temperatures are above 75 F, and monthly during cooler weather. Fertilizing is not necessary. Rejuvenate established plants by cutting longer stems back to side shoots close to the crown in early spring. Trim off the seedheads whenever they start to look weathered.

Other Species and Cultivars

T. camphoratum, camphor dune tansy, is native to the coastal sand dunes around San Francisco Bay. Growing to 1 foot tall and wide, it has deeper green foliage, yellow blooms, and is hardy in Zones 8 through 11. Do not plant *Tanacetum vulgare* in California; it is invasive.

Penstemon
Penstemon species

ZONES: 5 through 11
FORM: Upright open-branched with stiff flower stalks in spring or summer
GROWTH AND MATURE SIZE: quick growing to 2 to 6 feet x 1 to 2 feet
USES: Dry perennial gardens, focal point, midground, mass, drifts, color beds
SOIL: Natives prefer rocky, native soil; others need well-drained soil.
PESTS: Root rot in dense shade or with excessive summer water

With 500 penstemon species, it is no exaggeration to say that there are penstemons for every garden. In low elevation deserts in spring, the reliable Parry's penstemon (*Penstemon parryi*) sends up 3-foot-tall stalks with pink flowers, as does the stunning red-flowered firecracker penstemon (*P. eatonii*). Low and intermediate elevation deserts enjoy summer-blooming rock penstemon (*P. baccharifolius*), with slim red flowers above the deeply serrated leaves; and native Palmer's penstemon (*P. palmeri*) with 5-foot-tall stalks of fragrant, pale pink flowers. Coastal, valley, and mountain areas enjoy *P. spectabilis* with lavender purple blooms on 3- to 5-foot spikes.

Shared Spaces
Mix desert penstemons with annual wildflowers such as Mexican gold poppy or desert bluebells for a stunning spring color display. Plant generously to cover bare areas, fill in tree wells, and to line driveways, walkways, patios, and pool areas. Native penstemons do well in areas that receive minimal care. Hummingbirds are strongly attracted to penstemons, so plant them where you can enjoy these delightful visitors.

Cultivation
Water thoroughly after planting. Water every two to four days for two to three weeks, then every four to seven days until established. Water established low-desert penstemons every one to two weeks in summer; water other species weekly in summer. Water penstemon weekly while it's growing and blooming in high desert zones; rely on natural rainfall in winter. In temperate climes, water established penstemon once every two or three weeks, allowing the soil to dry out between watering. Fertilize sparingly to avoid excessive leaf growth. Prune spent bloom stalks anytime to encourage repeat blooming.

Other Species and Cultivars
P. baccharifolius Diablo™, rock penstemon, is a shrubby penstemon growing 2 feet tall and wide. Vibrant rosy red flowers are produced on short spikes intermittently through spring and summer. It extremely well-drained soil and enjoys a little afternoon shade in the low desert regions. It is hardy to Zone 6. 'Sweet Joanne' has huge flower spikes in brilliant clear pink, hardy in Zones 4 through 11.

Prince's Plume
Stanleya pinnata

ZONES: 4 through 10

FORM: Bushy, vase shape with long arching flower stems in spring

GROWTH AND MATURE SIZE: Quick-growing perennial, 30 inches x 12 to 18 inches

USES: Wildflower, succulent, dry perennial and rock gardens, focal point, sweeps, dry stream beds

SOIL: Dry, infertile

PESTS: Protect young plants from wildlife with wire mesh during the first season

Prince's plume is a tough desert wildflower with pale green basal leaves emerging from a woody crown in spring. Sturdy, wandlike stems end in showy racemes of yellow flowers. The foot-long clusters of blooms and the delicate filigree of stamens create plumes worthy of a prince. Long, slender seedpods called "siliques" droop from the stems as the flowers fade. Prince's plume grows wild in exposed, rocky, windswept places in soils that are typically high in selenium, but it adapts readily to the drier borders of desert gardens where conditions are less severe. It does best in minimally cultivated settings where it is an elegant antithesis to the badlands it calls home.

    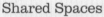

Shared Spaces

Prince's plume makes a striking contrast to threadgrass and Rocky Mountain penstemon in a xeric flower bed, or clustered for early color among desert penstemon, shadscale, purple fern verbena, and prickly pear cactus.

Cultivation

Plants started from seeds persist longer and grow more vigorously than potted transplants because their deep initial roots are not disturbed. To start seeds, rake the planting area to loosen the soil. Sow the seeds and rake them lightly into the surface. Germination takes less than a week when daytime temperatures are 70 F. Thin seedlings or space transplants a foot or more apart in groups of three or more for a strong show. Apply a 3-inch mulch of fine gravel. Water to a depth of 2 feet every two weeks when temperatures are above 75 F, and monthly during cooler weather. Plants grown from seeds sown directly in the garden in areas that receive 10 to 12 inches annual rainfall require no supplemental water after the first year. No fertilizer is needed. Trim off flower stalks before they set seeds to keep plants blooming longer, or wait until the seeds have disbursed in habitat gardens. Rejuvenate established plants by cutting off the previous season's growth close to the ground anytime from autumn to early spring.

Other Species and Cultivars

Stanleya pinnata var. *bipinnata* has finely divided lacy leaves that are particularly nice. *S. elata* grows larger to 4 feet x 3 feet, but it has smaller blooms.

Russian Sage
Perovskia atriplicifolia

ZONES: 4 through 11
FORM: Wide vase-shaped, bushy and sprawling with long flower spikes from spring through summer
GROWTH AND MATURE SIZE: Quick-growing perennial to 3 to 4 feet x 3 to 4 feet
USES: Border, focal point, drifts, accent
SOIL: Well-drained soil
PESTS: None

Russian sage is remarkably durable in all Southwestern zones. The delicate, feathery, pale gray leaves are widely spaced on the stems. The plant looks translucent, like a blue haze in the garden, and is especially visually cooling in a hot garden. Flowers range from a light sky blue to intense indigo and are held in long spikes at the ends of the stems from spring through summer. The combination of the waving blue flowers and the light, ghostly foliage gives the plant an ethereal quality that is entirely at odds with its tolerance of hot, dry conditions as well as the rigors of a mountain climate in winter.

Shared Spaces

Mix Russian sage with perennials such as plumbago and salvias. Plant generously to maximize the lovely foliage and bloom and to create a loose informal border or fill a barren spot in the garden in front of a deep green hedge. Russian sage is particularly effective planted around structures like a statue or fountain.

Cultivation

Water thoroughly after planting. Water every two to four days for two to three weeks, then every four to seven days until established. Mulch roots generously through summer to help keep roots hydrated. Water weekly in summer; every ten to fourteen days in winter in low deserts. Do not water in winter rain areas or if it is dormant. Fertilize with slow-release or organic fertilizer in early fall from the coast to the low desert, in late spring in the high desert. Prune to within a foot or two of the ground in early spring to remove winter-damaged stems or reinvigorate the plant. Cut spent blooms regularly through the growing season to help prolong the bloom. Russian sage reseeds in coastal and valley gardens

Other Species and Cultivars

'Blue Spire' has deep blue flowers. 'Blue Mist' has pale blue flowers. *P. atriplicifolia* 'Little Spire' is a multi-stemmed mounded dwarf to 2 feet tall, with smoky- blue flowers.

South African Geranium
Pelargonium sidoides 'Burgundy'

ZONES: 9 and 10
FORM: Low mounds with wispy stems holding blooms above the foliage spring through fall
GROWTH AND MATURE SIZE: Fast-growing perennial to 12 inches x 12 inches
USES: Foreground, border, mass, drifts, slopes
SOIL: Well-draining soil
PESTS: None

South African geranium is a low-growing, perennial evergreen with small burgundy flowers. These delicate looking blooms appear in clusters of six or more on stalks held several inches above mounds of heart-shaped blue-green leaves. Leaves are velvety and crenulated with edges that curl slightly to reveal silvery undersides. The color and texture of the leaves contrast with the flowers for an absolutely beautiful plant suitable for borders or containers. This geranium requires very little water, making it the perfect plant for a Mediterranean climate. In its native grassland, it dies back and goes dormant to survive the hot months of summer. Here it stays evergreen.

Shared Spaces

Mass South African geraniums for a long border edging or grow as a single tuft of leaves and flowers in any sunny flower bed. Or plant along the edge of a large pot and let the geranium cascade over the side. In a low-water perennial bed, combine with Mexican bush sage so its purple wands wave above burgundy flowers. Add tall grasses such as the blue-green leaved 'Fairy Tales' fountain grass.

Cultivation

Water well and mulch after planting. In cooler winter gardens, grow as a container plant and move to a protected spot for winter. Provide occasional deep watering from spring to fall and if there is a long dry spell in winter. Keep plants mulched. Only potted South African geranium needs fertilizer. Use a balanced organic fertilizer. Over time these geraniums can become leggy. In November or December, cut stems back to within a few inches of the ground. Winter rains will trigger a new growth cycle. Set cuttings into a moist potting mix and you'll soon have more lovely geraniums.

Other Species and Cultivars

The species *Pelargonium sidoides* is not as floriferous as 'Burgundy', but its flowers are nearly as lovely and are fragrant in the early evening. Heartleaf geranium (*Pelargonium cordifolium*) is shrubby, (4 feet x 3 feet) with soft green, heart-shaped leaves. Spring through fall, flowers are large and pink. Kidneyleaf geranium (*Pelargonium reniforme*) (10 inches x 12 inches) has bright magenta-pink petals that have ruby markings.

Spurge
Euphorbia species

ZONES: 7 through 11
FORM: Clumping mounds with flowers late winter through spring
GROWTH AND MATURE SIZE: Fairly fast-growing perennial to ½ to 4 feet x 1 to 5 feet
USES: Foreground, ground cover, border, succulent, dry stream, rock, and perennial gardens
SOIL: Well-drained soil
PESTS: None, but protect skin and eyes from its irritating and toxic milky sap

Spurge is a terrific plant with a dreadful name. There are more than 2000 kinds of spurges. Many are clumping perennials grown as ground covers and small shrubs. In mild climate gardens, spurges serve as a flower bridge, linking winter gardens to spring gardens. Flowers open in late winter, typically in bright chartreuse. By the time spring arrives, some species start to wind down, though some last into early summer. Look closely at spurge to see that outer bracts, not petals, are the showy parts. Spurge's upright or trailing succulent stems are clothed in deep green, burgundy, or blue-green foliage that add texture and contrast to the garden.

Shared Spaces

Spurge fits succulent gardens of aloes, agave, dragon tree, Mexican grass tree, blue chalk sticks, and red yucca. In a perennial bed, plant with purple-flowering sages, tall verbena, African geranium, and pink- or orange-flowered African daisy. Use spurges to edge beds, mix them into beds, or use them to fill empty spaces throughout beds. Use these same plants with other spurges in large container plantings.

Cultivation

Water well and mulch after planting. Water these very drought-tolerant plants regularly the first summer and only occasionally in summer after that. In coastal gardens, spurges often reseed into dry areas of the garden and do just fine. In hotter gardens, some deep watering in the growing season produces more flowers. No fertilizer is needed. After flowers fade, seedpods shoot their seeds into the air with a loud "pop!" If you start with just a few plants, you'll soon have a patch. Pull up unwanted seedlings to share.

Remove spent flowers and stems before winter. New stems will sprout from the base.

Other Species and Cultivars

Euphorbia 'Ascot Rainbow' has cream, lime, and green flowers with cream and green-blue foliage that has a reddish pink tinge in winter. It grows 20 inches tall and wide. 'Ruby Glow' is compact with foliage that turns brown to red in fall. Hardy in Zones 6 through 11. *Euphorbia myrsinites* has wonderful geometric foliage on octopus-like stems reaching 6 inches tall by 2 feet wide.

Sticky Monkey Flower
Mimulus aurantiacus

ZONES: 8 through 11
FORM: Upright and open-branches lined with blooms spring into summer, sometimes in fall
GROWTH AND MATURE SIZE: Fast-growing perennial to 1 to 3 feet x 2 to 4 feet
USES: Dry perennial garden, sweep, slopes, midground
SOIL: Tolerates many soils as long as water is limited.
PESTS: Good air circulation prevents fungal diseases; watch for aphids

Sticky monkey flower grows naturally throughout California. Other *Mimulus* species are not as drought tolerant, being native to wetter regions. This 2- to 3-foot-tall and wide perennial is a fast grower with sticky, narrow green leaves; in undisturbed areas, it has large creamy yellow-orange, five-petal flowers pollinated by insects. Interestingly, in areas where humans have significant impact on the environment, the same monkey flowers produce smaller red flowers pollinated by hummingbirds. Though monkey flower plants are not long-lived, their variety, their beauty, and their profuse flowering with almost no water or care make them ideal garden plants.

Shared Spaces

Sticky monkey flower is a good choice for coastal, inland valley, foothills, and low elevation mountain gardens. Combine sticky monkey flower with California poppy, native sages, native fescue, and flannel bush. Add monkey flower to a dry Mediterranean garden with grevillea, winter cassia, sunrose, and rockrose. To stem erosion on a slope, plant sticky monkey flower with California fuchsia, California lilac, and manzanita.

Cultivation

Water deeply and mulch after planting. Deep water occasionally through the first spring and summer to establish. Stop watering when branches turn brown in summer. Once established, monkey flower survives on rainfall alone, especially in mild coastal and cool northern gardens. In hotter climates, provide an occasional deep drink in summer. Individual sticky monkey flower plants last only a few years. Pinch branch tips to keep plants bushy. In the hottest summer months, plants may turn brown and go dormant. Cut back the soft wood but not the harder wood of the branches. They will resprout in fall.

Other Species and Cultivars

'Apricot' (3 to 4 feet tall) has soft apricot-colored flowers. *Mimulus* 'Ruby Silver' (2 feet x 2 feet) has many deep ruby flowers. 'Trish' (1 to 2 feet x 1 to 2 feet) has soft pink blooms with yellow throats. 'Jack' (1 to 2 feet x 1 to 2 feet) has deep burgundy flowers. Orangey azalea-like flowers of *Mimulus bifidus* are the largest monkey flowers.

Torch Lily
Kniphofia uvaria

ZONES: 5 through 11
FORM: Tall, fountainy leaves with upright bloom stalks in spring through summer
GROWTH AND MATURE SIZE: Moderate growing perennial to 30 inches x 24 inches
USES: Border, focal point, foreground in dry perennial bed, sweeps, mass
SOIL: Well-drained soil; also heavy clay as long as it isn't too wet; tolerates saline soil
PESTS: Protect from rabbits until established

Torch lily is a South African high-altitude native with coarse, grassy leaves and flame-like flower spikes. Leaves grow to 2 feet long, arching over so that the leafless flower spikes stand well above the clumps of leaves. The 6-inch flower spikes top stout 30-inch flower stems. The tightly clustered, tubular flowers are soft coral-orange at the tips blending to yellow at the base. Established plants' deep, pencil-thick roots account for torch lily's drought and heat tolerance. 'Alcazar' is more cold hardy (possibly to dry Zone 4), vigorous, and deeper in color. 'Border Ballet' is shorter, to 2 feet tall, in a mix of colors including pink. 'Primrose Beauty' is yellow.

Shared Spaces

Mix torch lily in xeric perennial beds with 'Moonshine' yarrow, valerian, 'Powis Castle' artemisia, and salvias; or try it clustered in the foreground of shrub borders with dwarf or woolly butterfly bush, English lavender, and rosemary. Plant the species to weave a tapestry with easy-to-grow seedlings that range in color from all orange or all yellow to flame-like bicolors.

Cultivation

Space plants several feet apart, and mulch with three inches of organic compost, shredded bark, pecan shells, or fine gravel. Water to a depth of 30 inches every two weeks when temperatures are above 75 F, and monthly or less during cooler weather or in heavy soils. Work slow-release fertilizer into the soil when planting or dividing clumps to help new starts root. Fertilizer is not necessary once plants are well rooted. Trim off flower stalks at their base as they fade. Clean up established plants by cutting dead leaves close to the ground from autumn to early spring. Lift, divide, and reset plants when clumps become so crowded that they don't bloom well.

Other Species and Cultivars

Kniphofia caulescens has gorgeous blue-green rosettes of foliage with red and yellow late-summer blooms. It reaches 4 feet tall and 3 feet wide, and is hardy in Zones 4 through 11. 'Little Maid' is an all-yellow dwarf, 1 foot x 1 foot.

Western Mugwort
Artemisia ludoviciana

ZONES: 6 through 11
FORM: Upright bushy shrub with inconspicuous flowers
GROWTH AND MATURE SIZE: Quick-growing perennial to 2 to 4 feet x 3 to 5 feet
USES: Border, dry perennial garden, succulent garden border, midground, ground cover, mass
SOIL: Well-drained, alkaline soil including rocky, native soil
PESTS: Root rot if overwatered or planted in poor draining soil

American native western mugwort was exported to England more than one hundred years ago and grown there for decades as an ornamental. European breeders have sent us back cultivars such as 'Silver Queen' and 'Silver King'. But gardeners can still find the shorter, spreading forms that rule the natural world. Flowers hardly count in this species; it is grown for the irregularly dissected, aromatic, pale foliage. In the garden, western mugwort provides a calming presence; the foliage lights up dark corners and provides excellent contrast when used in colorful perennial plantings. *A. tridentata* is more cold tolerant, and is found growing naturally in high desert regions.

Shared Spaces

Western mugwort mixes well with salvias, red justicia, and globemallow for color and textural contrast. Mix with succulents or in outer areas of the garden that receive minimal care. Mugwort's spreading habit makes it a good choice for erosion control on steep slopes.

Cultivation

Water thoroughly after planting. Water every two to four days for two to three weeks, then every four to seven days until established. Water weekly in summer, although established plants can grow on much less.

Western mugwort gets floppy and leggy in deep shade or when overwatered. Plants are dormant in winter in cooler climes, so reduce watering to once a month or rely on natural rainfall. No fertilizer is needed. Prune to remove winter-damaged stems and reinvigorate in early spring. This species spreads by rhizomes that form 2- to 3-foot-wide clumps. Divide in early spring, discard oldest sections, replanting the newer ones.

Other Species and Cultivars

Artemesia californica is the California sagebrush, a 3- to 4-foot-tall shrubby perennial that lends its musky perfume to foothills, scrub, and chaparral environments. Drought tolerant and gray-leaved, it is hardy to 15 degrees. *A. filifolia* grows to 3-foot mounds, (not recommended for low desert zones). *A. arborescents*, silvery sagebrush, grows 6 feet x 8 feet and is hardy to 25 degrees. *A. versicolor* 'Seafoam' is hardy in Zones 4 through 11 and grows small at 8 inches x 24 inches. *A. abrotanum* 'Tangerine' is a 3-foot mound with feathery, fragrant deep green foliage.

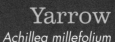

Yarrow
Achillea millefolium

ZONES: 5 through 11
FORM: Flattened mounds of feathery foliage with arching flower stems from early spring through summer
GROWTH AND MATURE SIZE: Fast-growing perennial to 2 to 3 feet x 2 to 3 feet
USES: Foreground in perennial beds, sweeps and drifts, ground cover
SOIL: Well-drained soil
PESTS: None

Yarrow are glorious low-growing perennials in spring and summer gardens of the Southwest. Flower stalks are usually tall, although dwarf forms have been developed, with airy, dill-like foliage. Clusters of tiny flowers are held above the foliage in large, flat heads, each with hundreds of blooms. Yarrow comes in a rainbow of colors, and many are one color early in the season, another color as they age. Established plants spread by runners and some forms self-seed freely. Alert gardeners often find new color variations from among those seedlings. 'Garden Pastels' is just that, and the 'Galaxy' strain has darker tones. 'Debutante' is white with red accents.

Shared Spaces
Use yarrow as background for plantings of phlox, *Caryopteris*, Russian sage, and salvias. Plant generously to create drifts or fill barren spots in the garden. Mix yarrow with succulents such as yuccas and agaves for contrast and color. Deep-colored varieties are especially effective with ornamental grasses.

Cultivation
Prepare beds for seed by adding slow-release or organic fertilizer to the bed and working it in gently with a rake or fork. Broadcast seed evenly and cover lightly, pressing the soil with a rake to prevent seeds from washing away. Water every day or two until seeds germinate, then water every four to seven days until established. When starting with transplants, water thoroughly after planting. Water every two to four days for two to three weeks, then every four to seven days until established. Apply generous amounts of mulch in summer. hold in moisture. Water established plants weekly in summer, monthly or less in winter, and none in the rainy season. No supplemental fertilizer is needed. Harvest spent flowering heads to use in dried arrangements. Cut back to the ground in fall after bloom is done. Divide every two or three years to keep plants from becoming overgrown.

Other Species and Cultivars
'Moonshine' has silver gray foliage and lemon yellow flowers; hardy in Zones 3 through 9. *S. serbica* is slower growing (4 inches x 15 inches) and has white blooms with yellow centers. 'Paprika' has red flowers.

Grasses & Grasslike Plants

In the Southwest, the traditional lawn is vanishing and it isn't a moment too soon. A lawn is one of the thirstiest, greediest, most resource intensive, and high maintenance of all garden features. There are no other garden plants that require monthly fertilizer, weekly "pruning" (mowing) with power tools that use fossil fuels and generate greenhouse gases, and watering several times a week simply to keep them alive.

Gary Mallory, owner of Heads Up Landscaping in Santa Fe and Albuquerque, New Mexico, has watched the trend move away from lawns in his landscape contracting business. In the late 1970s and early 1980s, Heads Up installed 15 semi-truckloads of turf *every week*. Today, Mallory says, if his company installs a single semi-load of turf in a week, that's a lot. And, that turf most often is installed on athletic fields, not in home gardens.

Athletic fields, community parks, and high-use common areas in housing developments (but not parkways and walkways) are reasonable places to use turf; they are places that get a tremendous amount of use by many, many people. If you have very small children who like to roll and tumble outdoors, then it makes sense to have a small lawn, about as much space as they need. Otherwise, lawns are much like residential swimming pools (and coincidentally, use about as much water). They are pretty to look at, but the amount of use they get simply doesn't justify having them in our arid climates.

And if you are concerned about where your dog will do to do his or her duty, please don't worry. The dog won't explode if you remove the lawn (we know this from personal experience).

No lawn, however does *not* mean no grasses. Nor does it mean no sea of green. It simply means rethinking your space. It means using low-water ornamental grasses rather than thirsty turf grasses. And it means creating seas of green that, more like true seas, have waves and mounds and ups and downs. It means meadows and praries of grasses mixed with wildflowers and with bulbs. And it means planting gardens of trees, shrubs, perennials, annuals, and ornamental grasses in place of a lawn. No lawn is a beautiful thing!

This chapter focuses on of ornamental grasses and other plants whose shapes are much like grasses. These plants play many roles in the garden. They serve as ground covers, cover drainage swales and slopes, or accent boulders.

Water-wise ornamental grasses send their roots deep into the soil, anchoring it down, standing tall and willowy in the hottest and coldest of winds. Their blades are green, blue-green, gold, or bronze. The true ornamental grasses send up tall flower stalks topped in feathery plumes in spring or summer. They mix beautifully with shrubs, trees, succulents, and perennials. Ornamental grasses and their allies add texture and movement to the garden as they wave in a gentle breeze.

In some parts of the Southwest, gardeners are experimenting with blue grama grass ground covers (*Bouteloua gracilis*), especially for areas that don't get much foot traffic. Blue grama is a Southwest and Great Plains native grass with pale blue-green blades that forms dense clumps. Blue grama can be planted from seed or from plugs, which are tiny plants that you literally plug into the soil.

In California, the hot new meadow grasses are not grasses at all, but grasslike plants in the sedge family. California meadow sedge (*Carex pansa*) and California field sedge (*Carex praegracilis*) are nearly indistinguishable to the novice but the pros will tell you that California field sedge is slightly taller than California meadow sedge. Either way, both make good low-water, low-care meadows that can be left as billowy, green seas or mowed to look somewhat lawn-like and tolerate traffic.

These sedges are usually available as plugs, four-inch pots, or one-gallon containers. Plant plugs ten inches apart and they will fill in within a year or two.

Perhaps the greatest challenge with meadows and grasslike ground cover plantings is managing weeds. In that first year or two as the plants fill in, the empty spaces are prime real estate for weeds. Plan on spending some time sitting amid the grass, looking to distinguish between weeds and young grasses, then weed away. By year two or three, the grasses will have crowded out the weeds and you can focus your attention elsewhere.

It is that simple.

Beargrass
Nolina species

ZONES: 5 through 11
FORM: Broad clumps with tall flower spikes in spring or summer
GROWTH AND MATURE SIZE: Quick-growing perennial grass to 2 to 5 feet x 4 to 10 feet
USES: Slopes, dry streambed, boulder accent, succulent and native plant gardens, mass
SOIL: Fast-draining soil
PESTS: Stressed by overwatering

Young seedlings of beargrass look like rather coarse-bladed clumps of grass, but unlike true grasses, the foliage is thick and fleshy. Beargrass leaves are slender, less than 1 inch wide and 3 to 5 feet long. Triangular if viewed as a crosssection, the leaves arch gracefully to form clumps. Tiny individual flowers appear by the hundreds on densely branched, plumelike flower spikes. *Nolina texana* leaves are ½ inch wide, up to 3 feet long in clumps 4 to 5 feet wide. Densely clustered flowers are massed on 6-inch heads. It's hardy to Zone 5 if established early in summer and kept dry in winter. Many are protected species, so do not collect seeds from wild plants.

Shared Spaces
Native to the Southwest, beargrass is almost always found on slopes in large groups in rocky terrain. Plant it among boulders in accent groupings with other succulents and cacti as well as mesquite, live oaks, prostrate sumac, cliffrose, fernbush, desert marigold, and sand lovegrass. Because the leaves are not sharp, beargrass is often used for a tropical look around swimming pools.

Cultivation
Beargrass are usually transplanted from 1- or 5-gallon-sized containers into the garden in early spring through fall in warmer climates and in spring through summer in higher elevations. Loosen the soil well, and don't let plants settle by burying the crown deeper than they had been growing. Mulch with gravel. Water transplants sparingly, just often enough that the soil doesn't dry out completely between watering. When plants are well rooted after a few years, water deeply during the growing season once or twice a month. Keep plants dry in winter to avoid root rot. No fertilizer is needed. If plants are growing where seed litter might be a problem, prune off the flower stems after the plants bloom. If feeding wildlife is a priority, leave the seedheads on until the birds have harvested their fill. Trim the dried basal leaves off in more cultivated garden settings.

Other Species and Cultivars
Nolina erumpens has stiffer leaves than *N. texana* with flower stems almost as tall as *N. microcarpa*.

Big Bluestem
Andropogon gerardii

ZONES: 4 through 11
FORM: Upright, narrow clumps with silky flower heads June through September, persistent through fall and winter
GROWTH AND MATURE SIZE: Quick-growing to 4 to 5 feet x 2 feet
USES: Groupings, screen, background, mass
SOIL: Well-drained soil
PESTS: None

The seemingly endless expanses of bluestem undulating in the wind are the awe-inspiring amber waves sung of in "America the Beautiful." Big bluestem is a primary component of the tallgrass prairie that has all but disappeared from the Great Plains. It is a warm-season bunchgrass that naturally ranges in color from pale green to silver-blue. Its silky flower heads are tawny purple and the seedheads are fluffy and bronze-colored, branched in three parts like a turkey's foot. Big bluestem is big, shooting up to 5 feet tall in a few short months; individual plants are columnar in form and sway in the slightest breeze.

Shared Spaces
The bold presence of big bluestem is even more emphatic when plants are grouped in front of a wall or tall fence. Since it should be cut down near the ground each spring, it is best paired with evergreen companions such as Arizona rosewood, 'Tuscan Blue' rosemary, and burkwood viburnum, which provide interest while the grass regrows.

Cultivation
Transplant container-grown starts 3 to 5 feet apart loosening the soil well so the plants can root out easily. No amendments are needed. Water transplants to a depth of 2 feet once a week when temperatures are 90 degrees Fahrenheit or above, every 2 weeks when temperatures are 60 to 90 degrees Fahrenheit, and monthly during cooler weather. No fertilizer is needed. Trim old leaves down close to the ground in late spring so the new leaf blades don't have to push though dead stems for light.

Other Species and Cultivars
'Champ' is a selection adapted to drier conditions in sandy soils and fine-textured clay.

Blue Fescue
Festuca glauca

ZONES: 4 through 11
FORM: Clumping
GROWTH AND MATURE SIZE: Moderate-growing evergreen grass to 4 to 12 inches x 12 inches
USES: Meadow, mass, understory, accent, rock garden, dry streambed
SOIL: Well-draining soil; no soggy soils
PESTS: None

Fescue is a perennial bunching grass that forms rounded tufts of narrow blades. In summer, the tufts are topped with wands of wheatlike flowers that blow in the breeze. Some members of these evergreen, cool-season grasses have handsome deep green blades, but the blue fescues are the ones that always catch your eye. They look lovely planted as a sea surrounding the trunk of a pine or other deep green-leaved shrub or tree. If you are trying to create an Asian feel to your garden, plant blue fescue in a large, rectangular area, setting plants out on a diagonal grid. Keep the fescue trimmed to maintain its geometry.

Shared Spaces
Blue fescue's tones soften the garden. Plant in clusters of odd numbers of plants (3, 5, 7) for a natural look, or mass plant for a meadow. Plant blue fescue into garden borders or mass on hillsides to control erosion. It's an excellent choice for edging a walkway or flowerbed, or planting between pavers.

Cultivation
Spacing depends on the variety. Water deeply and mulch well at planting. After that, water every three to four days for a month; then every seven to ten days through the first summer. If needed, apply time-release fertilizer in spring. Cut back established plants to within a few inches of the ground in early spring. Divide overgrown clumps in fall.

Other Species and Cultivars
'Sea Urchin' is compact, to 8 inches x 12 inches with brighter steel-blue foliage. 'Boulder Blue' is intense blue, upright at 15 inches x 12 inches. 'Siskiyou Blue' (18 inches x 15 inches) prefers part shade in cooler gardens. 'Meerblau' grows 8 inches x 12 inches, has blue-green foliage, and no flowers. 'Azurit' has silver-blue foliage on 12-inch mounds. California fescue (*Festuca californica*) is a 2-foot mound, silvery to greenish blue with blue flowers. Atlas fescue (*F. mairei*) produces 2½-foot-tall gray-green mounds. Do not plant tall fescue, *Festuca arundinacea*, in California. It is an invasive weed.

Blue Grama Grass
Bouteloua gracilis

ZONES: 4 through 11
FORM: Flat-topped clumps or dense even blades
GROWTH AND MATURE SIZE: Fast-growing winter dormant grass; mow 3 to 4 inches
USES: Lawn, meadow, ground cover, dry stream or perennial bed, slopes, erosion control
SOIL: Well-drained soil
PESTS: None

One of the most drought- and heat-tolerant of the native grasses is blue grama grass, which comes from the low- and mid-elevation areas of the Southwest and Great Plains. This modified bunchgrass has pale green blades, is fast-growing, and is long-lived on most soils. If it's given no supplemental watering, it grows as individual clumps that make a beautiful mounding grass ground cover. When seeded heavily and watered, it forms a dense sod, making it one of the better grasses for a native lawn, prairie, or meadow. In winter, blue grama goes dormant and may look dead, but come spring conditions, new green blades appear.

Shared Spaces

Blue grama may be used either as a meadowy lawn or as a wilder prairie ground cover, but in small gardens self-sowing can be a nuisance if allowed to go to seed. Keeping the seedheads mowed will help.

Cultivation

Once nighttime temperatures are consistently at 50 F, the ground is warm enough to seed blue grama grass. For a dense cover, sow onto prepared soil at a rate of 4 pounds seed per 1000 square feet of space. Rake the seed ¼ to ½ inch into the soil. Once the grass is 4 to 5 inches tall, decide whether you prefer a grassy ground cover or a mowed lawn. Mow no shorter than 4 inches, every three weeks in hot summer months. Mowing shorter creates a stiff, bristly stubble. Water deeply once a week when temperatures are 85 F or above, every two weeks when temperatures are 70 to 85 F, and monthly during cooler weather. Apply 1 to 2 pounds of nitrogen fertilizer per thousand square feet in spring. In hard freeze areas, mow to two inches and rake heavily in late March to remove thatch and expose the soil to more sun in order to accelerate the recovery process.

Other Species and Cultivars

'Hachita' has a fine texture and dense growth favored for a more manicured meadowy lawn. 'Lovington' and 'Alma' were both developed from blue grama grasses native to New Mexico.

Blue Oat Grass

Helictotrichon sempervirens

ZONES: 4 through 10

FORM: Low-clumping

GROWTH AND MATURE SIZE: Fast-growing evergreen grass to 18 inches x 18 to 24 inches

USES: Understory, accent, drifts

SOIL: Well-drained soil; compost may make sandy soil more water retentive and clay soil more permeable

PESTS: Susceptible to rust when grown in deep shade at higher elevations; rabbits may munch new growth

Its soft color, fine texture, and controlled growth make cool-season blue oat grass an excellent garden companion for a wide range of plants. The clumping, rather stiff, steel-blue foliage holds its color throughout winter. Leaves are slender, 1/8-inch wide, and grow in tight, 18-inch-tall bunches held in a narrow 18- to 24-inch-wide fan shape. The seedheads are loose panicles borne on stems twice the height of the leaves; the flat seeds resemble oats and dry a pale straw color. Most of the seeds are empty, which prevents weedy self-sowing. It is fairly heat-and drought-tolerant once it's established. The narrow leaves limit evaporation, and the pale leaves reflect heat.

Shared Spaces

Blue oat grass makes a subtle color foil for gayfeather, purple coneflower, and penstemon. It is appealing clustered between evergreens. It can also be part of a tone-on-tone scheme with partridge feather and artemisias. The winter contrast with the rust seedheads of 'Autumn Joy' sedum is striking.

Cultivation

Transplant or divide in cool weather when daytime temperatures stay below 75 degrees F. Set plants at the same depth they were in the nursery container. Space plants 2 to 3 feet apart, in groups of three or more. Apply organic mulch or gravel mulch when plants are grown in the shade or along dry streambeds. Water to a depth of 2 feet once a week when temperatures are 85 F or above, every two weeks when temperatures are 60 to 85 F, and monthly during cooler weather. Fertilizer is not necessary, but where in warm locations where plants are watered frequently, apply a small amount of a lawn fertilizer Cut leaves close to the ground in early spring, and trim off the flower stalks as soon as they start to dry.

Other Species and Cultivars

Plant the species; blue oat grass is especially good mixed in perennial beds as it rarely self-sows. *H. sempervirens* 'Sapphire', or sapphire blue oat grass, has wider foliage with a brighter blue color. It grows 24 inches x 24 inches and is hardy in Zones 4 through 10.

Buffalo Grass
Buchloe dactyloides

ZONES: 3 through 11
FORM: Short, clumping, spreading by stolons
GROWTH AND MATURE SIZE: Slow-growing winter dormant grass; if mowed, mow to 2 to 4 inches
USES: Lawn, meadow, prairie, overgrowth for bulbs
SOIL: Heavy or well-amended soil
PESTS: None

Buffalo grass is native to the short grass prairies of the Great Plains as far south as New Mexico. Blades of buffalo grass are blue-green to pale green during summer but fade to a warm, golden-brown through winter when it is dormant. Buffalo grass is a short bunch grass that spreads slowly from stolons. It is becoming widely used as a turfgrass alternate in intermediate and high desert zones for its durability and low-water use. 'Prairie' and '609' are female selections that grow to 8 inches tall, while 'Cody' and 'Tatanka' are shorter. 'Topgun' and 'Plains' are planted from seed and are dense, short-leaved grasses with darker blades.

Shared Spaces

Mix with faster-growing blue grama to establish a lawn quickly. Use a buffalo grass lawn as a frame for colorful perennials and annual beds. The fine texture makes it useful for play areas for children and pets.

Cultivation

Broadcast seed (2 to 4 pounds per 1000 square feet) or set in plugs. Water every day or two to keep the bed evenly moist until seeds begin to germinate, then water weekly until the lawn is well established.

Apply lawn or organic fertilizer in spring. An iron and sulphur fertilizer may be applied in late summer to help green up the lawn, but do not use nitrogen-based fertilizer then. Water established lawns weekly when temperatures are above 85 F, every two weeks when they are between 70 and 85 degrees F, and monthly thereafter. Buffalo grass does not need to be mowed. If you choose to mow, mow to 2 to 4 inches tall, often enough that you remove no more than 1 inch each mowing. Mow short in early spring to encourage new green growth. If buffalo grass is underplanted with spring bulbs, rake carefully instead.

Other Species and Cultivars

'Prairie Thunder' was developed for increased seedling vigor. Adapted to Zones 3 through 11, it is the most cold tolerant of the warm-season grasses. 'UC Verde' is growing in popularity in California. It's dormant from late fall into spring.

Deer Grass
Muhlenbergia rigens

ZONES: 5 through 11
FORM: Large fountainlike to round at maturity
GROWTH AND MATURE SIZE: Fast-growing evergreen grass to 4 feet x 4 feet
USES: Mass, focal point, screen, border, ground cover
SOIL: Well-drained, fertile, heavy clay, or rocky, native soil
PESTS: None

Deer grass is a large, narrow-leaved bunchgrass that is extremely drought tolerant, immune to heat and aridity, and rarely invasive. The countless, light green leaves form a fountain of a plant that, when mature, is nearly round. Tan, flowering spikes shoot up in late summer, arch over, and fade to a reddish hue as they age. Pink muhly (*Muhlenbergia capillaris*), is shorter Zones 5 through 8, with striking, airy purple plumes in fall. *M. lindheimeri* has wider leaves with a bluish caste that turns delicate silver after the first frost. *M. emersleyi* has deep green leaves topped with purple to red-flowering stalks in late summer and fall.

Shared Spaces

Deer grass is striking when planted in mass groups, almost as a ground cover for large areas. Plant generously for an informal border, to create a low screen, or line walkways and drives. Its tremendous drought and heat tolerance make it a good choice for succulent beds or for other areas that receive minimal care. The soft form and striking autumn color make it particularly effective near seating areas, patios, or around pools. In smaller gardens, use as a specimen or focal plant, or place in large containers.

Cultivation

After planting, water thoroughly. Water every two to three days for a month, then weekly through the first summer. Apply slow-release or organic fertilizer annually in spring. Water established plants every two to three weeks in summer when temperatures exceed 70 degrees F. In higher elevation regions, water monthly in summer although well-established plants thrive on natural rainfall. In all zones, rely on natural rainfall in winter. Deer grass is evergreen in low zones, but is semidormant in winter in high zones. Prune severely, to within a few inches of the ground, in early spring to remove spent flowering stalks, dead leaves, and reinvigorate the plant. Pink muhly does not require pruning.

Other Species and Cultivars

M. emersleyi El Toro™, bull grass, is a clone selected for its showy rosy-purple panicles. Compact-growing to just 2 feet x 2 to 3 feet, it is hardy to Zone 6. Its blue-green foliage is wider than other muhlies.

Dwarf Fountain Grass
Pennisetum alopecuroides

ZONES: 5 through 10
FORM: Arching mound
GROWTH AND MATURE SIZE: Quick-growing evergreen grass to 1 to 2 feet x 1 to 2 feet
USES: Small borders, perennial and dry stream-bed gardens, focal point, meadows, drifts
SOIL: Not fussy
PESTS: Protect new transplants from rabbits with wire mesh or repellents until rooted

Fountain grass is much more consistent and cold hardy than the other *Pennisetum* species. The slender, bright green leaves form an arching mound, and bushy spikes of rosy-brown flowers 5 to 8 inches long and 1 inch wide begin pushing up through the foliage. Late summer and autumn are the height of the season for this showy grass, when the color fades to pink-blushed tan and the silken texture of the flowers becomes fluffier. 'Hameln' has arching leaf blades ⅛-inch wide and 20 inches long with buff-ivory flowers. 'Little Bunny' forms a 1-foot mound; the short flower spikes are buff tinged with pink.

Shared Spaces
Hardy fountain grass grows large enough to balance tall trees and shrubs in borders, yet it is subdued enough to mix with perennials such as salvias, Jerusalem sage, and gayfeather. After frost, the muted tan color contrasts the deep sable cones of black-eyed Susan.

Cultivation
To plant dwarf fountain grass, turn a 3-inch layer of compost into the soil first. Plant fountain grass 2 to 3 feet apart, leaving space between plants. These plants have a lovely texture that is best seen when they are not crowded. Water established plants to a depth of 18 inches every two weeks when temperatures are above 65 F; water monthly during cooler weather. Use chelated iron or a granular iron-and sulfur fertilizer if leaves yellow in summer's heat. Cut plants down close to the ground when they start to look weathered in fall, or leave them and enjoy their winter silhouettes.

Other Species and Cultivars
'Red Riding Hood' is compact with dark purple foliage, perennial in Zones 9 through 10, annual elsewhere. 'Princess Molly' has burgundy leaves, 14 inches tall, perennial in Zones 8 through 10. 'Red Head' grows 3 to 4 feet x 3 feet, perennial in Zones 5 through 9, and has green foliage with long smoky-purple plumes. Leaves turn golden in fall. Do not plant the following invasives: crimson fountain grass (*Pennisetum setaceum*), feathertop grass (*Pennisetum villosum*), or buffle grass (*Pennisetum ciliare*). Kikuyu grass (*Pennisetum clandestinum*) is invasive only in California.

'Jose Select'
Tall Wheatgrass
Elytrigia elongata 'Jose Select'

ZONES: 3 to 8
FORM: Tall, open vase-shaped
GROWTH AND MATURE SIZE: Fairly quick-growing evergreen grass to 5 feet x 2 feet
USES: Focal point, drainage swales
SOIL: Well-drained soil, lean
PESTS: None

'Jose Select' tall wheatgrass has traveled the globe to find its way into Southwestern gardens. This Eurasian native was selected because it tolerates very alkaline soils, is long-lived, and is heat- and drought-tolerant. It was first introduced in the western United States in 1965 as a pasture grass, where it established quickly with a modest amounts of water. 'Jose Select' is a cultivar with strong ornamental merit as well as practical uses. It makes narrow clumps of dark green leaves that grow robustly and stately. By late summer, thick seed spikes stand 5 feet tall. Frost gradually turns the whole plant a golden yellow, and it persists through winter unbowed by snow.

Shared Spaces

At lower elevations, use in drainage swales or against north- and east-facing walls with afternoon shade. Its tall, stiff profile can be used as a series of exclamation points in the garden. Like exclamation points in prose, a few go a long way toward adding emphasis; too many and the effect can be rather strident. Against a weathered coyote fence or stone or plaster wall, the pale golden seedheads are a dramatic accent. Mixed with hollyhocks, they can take over the show when flowers are finished for the season.

Cultivation

Loosen up the soil well and set plants or divisions out at least 4 feet apart so each stands independently of the others. Planting seed in large areas is usually done mid-August through October in desert areas. Use 16 pounds of seed per acre. Water plants deeply once a week when temperatures are above 85 F, every two weeks when temperatures are 65 to 85 F, and monthly during cooler weather. Water established plants to a depth of 2 feet. Fertilizing is not necessary. In spring, cut the previous year's growth down as close to the ground as possible without scalping the grass crown. Stripping the seeds off the stems as they ripen will keep plants from becoming weedy.

Other Species and Cultivars

Because 'Jose Select' is a cool-season grass, it naturalizes best at elevations above 6000 feet, where summer heat isn't extreme, and rainfall and snow are more plentiful.

New Zealand Flax
Phormium species

ZONES: 8 through 11
FORM: Structured open vase-shaped
GROWTH AND MATURE SIZE: Moderately growing evergreen to 1½ feet to 8 feet x 1½ feet to 18 feet, depending upon variety
USES: Border, sweeps, mass, focal point, perennial and dry streambeds, background to foreground
SOIL: Well-drained soil
PESTS: Mealybugs and snails hide in leaves

Every garden needs strong foliage plants, and New Zealand flax fits that bill perfectly. Its fans of strappy and sometimes arching evergreen leaves come in countless shades of olive green to red, yellow, bronze, nearly purple, chocolate, and bright green—often in combinations. Though summer brings tall spikes of dark-colored flowers shaped a bit like tiny bird of paradise blooms, it is the New Zealand flax's low maintenance and colorful leaves that make it such a great garden plant. There are dozens of varieties, from 18-inch dwarfs to 8-foot giants, all a bit taller than wide. These tough plants are tolerant of fairly harsh conditions as long as they get lots of sun.

Shared Spaces

In a mass planting, be sure to allow enough space for the plant's natural widths. Flax's strong profile fits all garden styles. Plant the largest varieties as a background with trees and shrubs. Edge flower borders or assemble container plantings of tiny 'Jack Sprat' and medium-sized 'Shiraz' with chartreuse-leaved 'Golden Spirit' smoke tree. Or combine yellow-leaved 'Yellow Wave' with red-leaved redbud 'Forest Pansy'.

Cultivation

Water well after planting and apply coarse chips or a rock/ gravel mulch. New Zealand flax tolerates long dry periods but looks better with occasional deep water in summer along the coast and in inland valleys. No fertilizer is needed. As New Zealand flax mature, some varieties tend to revert to the green or bronze color of their hybrid parent. Simply cut the offending sprout (or leaf) off at its base. Divide plants if they grow too large for their spot or if clumps die out in the center.

Other Species and Cultivars

There are dozens of cultivars and hybrids to choose from, so be sure to match size to space. *Phormium cookianum* 'Black Adder' has three-foot-tall burgundy-black leaves. *Phormium tenax* 'Atropurpureum Compactum' is 5 feet tall with bronze foliage. Smaller cultivars include 'Apricot Queen' at 3 feet tall with juvenile apricot foliage that turns pale yellow with green margins at maturity; *P. cookianum* 'Creamy Delight', which has creamy yellow centers edged in green and red margins (2 feet); and 'Evening Glow', 3 feet tall with bright red centers edged in bronze foliage.

Sedge
Carex species

ZONES: 5 through 11
FORM: Clumping with wiry stems
GROWTH AND MATURE SIZE: Quick-growing evergreen to 6 to 24 inches x 16 to 24 inches
USES: Mass, drifts, rock gardens, dry streambeds, filler, ground cover, slopes, lawn, meadow
SOIL: Any soils
PESTS: None

Want a lawn that you don't have to mow? There are creeping sedges fit the bill. Sedges look like grasses and grow like grasses, but they are not grasses. Instead they are related to papyrus and edible water chestnut. Want color in your garden beds without relying on the seasonal come-and-go nature of flowers? There are clumping sedges for that purpose. Some sedges have long billowy leaves that resemble long-haired "Cousin It" from the 1960s television series *The Addams Family*. Others have shorter blades that hearken back to the spiky punk hairstyles of the 1980s. Either way, once you grow sedge in your garden, you'll be hooked.

Shared Spaces

Plant *en masse* and leave unmowed for a naturalistic meadow. Plant colorful clumping sedges to spill over walls, to grow between stepping-stones, to mix in containers, or to edge garden beds. Mix orange sedge with blue fescue and surround both with creeping woolly thyme, which blooms palest pink in spring. Plant creeping sedges to stabilize slopes, as a ground cover, a formal lawn, or meadow.

Cultivation

Plant fall through spring, in part to full sun near the coast and in some shade in valleys and deserts. Plant from pots or plugs (small plants). Water deeply and mulch well. Along the coast, water occasionally in summer. In low and high deserts, water when the soil is dry 3 inches down. No fertilizer is needed. Dead blades turn wheat colored and loosen from the center. To remove them, gently comb the plants with your fingers or a wide-tooth comb. Cut back once in fall or mow monthly for a more traditional lawn. Transplant or share unwanted seedlings.

Other Species and Cultivars

European native Berkeley sedge (Carex divulsa, also sold as Carex tumicola,) produces tall, graceful clumps of bright green blades, 12 to 18 inches tall. Blue sedge, Carex glauca, is very short, just 6 inches tall with narrow blue blades. Plants spread slowly on a low-water diet, faster with more water. Eventually, they knit together into a tufted blue carpet.

Silver Grass
Miscanthus sinensis

ZONES: 5 through 11
FORM: Clumping with arching blades; feathery plumes rise above foliage in late summer or early fall
GROWTH AND MATURE SIZE: Winter dormant but quick-growing to 2 to 8 feet x 1 to 6 feet
USES: Accent, focal point, background, mass, drifts, meadow, dry streambed
SOIL: Well-drained soil
PESTS: None

For more than 100 years, this tall stately grass has graced Japanese gardens, lending its graceful and textural blades to sophisticated compositions. In Southwestern gardens, silver grass works in both formal and informal gardens. Different varieties have different colored blades, from silver to striped (vertical or horizontal) to deep green; some are broad and some are narrow. This clumping grass has large feathery flowers that rise above the blades in late summer or fall. As is typical with warm-season grasses, silver grass goes dormant in winter, at which point flowers and blades turn the color of wheat, sometimes with reddish overtones.

Shared Spaces

Plant silver grass as an accent, as a screen, or as a background plant. Grow it as a tall element in a meadow of sedges, or place it in a large pot and underplant with trailing nasturtium, cape fuchsia, or germander sage. Harvest flowers for dried arrangements.

Cultivation

Water deeply after planting and mulch thickly. Silver grass tolerates both wet and dry conditions, but growth slows and plants flower a bit less when grown on the drier side. Water regularly and deeply (wet the soil about 6 inches deep) through the first two summers until plants send roots deep. After that, water when top 3 inches of soil are dry. Blades dry to a straw color by late fall. Cut them back or enjoy until new blades sprout in spring. The new blades will eventually hide the old. To cut back, loop twine around the circumference of the blades, about 8 inches above ground. Tighten the loop, then tie it off. Cut the sheaf, leaving 2 to 3 inches of stubble. Silver grass can reseed in areas of the garden that stay constantly moist.

Other Species and Cultivars

'Gold Breeze' (to 6 feet) has dense gold stripes across fluid apple-green leaves with showy red blooms. 'Gracillimus', maidenhair grass, has copper-colored plumes on green foliage that reaches to 6 feet tall. 'Little Zebra' has bright gold-banded foliage with spikes of purple-red flowers and upright foliage to 3 to 4 feet tall.

Bulbs

Whether you live in the Southwest mountains, deserts, valleys, or along the coast, you can have a fabulous display of daffodils or dozens of other climate-appropriate bulbs, rhizomes, tubers, or corms, all plants that we typically lump together into the "bulb" category. What makes these plants distinct from others is that they store energy in roots, stems, and other plant parts that are underground.

Nearly all plants make energy in their leaves by the process called "photosynthesis." Bulbs use much of their energy to make leaves and flowers during the growing season. Once they finish flowering, the leaves continue to photosynthesize. The energy they make moves down the leaves to be stored in their underground storage structures. With true bulbs, the storage structure is the "bulb" part of the plant. With plants like iris, the rhizome—technically an underground stem—stores the energy. Corms and tubers are different kinds of underground stems that store energy as well.

This post-bloom, energy-storage period is critical to bulb survival. That's when the leaves make the energy they need to sprout and bloom the following year. If you cut the leaves off when they are green the chances are your bulbs will disappear forever.

Hybrid tulips and other bulbs that we inherited from Northern Europe and Asia are a pretty thirsty bunch. But there are plenty of beautiful water-wise bulbs native to the Southwest, South Africa, and the Mediterranean that are extremely easy to grow and tolerate about any soil as long as it drains well. These bulbs require very little, if any, fertilizer and no attention other than removing spent leaves and occasionally dividing clumps that grow very wide.

A few of the bulbs in this chapter are critter delicacies. Crocus and grape hyacinth, for example, are sometimes munched on by gophers from the bottom and bunnies from the top. Protect these bulbs by planting them in a wire mesh "gopher basket" and sprinkle the soil with bloodmeal in early spring.

Other bulbs such as naked ladies, daffodils, allium, and iris are not on the critter cuisine list. They are some of the best bulbs for low maintenance gardens and large open areas that are hard to protect.

Nearly all water-wise bulbs become dormant or slow their growth during some parts of the year. Their "downtime" helps them conserve both water and energy. They are still alive and appreciate *some* moisture, but give them too much water and they will rot. Plant bulbs such as baboon flower and blazing star into well-drained beds of low-water perennials and annuals. Naked ladies and other bulbs that need absolutely no water when they're dormant are better planted in a location away from all irrigation. Simply let them live life on their own; a bulb grower's dream!

Bulbs are wonderful layered with other plants in the garden. Plant bulbs where they land, making sure their growing tips face up before covering them with dirt. As a rule of thumb, the pointed ends face up—that's where the shoots will emerge—while flattened ends—where the roots will emerge—face down. If in doubt, plant them sideways. The bulbs will figure out which way is up and which is down.

To extend the show, overplant bulbs with ground covers, annuals, and perennials that bloom in different seasons. The bulbs will be in center stage during their peak bloom period while the other plants will steal the show after the bulb blooms and foliage begins to wane.

In these pages, we include bulbs primarily from dry climates around the world. Not all of them are adapted to the arid conditions of the entire Southwest but there are low-water bulbs for every part of the region.

Baboon Flower
Babiana species

ZONES: 9 and 10
FORM: Short foliage with one-foot-tall flower stems in mid- to late spring to early summer
GROWTH AND MATURE SIZE: Small to 6 to 12 inches, summer dormant, naturalizing over a few seasons
USES: Foreground, mass, drifts, small accent, meadows
SOIL: Any soil
PESTS: Deter hungry squirrels, rabbits, and rodents

South African bulbs bring so many bright colors to the garden that they can sometimes become overwhelming. One group, however, blooms in deep tones that balances the others. These are baboon flowers, named because their underground corms are a favorite treat of wild baboons. The most common baboon flowers open in shades of blue, purple, magenta, or red. Less common (but no less beautiful) types bloom white or pale yellow. These are petite plants with short, deep green, lance-shaped leaves and several flower stalks only a foot tall holding five or more 1½-inch cup- or star-shaped blooms. In a dry garden, baboon flowers naturalize over a few years.

Shared Spaces
Expect bulbs to naturalize, settling in tiny spaces between plants, sidewalk cracks, and other open spots within a few years. Add to a meadow planting, tucked in among tufts of ornamental grasses and sedges. Baboon flowers can fill a container after a few seasons, or mix with other summer dormant bulbs and plants such as tall bugle lilies, species *Gladiolus*, or annual California poppies.

Cultivation
Amend the soil with organic compost and bonemeal. Set corms 3 to 4 inches deep and 4 to 6 inches apart. Water well after planting, and mulch. New leaves appear with cool fall weather. Baboon flowers in the ground survive on rainfall in most coastal gardens. In hot inland and desert gardens, water deeply once or twice monthly in the growing season. Stop watering when bulbs go dormant in summer. Topdress with bonemeal or organic bulb fertilizer when new leaves appear. Allow leaves to dry on the bulb after flowering. Cut (don't pull) leaves once they are completely brown and dry.

Other Species and Cultivars
Babiana angustifolia has violet to blue flowers with maroon markings near the base of petals; *Babiana nana* has rose-scented, pale purple or blue flowers with white markings inside the petals. For magenta, purple, or blue blooms, try *Babiana stricta* or varieties 'Brilliant Blue' and 'Purple Haze'. For fragrant white flowers, plant 'Pearly White' and 'Alba'. For magenta or wine-red flowers, try *Babiana villosa*, which also tolerates clay soil.

Blazing Star
Tritonia crocata

ZONES: 8 through 11
FORM: Upright sword-shaped leaves lined with blooms in midsummer
GROWTH AND MATURE SIZE: Summer dormant, naturalizing, 1 to 2 feet x 1 to 2 feet
USES: Border, drift, meadow, midground in bulb garden, dry perennial bed
SOIL: Well-drained soil
PESTS: Occasional aphids, whitefly; watch for slugs and snails

One of the loveliest South African bulbs available in nurseries is blazing star, an iris relative that has many species. The blazing stars most widely available are varieties of *Tritonia crocata*, with one-foot-tall, sword-shaped leaves forming fans. Each fan produces several tall, slender stems lined in 2-inch flowers that open from the bottom to the top. Flowers come in shades of pale pink, apricot, orange, lipstick red, or salmon. Each petal tends to be darkest towards the center, paler towards the edges. Contrasting yellow streaks are at the base, while stamens are tipped yellow. This perennial, summer-dormant bulb (really a corm) is native to the drier areas of the country.

Shared Spaces

Create a low-water, all-season, orange-flowering garden with California poppy, 'Salmon Run' blazing star, 'Seashell' bugle lily, 'Pumpkin Pie' African daisy, and 'Apricot Sunrise' anise hyssop. For texture, add succulent flapjack plant with its very round green leaves edged in burnt orange, and *Aloe marlothii*, whose wintertime candelabra has bright orange flowers.

Cultivation

Where winter temperatures stay above 20 F, plant dormant corms in early fall. Otherwise wait until early spring. Choose a spot where blazing star will get water in the growing season but not in summer. In the ground, plant 3 to 4 inches deep and 3 to 6 inches apart. After planting, water well and mulch. For container culture, space corms 3 inches apart. Mulch with rounded gravel. Water deeply during the growing season when the top several inches of soil dry out. Stop watering after May. Store containers where they won't get winter water. When new growth appears, topdress with a layer of compost. If you dig dormant corms, brush off the dirt and store them in a cool, dry location. Allow leaves to dry on the plants after bloom fades. Cut back leaves once they are completely dried out and brown.

Other Species and Cultivars

'Avalanche' has bright white flowers. 'Salmon Run' has salmon-colored flowers. 'Fruit Salad Mix' is a mixture of pale peach, apricot, lipstick red, and salmon-colored flowers. 'Embers' has bright coral-red blooms while 'Bermuda Sands' has pale pink flowers.

Blue-eyed Grass
Sisyrinchium bellum

ZONES: 8 through 11
FORM: Flower stems 2 to 4 inches above narrow foliage in late spring to early summer
GROWTH AND MATURE SIZE: Small, summer dormant, sometimes naturalizing to 6 to 18 inches x 6 to 12 inches
USES: Meadow, rock garden, foreground, drift, between pavers
SOIL: Adaptable to all soils; unamended soils are fine.
PESTS: None

Sometimes the smallest plant adds just the right touch to a garden. Blue-eyed grass is a tiny member of the iris family with narrow grasslike leaves that form small tufts. It spreads by rhizomes. The name "blue-eyed grass" comes from the many star-shaped flowers that rise from tufts in spring. Each little flower (about half an inch across) opens blue to purple with a yellow eye in the center. Blue-eyed grass is native to woodlands, chaparral, and sage scrub habitats. Like so many other Southwest natives, blue-eyed grass goes dormant briefly in the heat of summer. In a garden setting, it often naturalizes, which is nice, especially in an informal garden.

Shared Spaces

Diminutive plants like blue-eyed grass show best when used in small areas, such as tucked in among rocks or planted between pavers in a walkway. Blue-eyed grass tolerates a surprising amount of foot traffic. Alternatively, use blue-eyed grass as an accent or surprise element, for example as a bit of visual spice in a sedge meadow. Combine blue-eyed grass with California poppy to underplant redbud, California lilac, and flannel bush (the blue and yellow combination is exceptional). In a container garden, mix with native penstemon, sticky monkey flowers, and native sage.

Cultivation

Water well after planting and mulch thickly. Blue-eyed grass can also be grown in containers with well-draining potting soil. These little iris cousins survive on rainfall alone along the coast, but in hot inland and valley gardens, they look better with twice-weekly, deep watering in summer. No fertilizer is needed. Groom plants to remove spent flowers, brown leaves, and leaf litter. Dormant plants can be divided every few years.

Other Species and Cultivars

S. graminoides has deep blue blooms with yellow throats, grows to 20 inches tall, and is hardy in Zones 5 through 8. *S. striatum* has small creamy yellow flowers. Leaves persist in winter, giving frosty winter interest. 'Rocky Point' has purple-blue flowers; 'Raspberry' is 16 inches tall with purple flowers streaked raspberry pink. 'E.K. Balls' is only 4 inches tall, but has mauve-colored flowers.

Clivia
Clivia miniata

ZONES: 9 through 11
FORM: Thick, long fleshy leaves and tall stems with large tubular flowers winter through spring
GROWTH AND MATURE SIZE: Slower to multiply, evergreen, growing to 1 to 2 feet x 1 to 2 feet
USES: Mass, sweeps, focal point, midground, shady perennial bed, understory
SOIL: Well-drained soil
PESTS: Watch for snails in crevices between leaves

Clivia are the shining lights of dry shade gardens. Their deep green, tongue-shaped leaves grow 1 to 2 feet long, forming fans. The most common clivia are hybrids of *Clivia miniata*. They have thick, fleshy green flower stems that rise from the center of their leaf fans. Each stalk is topped by a cluster of tubular flowers in shades of red-orange to coral, and even pale golden yellow from winter through spring. When flowers fade, the show continues with large colorful berries that start out green and ripen to red, orange, yellow, purple, and even pink. Their shallow roots don't mind being planted in shallow soils around the roots of trees and shrubs.

Shared Spaces

Mass plant clivia in a shade garden, beneath Japanese maple, and alongside flowering maple giant dracaena, and king palms. Potted clivia is perfect for a shady spot on the patio or to add architectural interest to a shady flower bed.

Cultivation

Water well and mulch after planting from nursery containers. For container culture, choose a large pot so plants can grow undisturbed for many years. Use a well-draining organic mixture.

Plants tolerate moist soils in the summer but prefer to be drier in the cool months. If you have a choice, err on the dry side. Apply balanced organic fertilizer in early spring. Groom to remove spent leaves and old fruit stalks. Clivia prefer to be crowded, so don't be anxious to divide them. When you do divide them, replant new divisions. Avoid cultivating around or otherwise disturbing clivia roots and rhizomes.

Other Species and Cultivars

Hybrid 'San Marcos Yellow' blooms yellow on 2-foot stalks.

'French Hybrid' flowers are dark orange. 'Arturo's Yellow' or 'Yellow Charm' have butterscotch-yellow flowers followed by yellow fruits. 'Orange Variegated' has lovely green and pale yellow striped leaves. *C. nobilis* has long notched leaves and hanging clusters of long tubular orange flowers with striking green tips. *C. caulescens* leaves end in a narrow point with clusters of tubular flowers in pale red with green tips. *C.* x *cyrtanthiflora* is a hybrid with pendulous orange flowers and is hardy to 26 F.

Crocus
Crocus species

ZONES: 4 through 9
FORM: Narrow, straplike foliage with short stems holding large blooms in early spring or autumn
GROWTH AND MATURE SIZE: Summer dormant, fast growing to 4 inches x 4 inches
USES: Foreground, mass, drifts, rock gardens, understory, borders, meadows
SOIL: Gritty decomposed granite and sand are ideal; clay will do if it's not too wet
PESTS: Rabbits

Species and hybrid crocuses frame the garden season like colorful bookends. Dutch crocus (*Crocus vernus*) bloom white, yellow, and purple as the welcome first sign of the coming of spring. The violet-purple flowers of autumn crocus (*Crocus speciosus*) appear in early fall to mark the mellow ebb of the warm-weather season. Deep purple *Crocus chrysanthus* has small flowers that appear earlier than the hybrids. *Crocus sativus*, saffron crocus, blooms in early fall, too, with deep purple, cupped blooms, yellow anthers, and three-lobed scarlet stigmas. It takes 4000 flowers to harvest an ounce of saffron. *C. sativus* is hardy in Zones 6 through 9.

Shared Spaces

Crocuses make beautiful additions to rock gardens among soapwort, Greek yarrow, fleabane, and stonecrops; group them along paths and the edges of perennial borders with blue fescue, desert zinnia, or blue spurge. Or plant them in broad sweeps in buffalo grass or sheep's fescue lawns.

Cultivation

Plant Dutch crocuses in autumn when the soil has begun to cool down and the days grow noticeably shorter. Plant autumn crocuses in August; they bloom soon afterwards. For natural-looking drifts, put the corms in a box and gently toss them out across tilled soil. Dig them in, pointed side up, 2 inches deep and at least 4 to 6 inches apart or where they fall. Water once a week to a depth of one foot while the corms are actively growing. When crocuses are dormant, the water given to the companion plants will keep the resting corms viable. Work bulb food into the soil at planting time and reapply each spring. Trim off spent flowers, but leave the foliage until it withers naturally.

Other Species and Cultivars

C. chrysanthus can be scented and has many cultivars in yellow ('Advance'), purple ('Blue Pearl', 'Ruby Giant'), creamy white ('Romance'), and combinations. Greek crocus (*C. goulimyi*) is an autumn species that is unmatched for its fragrant, intense blue-purple blooms suffused with pink. It is the least cold hardy of the species mentioned here, reliable only in Zones 7 through 9.

Daffodil
Narcissus species

ZONES: 5 through 11
FORM: Green narrow leaves with long stems holding clusters of large blooms in spring
GROWTH AND MATURE SIZE: Fast growing, naturalizing, summer dormant to 6 to 8 inches x 4 to 8 inches
USES: Sweeps, drifts, border, accent
SOIL: Well-drained, fertile soil
PESTS: Gophers find the bulbs irresistible

Prized for their early and prolific bloom, daffodils do remarkably well in all zones of the Southwest. The tubular petals open like wide-mouthed trumpets and are surrounded at the base by a ruffled collar of sepals. In good garden soil, these are long-lived bulbs; they multiply generously, but are rarely invasive. For low and intermediate zones choose between the *Cyclamineus* types, with their swept back petals and one bloom per stalk or the Jonquilla type, with narrow leaves and one to five blooms per stem. The Tazetta types are the best for the hot desert regions and also work well in milder climates—they require no winter chill and have up to twenty flowers per stem.

Shared Spaces

Daffodils, especially the multiflowered Tazetta types, mix well with spring-blooming penstemon, red justicia, and other bulbs such as alliums and freesia. Use daffodils to create an informal border or edge for a larger bed, along a drive, or walkway. Daffodils make excellent plants for containers. Those known as paperwhites require no chilling period and are extremely easy to force into late winter bloom for indoor or holiday enjoyment.

Cultivation

Plant in fall in all but the coldest zones. Plant varieties that need a chill in high elevation gardens. Water thoroughly after planting. Water weekly until leaves or flowers emerge, but in heavy soils water when the soil dries out a bit. Apply slow-release or organic fertilizer annually in fall in the low desert; in early spring in colder zones. Water blooming daffodils every week or two, depending on the temperatures and soil. Keep dormant bulbs damp as you would any deciduous plant, but not continuously wet. Remove dried yellow leaves when they can be pulled away easily by hand. Cut flowers anytime.

Other Species and Cultivars

Combination daffodils are stunning with 'Vanilla Peach' petals accented with a ruffled peach corona; 'Pink Parasol' with crepe-paper white petals and a creamy peach corona; 'Mount Hood' is white on white; 'Centannees' has tipped yellow petals with an orange sherbet center. Butterfly daffodils have broad split cups that look like butterflies with their wings in open splendor. Double daffodils are ruffled like a rosette. The options are endless.

159

Daylily
Hemerocallis hybrids

ZONES: 5 through 11

FORM: Clumps of arching leaves with two or more blooms above the foliage from spring to midsummer

GROWTH AND MATURE SIZE: Fast growing, evergreen or deciduous, naturalizing to 1 to 5 feet x 1 to 5 feet

USES: Borders, perennial bed, understory, sweeps, drifts, mass, midground

SOIL: Well-amended, well-drained soil

PESTS: Slugs, snails

Daylilies form clumps of strappy green leaves that arch from a center fan. From spring onward, two or more (depending on the variety) lily-shaped flowers, in shades of yellow, orange, raspberry, burgundy, nearly purple, and blood red, form at the tips of stalks that rise above the leaves. The topmost flower opens first, then those below in sequence, but only for a day each. Plants may make several stalks, so the overall effect is lots of flowers over a long period of time. There are countless hybrids available— tall, short, different flower colors, spring bloomers, repeat bloomers, those that go dormant in winter, and those that are evergreen (depending on your zone).

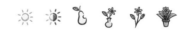

Shared Spaces
Plant daylily in just about any style garden, in traditional perennial beds, parking lot planters, tropical landscapes, or Mediterranean gardens. Combine with fine-leaved plants such as penstemon or with broad- or round-leaved plants such as sages and flowering maple. Tall daylilies fill that midborder space against a background of shrubs such as lilac, butterfly bush, and 'Silver Sheen' *Pittosporum* Use sweeps of dwarf daylily to edge the front of flower beds.

Cultivation
In hottest climates or when growing deep color flowers, plant in part shade so colors don't fade. Water thoroughly after planting, and mulch. Water deeply to keep soil moist the first two years until plants are established. Then water when the soil is dry several inches down from the surface. Daylilies more drought tolerant in valley and coastal gardens than in deserts. Unfertilized plants bloom, but organic fertilizer applied in early spring promotes more blooms. Divide rhizomes when clumps get overly large.

Remove spent leaves and flower stalks through the year.

Other Species and Cultivars
Repeat bloomers include 'Flamboyant Edge', evergreen, 6-inch double-flowering soft pink bloom with lavender eye and edges; 'Happy Returns', a strong naturalizer with fragrant lemon yellow flowers; 'Black Emanuelle' deep purplish black blooms growing to 30 inches; color combinations 'Kansas City Kicker' (lavender and pink); 'Cherry Valentine' (magenta and pink). Hundreds of choices!

Forest Lily
Veltheimia bracteata

ZONES: 9 and 10

FORM: Rosettes of long leaves with tall stems holding tubular clusters from winter to early spring

GROWTH AND MATURE SIZE: Quickly naturalizing, summer dormant, to 18 inches x 30 inches

USES: Dry shade garden, understory, focal point, mass, drifts, interior

SOIL: Humusy, well-drained soil

PESTS: Slugs, snails

Gardeners are forever looking for bulbs that grow in dry shade. Forest lilies fit that bill perfectly. These winter- to early-spring bloomers look soft and somehow more sophisticated than their brightly colored springtime bulb buddies. They make lush rosettes of almost succulent leaves, 10 to 12 inches long with undulating edges. From the center of each rosette rise 1- to 2-foot-tall flower stalks topped with a cluster of tubular flowers, arranged almost like a red-hot poker, and opening in shades of pink, rose, salmon, and occasionally pale yellow, all with an attractive green blush. After the flowers fade, leaves soon follow, allowing the bulbs to sleep through the hottest months of summer.

Shared Spaces
These bulbs are from the forests of South Africa and grow well in the shade of tall trees, with shade tolerant agaves, and hellebore. They can also be grown as houseplants.

Cultivation
Set bulbs at or just below the surface of the soil. To grow in a container, start with a pot large enough to accommodate growth for several years. Set the pot where it will get a few hours of direct morning sun or in daylong indirect light. Indoors, choose a spot with medium light. Water pots during the growing season, and allow them to go dry when plants are dormant. Mulch in-ground bulbs with organic mulch, and containers with pebbles. Feed sparingly with organic fertilizer early in the growing season (follow label directions). Provide an occasional deep drink when winter rains are sparse. Water to keep soil moist once rains end until plants go dormant, then stop watering until new leaves appear. Remove leaves only when completely dry, and avoid digging around or disturbing bulbs and roots.

Other Species and Cultivars
'Lemon Flame' has pale or greenish yellow flowers. Sand lily (*Veltheimia capensis*) is similar to forest lily but takes full sun, a bit more water, and flowers earlier in the year. Sand lily leaves are shorter and blue-gray; flowers are deeper pink and occasionally white.

Freesia
Freesia species

ZONES: 9 through 11
FORM: Fan of flat leaves with wavy stems holding tubular flowers in early spring
GROWTH AND MATURE SIZE: Summer dormant, quickly multiplying to 3 to 6 inches x 3 to 6 inches
USES: Foreground, border, drifts, succulent companion, perennial bed filler
SOIL: Any from well-drained, fertile to heavy clay soil; favors rocky, native soil
PESTS: None

While familiar to gardeners along coasts and inland valleys, Southwest gardeners may be surprised at how easily freesia grow in their gardens. This South African species is popular in the floral trade, thanks to its wide range of colors and forms, including double flowering. All are fragrant, some extravagantly so. In early spring, a fan of flat leaves emerges, followed by a nodding head of wide, tubular flowers in red, blue, lavender, purple, white, or yellow. Individual flowers remain open for a week or more, and the entire blooming sequence lasts about six weeks. Diminutive *Freesia alba* has white flowers that fill the spring garden with a sweet, spicy aroma.

Shared Spaces
This colorful species is an outstanding addition to spring plantings. Because freesia grows well in dry conditions, mix them with succulents such as aloes and agaves. Use freesia to fill barren spots in a newly planted garden. Freesia grows well in containers or planters either individually or mixed with other bulbs, annuals, or perennials. This reliable rebloomer, with its dry summer dormancy, is a perfect choice for a garden that is left on its own for the summer.

Cultivation
Set the corms 2 inches deep with the pointed end facing up. Cover completely and water thoroughly. Water every two to three weeks until the leaves emerge and then increase watering to once every seven to ten days. Water weekly when the plant is flowering, and continue to water every seven to ten days while the leaves remain on the plant, or in heavy soils, allow the soil to dry a bit between waterings. Apply slow-release or organic fertilizer annually in fall. Freesia can be kept entirely dry when it's dormant. Leaves continue to grow for a month or more after blooming. Allow them to dry naturally and remove them when they can be pulled away easily by hand. Cut flowering stalks anytime. Corms multiply quickly and may be divided every three or four years.

Other Species and Cultivars
Singles are 'Aladdin' (yellow), 'Cote d'Azur (blue), 'Elegance' (white), 'Oberon' (red), and 'Tonga' (pink). Double varieties are 'Priscilla' (orange-red), 'Purple Rain' (lilac), and 'Volante' (white).

Gladiolus
Gladiolus species

ZONES: 7 through 11
FORM: Tall swordlike leaves with tall stalks holding tubular flowers in late winter or spring
GROWTH AND MATURE SIZE: Species summer dormant and naturalizing to 1 to 3 feet x 6 inches
USES: Drifts, borders, dry perennial garden
SOIL: Excellent drainage
PESTS: Protect from hungry squirrels, rabbits, and rodents; watch for whitefly

Delicate looking, tough-growing species gladiolus are the wild gladiolus of Africa and southern Europe, and ancient parents of the fancy nursery hybrids. "Gladiolus" is derived from the Latin word *gladius*, meaning "sword shaped," and refers to the sword-shaped leaves that sprout in fall. Spring blooms follow, with tall stalks of delicate 3- to 4-inch, star-shaped tubular flowers whose colors range from subtle tones of cream, mauve, and pale blue to screaming hot orange, white, purple, coral, and yellow. Flowers are speckled and streaked in contrasting colors; some are fragrant. After blooms fade, leaves persist for a time.

Shared Spaces
Species gladiolus flowers add a graceful touch to any water-wise flower bed. These early spring bloomers are beautiful when grown with lavenders, rosemary, ornamental grasses, and soft foliage ground covers such as ornamental oreganos.

Cultivation
Set bulbs (technically corms) 4 inches deep and 5 inches apart. In pots, space just as deep and a bit closer together. Water well and mulch. Plants bloom best with an application of organic bulb fertilizer when leaves first appear. Water when the top several inches of soil are dry, during the growing season only. Withhold summer water so corms dry out. Allow leaves to dry on the corm after flowering. Cut (don't pull) completely brown and dry leaves. If you don't have a spot free from summer water, grow gladiolus in pots, nestled in the garden to look as if they are permanent. After one bloom fades, move the pot to a shaded spot and stop watering until new growth appears the next fall or winter.

Other Species and Cultivars
Yellow marsh Afrikaner (*Gladiolus tristis*) is an early bloomer with tall narrow leaves and slender ivory flowers with a sweet fragrance. Next blooming is sword lily (*Gladiolus byzantinus*), with hot pink flowers having white markings. *G. oppositiflorus*, wildflower salmon gladiolus, is cold hardy to Zone 5 with heavy mulch in winter. Reed bells (*Gladiolus gracilis*) are fragrant in pale blue or lavender with magenta purple streaks and speckles with a touch of yellow.

Grape Hyacinth
Muscari armeniacum

ZONES: 4 through 9
FORM: Grassy foliage with short stalks and grape-cluster blooms in earliest spring
GROWTH AND MATURE SIZE: Summer dormant, reseeds and naturalizes, to 6 inches x 6 inches
USES: Rock garden, edging, ground cover, understory, foreground, drifts
SOIL: Any, as long as it doesn't stay too wet
PESTS: Squirrels and pocket gophers; plant in enclosed spaces

Grape hyacinths are by far the easiest and most reliable spring bulbs for naturalizing in the Southwest. Their grassy foliage appears in late summer and remains green through winter. The bloom stalks, resembling tiny clusters of grapes, start poking through the leaves after the crocus fade, just in time to contrast with the earliest species tulips. Both 'Blue Spike', a medium blue, double-flowered form, and 'Saffier', a dark blue selection, are sterile, making them good choices for small protected spaces where more robust species might become weedy. *M. neglectum* is prolific and has longer leaves with lower florets that are dark blue with white rims, while the florets at the tip of the spike are pale blue.

Shared Spaces

Grape hyacinth reseed and spread to form a dense seasonal ground cover. Use them as edging for paths and perennial borders, or as an alternate-season ground cover interplanted with dwarf plumbago or 'Rosy Glow' sedum. Plant three bulbs for every plumbago or sedum. Because the leaves are dark green throughout fall and winter, grape hyacinths look weedy in dormant buffalograss, but are lovely in sheep's fescue lawns.

Cultivation

Space bulbs 6 to 10 inches apart, pointed side up, 2 to 3 inches deep; use a 6-12-6 or 5-10-5 fertilizer at planting time. Prolong spring blooming by watering weekly; while bulbs are dormant, water their neighbors to keep the bulbs viable. Resume watering every week or two, more often in the low desert, less in partial shade and in higher elevation gardens, in late summer and fall when the leaves reappear. In winter, water often enough to keep the ground from drying out completely if there is no rain or snow. Once established, no fertilizer is necessary. Trim off the spent flowers to prevent reseeding, but allow leaves to continue photosynthesizing until they wither. Thin established beds and replant culled bulbs elsewhere in late summer when leaves reappear. When bulbs are growing in lawns, avoid mowing until bulb foliage fades.

Other Species and Cultivars

'White Magic' has clear white blooms. 'Ocean Magic' has soft blue flowers. 'Bi-color Blue' has two-toned spikes of blue-purple with soft blue tips.

Iris
Iris species

ZONES: 4 through 10
FORM: Swordlike foliage; tall stalks of large blooms in early spring
GROWTH AND MATURE SIZE: Fast-growing, multiplying, winter deciduous, to 8 to 36 inches x 18 to 36 inches
USES: Drift, understory, perennial bed, focal point, midground to background, borders
SOIL: Well-drained soil, infertile sandy or gritty
PESTS: Iris borer, remove infested plants; wash off aphids with soapy water

Bearded iris (*Iris germanica*) grow easily and bloom briefly but spectacularly in May in nearly every color imaginable. Their flowers stand four feet tall. Some bloom again in fall if temperatures are mild. Siberian iris have smaller blooms in shades of dark violet-blue, pale blue, and white, showing later in spring on slender 30-inch stems. The plants tolerate quite a bit of shade. Several bulbous types grow well. Juno iris (*Iris bucharica*) grows 12 to 16 inches tall. It produces five or more blooms to a stem in a blend of yellow, cream, and rust above corn-like glossy green leaves. Two extremely cold-hardy dwarf iris are *Iris danfordii* and *Iris reticulata*.

Shared Spaces

Plant iris in single color groupings of three or five spaced 18 inches apart for a strong color display, or mix colors for a rainbow effect. Combine bearded iris with daylilies, 'Moonshine' yarrow, or ornamental grasses to hide fading foliage. Use Siberian iris as accents between flowering or evergreen shrubs. Plant dwarf iris in buffalo grass meadows for early color.

Cultivation

Plant rhizomes shallowly, leaving the shoulders exposed, especially in heavier soil and colder locations. Siberian iris need humusy soil and more water when first planted. If drip irrigating, place emitters to the side of the plant, not right above the rhizome. Water bearded iris thoroughly once every week or two until six weeks or so after flowering. Water monthly while the plants are dormant. Siberians prefer weekly watering while in bloom if in well-drained soils, twice a month while leafy, and monthly while dormant. Allow water to penetrate slowly to 18 inches. Slow-release fertilizer worked into the soil at planting keeps iris healthy until they need dividing. Lift and divide rhizomes every five years. Divide and reset established plants in late July and early August.

Other Species and Cultivars

I. spuria are 6 feet tall with large flowers late in the season, while California's native Pacific coast hybrid iris are a diminutive 8 to 24 inches tall and very early blooming in many shades. *I. pallida* 'Variegata' has fragrant late-spring blue flowers. Avoid *Iris psuedocorus* in California where it is invasive.

Mariposa Lily
Calochortus species

ZONES: 4 through 11

FORM: Grasslike foliage topped with cup-shaped blooms from spring to early summer

GROWTH AND MATURE SIZE: Summer dormant, fast growing to 4 to 36 inches x 4 inches

USES: Drifts, meadows, rock garden, understory

SOIL: Well-drained soil; some tolerance for clay

PESTS: Protect bulbs from hungry critters

Mariposa lilies are gorgeous flowering bulbs native to the West Coast from Baja to British Columbia. The genus name *Calochortus* is Greek for "beautiful grass," evidently a reference to their narrow, green, grasslike leaves, topped by three petals that form cup-shaped, nodding, or starlike flowers, typically 3 to 4 inches across. The petals of cup-shaped mariposa (Spanish for "butterfly") lilies are often marked at their base with speckles, freckles, and mysterious looking "eyes." Mariposa lilies bloom in white, lavender, pale pink, bright pink, rose, burgundy, orange, and bright yellow with burgundy markings.

Shared Spaces

In the ground, grow mariposa lilies in an open meadow, a rock garden, or as an understory to shrubs and trees. Grow mariposa lilies in containers to control water and keep bulbs from predators. Display them as potted plants during the bloom season or nestle the pots amid foliage in the garden so they look planted. After bloom, lift the containers and store dry for the following year.

Cultivation

Plant bulbs in late fall in a spot that gets no summer water. Plant 2 inches deep and 4 to 6 inches apart, with the pointed side up. Mulch well after planting. Keep soil moist until they bloom. Following bloom, allow the bulbs to go dry through summer. The dry dormant period is an important stage of the mariposa lily life-cycle. No fertilizer is needed. These plants require very little care. Remove leaves once they dry out completely.

Other Species and Cultivars

'Golden Orb' has buttercup yellow blooms with garnet markings. *C. superubus* has lavender pink with yellow edges and maroon brush marks. Butterfly mariposa lily (*C. venustus*) blooms white to bright pink, lavender, and burgundy. This bulb prefers bright shade. One of the easiest mariposa lilies is yellow mariposa lily (*C. luteus*). Its yellow petals are marked with burgundy deep inside the flower. Desert mariposa lily (*C. kennedyi*) takes part shade and has bright orange flowers (10 to 20 inches).

Naked Lady
Amaryllis belladonna

ZONES: 8 through 11
FORM: Strap leaves from fall through spring, tall stalks with clusters of tubular flowers in summer
GROWTH AND MATURE SIZE: Naturalizing and fast growing to 24 inches x 6 inches
USES: Background bulb garden, understory, focal point, border
SOIL: Well-drained soil
PESTS: None

Naked ladies are tough, showy South African bulbs that thrive on neglect. From fall through spring, they have tall, deep green, strappy leaves. In early summer, the leaves die to the ground. Then, in summer's heat, a 2- to 3-foot-tall flower stalk rises, topped by a cluster of up to twelve large, pink, trumpet-shaped flowers. Their fresh perfume fills the air in the afternoon. The name "naked lady" comes from the fact that, without any foliage, the flower stalks look naked. Flowers tend to be a deeper pink in cooler summer climates, paler pink in hotter areas.

Shared Spaces
Add naked ladies to low-water flower borders with perennial marigold, lavender, rosemary, blue hibiscus, honeybush, and bay. Combine with succulents for an interesting counterpoint. Use in an old-fashioned flower garden with lilac, iris, and geranium. For a classic Mediterranean garden, plant naked ladies with bougainvillea, yucca, agave, and purple-flowering Mexican bush sage.

Cultivation
Plant in summer when bulbs are dormant. Choose a spot in full sun or dry bright shade (especially in hot valley and inland gardens) with well-draining soil. Set bulbs a foot apart, leaving their shoulders at or above soil level. In cold winter gardens, bury bulbs completely. Set bulbs slightly closer in containers. Water well and mulch. When growing naked ladies in a container, choose one large enough to accommodate several years of growth to avoid interrupting the bloom cycle. Naked ladies thrive on neglect. They require little to no water and no fertilizer, yet reward you with fragrant blooms year after year.

Allow leaves to dry completely once the bloom fades; leave in place as mulch or move to the compost pile. *Note:* This bulb is poisonous if ingested.

Other Species and Cultivars
Naked ladies hybridized with other bulbs in the *Amaryllis* family produce flowers in shades of deep pink to white and even red. 'Cape Town' has deep rose-red blooms.

Ornamental Onion
Allium species

ZONES: 4 through 11
FORM: Tall, sometimes leafless stems produce round to drumstick-shaped blooms in summer
GROWTH AND MATURE SIZE: Naturalizing and quickly growing to 6 to 24 inches x 6 to 12 inches
USES: Drifts, mass, focal point, border, meadows
SOIL: Well-drained soil
PESTS: None

When you combine the words "ornamental" and "onion" into one phrase, it raises some questions. How can "ornamental" describe a plant that sleeps underground through winter and in early spring sends out small tufts of not-so-spectacular foliage? Just wait a bit longer, however, and the true show begins. Long, strong stems grow quickly to 6 inches or even 6 feet. Atop each are pom-pom blooms in deep, almost black, purple, sunshine yellow, clear snow white, and shades of red, maroon, pink, and even chartreuse, ranging in size from ½ inch to an enormous 5 inches across. Barely onion scented, beautifully ornamental—they live up to their name.

Shared Spaces

Ornamental onions are sometimes planted around roses and fruit trees as pest deterrents. Globular, rose-pink flower heads make an interesting foil for salvias and the blue spikes of veronica. Cluster with whiplash daisy in multiple groups of 5 to 9 bulbs. Interplant with yarrow and other bulbs in dry understory areas. Plant smaller flowering onions in drifts and use larger cultivars as focal points or background plantings in a perennial bed.

Cultivation

Seeds germinate best in cool soil in both spring and fall, or transplant from containers anytime during the growing season. Plant small bulbs in fall at 4 to 6 inches apart, larger bulbs 8 to 12 inches apart. If grown in the shade and mulched well, alliums may be watered once a week while in bloom, and every two weeks in summer after plants are well established. A little slow-release fertilizer may be worked into the soil at planting, but once established, they don't need fertilizing. Cut the old stems back to the ground some time before they begin to grow in spring.

Other Species and Cultivars

Drumstick onion (*A. sphaerocephalum*) has globular 2-inch-wide heads of tightly compressed wine-purple florets held 2 feet above the ground on slender, stick-straight stems. 'Mount Everest' towers to 3 feet with 3- to 4-inch white flower heads. 'Ambassador' has long-lasting foliage and enormous 8-inch blooms of dark purple flowers. *A. moly* 'Jeannine' has yellow blooms and spreads in broad clumps.

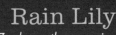

Rain Lily
Zephyranthes species

ZONES: 6 through 11
FORM: Masses of blooms cover narrow grasslike foliage in summer
GROWTH AND MATURE SIZE: Spreading over time and growing to 4 to 6 inches x 4 to 6 inches
USES: Borders, drifts, understory, perennial bed, meadows
SOIL: Well-drained soil
PESTS: None

In areas with good drenching rain in summer, rain lilies pop up out of the ground, bursting into bloom in pink, white, yellow, and light orange. Then they quickly fade, leaving only their leaves as a reminder that they will return once the rain returns. The large pink rain lily common to older gardens is *Zephyranthes grandiflora*. The tall, thin white flowers of *Z. drummondii* reach up to 12 inches in height and like most rain lilies, spread prolifically over time. The clear yellow flowers of *Z. citrina* bloom later in summer, as does the white-flowered evergreen species *Z. candida*. There are many hybrid forms, of which 'Ajax' is the most common.

Shared Spaces
Mix rain lilies with summer-flowering perennials such as salvia, gaillardia, lantana, or vinca. Rain lilies grow well in large containers or planters alone or in mixed plantings. Use evergreen species generously to form a loose, informal border or provide the edge for a large perennial bed. Most species of rain lily, and *Z. grandiflora* in particular, tolerate growing in a lawn.

Cultivation
Plant dormant bulbs in fall and container-grown plants either in fall or spring. Set container-grown plants in a hole that is the same size as the root zone. Water thoroughly after planting. Apply slow-release or organic fertilizer in fall and spring. Water established plants weekly in summer; rely on natural rainfall during winter. Plants will survive winter dormancy in beds that are regularly watered as long as there is good drainage. *Z. candida* should be watered every two to three weeks in winter. Leaves of rain lilies grow for only a short time after the blooming period and will dry and wither quickly. Remove when they can be pulled away easily in your hand. Evergreen species lose some leaves in summer and these can be removed by hand. Remove spent flowers anytime. Divide crowded clumps every four or five years in fall.

Other Species and Cultivars
Z. longifolia has thin, blue-green leaves and gold flowers and is native to Arizona. *Z. rosea* flowers pink. 'Apricot Queen' and 'Prairie Sunset' are yellow with pink and coral cast.

Spider Lily
Hymenocallis species

ZONES: 8 through 11
FORM: Long strappy leaves with tall stalks and large blooms from July to September
GROWTH AND MATURE SIZE: Multiplies slowly, deciduous or evergreen, quick growing to 1 to 4 feet x 1 to 3 feet
USES: Focal plant, summer borders, perennial beds
SOIL: Well-drained, even rocky, unamended, native soil
PESTS: None

Even amidst rocky soil and neglect, spider lilies thrive and light up dreary corners with their elegant, dangling white flowers. It is the common hybrid form of the large semievergreen plant with deep green strappy leaves. The flowers are extraordinary, with a filmy saucer uniting the thin draping petals on tall, sturdy stalks high above the foliage. Some of the smaller species *Hymenocallis maximillianii* or *H. littoralis* are deciduous in winter, growing and blooming only in the hottest part of summer.

Shared Spaces
The bulbs of the large, hybrid varieties increase in size over the years and produce many blooming stalks, making them especially dramatic as a specimen or focal plant. Mix with summer-flowering plants such as four o'clocks, California fuschia, and salvia. Smaller varieties do well in containers or planters, particularly in areas where it is too cold to leave them in the ground year-round.

Cultivation
Plant in spring or summer in desert regions. Along the coast and inland valleys, plant in fall and winter when bulbs are dormant. Place so that two-thirds of the bulb and all of the neck are above the soil surface. Cover and water thoroughly. Water weekly until leaves emerge. Spider lilies grow with or without additional fertilizer, but mulching the base of the plants helps keep them from drying out. Apply slow-release or organic fertilizer around the base annually in spring. Water established bulbs every seven to ten days in summer. Reduce watering to every other week in winter in well-draining soils. Remove spent flower stalks anytime. As leaves yellow and dry, they may be removed when they can be pulled away easily by hand. Spider lily bulbs multiply slowly and resent being disturbed.

Other Species and Cultivars
H. littoralis is a variegated spider lily having white fragrant blooms and dramatic striped foliage. *H. caribeae* is evergreen, reaching 18 to 24 inches tall with 3- to 4-inch white blooms. 'Sulphur Queen' has a citrus fragrance with yellow blooms.

Tulip
Tulipa species

ZONES: 8 through 10
FORM: Strappy leaves with many blooms above the foliage.
GROWTH AND MATURE SIZE: Multiplying, summer dormant, quickly growing to 6 to 36 inches x 3 to 6 inches
USES: Mass, drifts, border, perennial and annual beds, meadow
SOIL: More reliable in well-drained, fertile alkaline soil, or rocky, native soil
PESTS: None

Tulips sometimes seem like too much trouble—a big burst of overdone flowers over a too short time. Lady tulip (*Tulipa clusiana*), candia tulip (*T. saxatilis*), and *T. sylvestris* are exceptions. Hybrid tulips require a long chill period and exacting cultivation. These species tulips require only ordinary garden soil and minimal care, for which they reward you by multiplying rapidly and reblooming faithfully every year. Lady tulip has petals that are cream to yellow inside, red or coral outside. Candia tulip flowers are large and open in shades of pink, mauve, and lavender, often with bright yellow centers. *T. sylvestris* flowers range from lemon yellow to gold and are sweetly scented.

Shared Spaces

Mix species tulips with other spring-flowering perennials, bulbs, or annuals. These species are shorter than the hybrids and should be used in the front of a border or in groups. All grow extremely well in containers or planters either in mass or mixed with other bulbs or perennials. They spread by stolons (underground stems) and fill in small, barren corners or odd ends of beds.

Cultivation

Place bulbs so that the tip of the bulb is 2 inches below the surface, cover completely and water thoroughly. Water every week or two until the leaves emerge. Water growing and blooming plants weekly, more often if the weather is exceptionally hot or dry. Apply slow-release or organic fertilizer in fall and early spring. These tulips need a long, dry summer dormancy and can be left in the ground if they are kept dry or lifted and replanted if they are share space with actively growing plants. Leaves continue to grow for about a month after flowering and should be left to die back naturally. They may be removed when they can be pulled away easily by hand. Flowers may be cut anytime, and if they're picked early in the bloom cycle, they make good cut flowers.

Other Species and Cultivars

Species tulips quickly form colonies. *T. batalinii*, 'Bright Gem' is fragrant with sulphur yellow flowers; 'Red Gem' is red with an apricot glow. 'Lady Jane' has rosy-red petals edged in white; 'Cynthia' has red exterior petals edged with chartreuse, with a chartreuse-yellow interior.

Succulents

ucculents are plants that all store water variously in their leaves, stems, and roots as a way to survive long periods of dry conditions. They have sculptural, sometimes odd shapes; brightly colored branches; branching that's sometimes spines (cacti), sometimes thorns (succulents that aren't cacti), sometimes smooth; and amazingly beautiful flowers.

Gardeners new to the Southwest may be put off by succulents at first, but soon discover that they are just too easy and beautiful to ignore. Water-wise, virtually pest- and maintenance-free, and versatile in every way, these plants definitely are *not* just for desert gardens! Succulents are dependable, tough-as-nails plants that tolerate drought, heat, and wind. They wait silently for their needs to be fulfilled, are undemanding if ignored, and are not particular about their diet. Top all this off with their added gifts of flowers in bright glowing hues and their ease of propagation, and you have the perfect plant for the water-wise garden no matter where you live.

Still, not all succulents are suited to all dry environments. In the high desert, for example, even the most tough-as-nails succulents have their "happy places." At these elevations, *Sedum* 'Autumn Joy' and hens 'n chicks thrive in full sun, while agaves prefer part shade and manfredas prefer full shade in the low and intermediate deserts, and full sun along the coast and inland valleys. With some experimentation, you'll soon learn which succulents give the best show in your particular climate and microclimate.

Succulents play different roles in the garden as well. While larger-leaved stonecrops make good midground plantings, those with diminutive foliage fill pockets between native sandstone rocks or carpet the ground between steppingstones. For height in the garden, tall, rosette-crowned aeonium create a background planting resembling a grove of thick-stemmed miniature palm trees. No matter where you garden, how big your garden is, or what style it might be, there are succulents for you.

To plant a succulent in the ground, dig a hole two to three times wider than the plant's container and about as deep. Don't amend the soil. Remove the plant from its container and, with your pruners, cut an inch thick slit into the rootball, slicing from top to bottom. Make a few slits around the rootball.

If the plant is potbound and roots are thicker than a pencil, lay the rootball on its side, then use your pruners or a sharp knife to cut about an inch wide slice off the bottom of the roots, just as if you were cutting a slice off a loaf of bread. Then make the slits down the sides with your shears and remove the container. Set the plant in the hole just slightly higher than it sat in the container. Fill around the plant with unamended soil, then press gently around the base to remove air pockets. Mulch with several inches of smooth river rock, cinder rock, gravel, or coarse sand.

Once planted, succulents are best left alone other than occasional water and periodic grooming. When you water succulents in the ground or in a container, allow the soil to dry *completely* between waterings. Succulent mortality is most often a result of overwatering, so resist the urge to water until you have checked the soil with your finger. If it's dry down past the first joint of your index finger, it is time to water. Place the hose at the base of the plant and let the water drip slowly until it saturates down to the roots. Succulents do not need fertilizer. If you live in an area where you take your succulents inside in winter, you might want to feed them with a bit of granular slow-release or organic fertilizer when you take them out in spring

As tough as succulents are, not all are hardy in all parts of the Southwest. If you covet a species that is not cold hardy in your zone, grow it in a pot that you can move inside or under the eaves in winter. Or, plant it in the ground in spring, enjoy it through the warm months, then dig it up before the first frost. If your plant is too big or well rooted to dig, take cuttings and start a new plant as the cold weather approaches.

Propagating succulents is usually as simple as sticking a succulent branch into a pot of sandy potting mix. Some succulents even root from leaves set onto the surface of potting mix. Let the stem or leaf air dry for a few days before potting it. Water when you pot it, then don't water again until the soil is so dry that it's cracking on the surface. Then, water slowly and deeply.

Aeonium
Aeonium species

ZONES: 9 through 11
FORM: Some low, spreading clumps of rosettes, some tall-stemmed rosettes
GROWTH AND MATURE SIZE: Fairly fast-growing evergreen succulent to 1½ x 4 feet x 1 to 3 feet
USES: Midground, accent, water-wise perennial gardens, borders, rock and succulent garden
SOIL: Well-drained soil
PESTS: None

Gardeners are often challenged to keep their gardens interesting between bloom seasons. One approach is to incorporate evergreens with interesting leaf colors and textures. Aeoniums are just those plants. Aeoniums form rosettes of spoon-shaped leaves that, at first glance, look like big succulent flowers. Some aeoniums have bright green leaves; some are a deep burgundy, almost black. Then there are aeoniums with leaves of all shades and variations in between. In summer, aeoniums form stalks of tiny yellow flowers that are nice, but less impressive than their leafy rosettes. Most aeoniums multiply by making side shoots (pups), many forming broad colonies.

Shared Spaces

Aeonium are the mainstay of many succulent gardens. You can also use them in combination with other water-wise plants. Use 'Sunburst' to light up deep green cape rush. Plant burgundy 'Zwartkopf' next to bright green-leaved Jerusalem sage, red-hot poker, and drought-tolerant sages. Insert stems of aeonium into cracks in stone walls or plant them in containers. They look especially good in aged terracotta.

Cultivation

Aeoniums go into suspended animation in summer, so water sparingly or your plants will rot. The rains that arrive during their winter growing season should take care of their water needs, but water occasionally during a dry winter. No fertilizer is needed. Groom plants to remove dead leaves and spent flower stalks. There is no need to prune, but you can remove branches to shape.

Other Species and Cultivars

One of the most beautiful aeoniums, 'Sunburst', has pale yellow leaves striped in green and edged in pink. *A. arboreum* 'Zwartkopf' grows 3 to 4 feet tall with nearly black rosettes. 'Blushing Beauty' leaves are green with red blush. 'Cyclops' is a 4- to 5-foot-tall stem topped by a single rosette of deep burgundy and green leaves. *A. undulatum* forms a low colony of 8-inch bright green rosettes. Dinner plate aeonium (*A. tabuliforme*) forms rosettes only 2 inches tall that spread up to 18 inches in diameter, hence the name. This most striking aeonium is best grown in a wide container.

Agave
Agave species

ZONES: 5 through 11
FORM: Thick, stiff, usually prickly leaves form a rosette
GROWTH AND MATURE SIZE: Slow growing evergreen, ½ foot to 5 feet x ½ foot to 7 feet
USES: Focal point, perennial, succulent gardens, dry stream bed
SOIL: Well-drained, fertile soil to rocky, native soil
PESTS: Some are susceptible to agave snout weevil; replace the plant

Agaves have stiff leaves often tipped with spiny points arranged with tight regularity into a rosette. Cream to gold flowers line tall stalks. Many species produce "pups," and a few produce plantlets (called "bulbils") along the flowering stalk. The mother plant typically dies after flowering. There are agaves for all zones of the Southwest, from the native Parry's agave (*Agave parryi*) with gray leaves rimmed in maroon to the soft, unarmed, celadon-green leaves of foxtail agave (*A. attenuata*). Other choices include the large blue-gray *A. americana*; the solitary *A. victoriae-reginae* with rigid, dark green leaves marked in white; or the rapidly spreading *A. lophantha*.

Shared Spaces

Agaves provide interest and contrast to all gardens. Many species tolerate summer watering enough to grow with perennials. Their shallow root system and dramatic forms make agaves an excellent choice for growing in containers. Native species are especially useful in low-maintenance areas of the garden.

Cultivation

Water immediately after planting. Water every four days for the first month if temperatures exceed 90 degrees F. Most agaves do not need fertilizer, although tropical species benefit from slow-release or organic fertilizer once a year. Water established plants every two weeks in summer in low desert gardens; every month in cooler climates. Water sparingly over winter in all zones. Remove dead leaves or spent flowering stalks anytime. Resist pruning living leaves—it invites infection. If plants crowd a path or walkway, prune just the terminal spine for greater safety. Remove pups anytime.

Other Species and Cultivars

Variegated dwarf century plant (*A. desmettiana variegata*) (Zones 9 through 11) is slow growing to 3 feet tall and wide with blue-green foliage edged in bright yellow. Durango Delight™ is a moderate grower to 2 feet x 3 feet and is good for containers. *A. parryi* var. *truncata*, the artichoke agave (Zones 6 through 9), has 2- to 4-foot rosettes, forming clumps 5 feet across. *A. desmettiana* is dwarf (Zones 9 through 10) with bluish leaves that turn outward. *A. vilmoriniana*, octopus agave, has 3- to 4-foot long arching leaves that resemble—you guessed it—octopus arms.

Aloe
Aloe species

ZONES: 9 through 11

FORM: Thick leaves form clumps of rosettes

GROWTH AND MATURE SIZE: Moderately growing evergreen succulent to 1 to 5 feet x 1 to 5 feet

USES: Focal point, succulent, dry shade, rock, dry stream, and perennial gardens

SOIL: Well-drained, fertile soil to rocky, native soil

PESTS: Ants, mealy bugs; root rot if overwatered or in poorly drained soils

Aloes are one of the most beautiful succulents for gardens from the low desert to the coast. Their thick, glossy leaves may be dark green, pale blue-gray, or nearly white. Winter-blooming flowers occur on long stalks in soft shades of coral, pink, and red. Coral aloe (*Aloe striata*) has wide, light green leaves bordered in pink and dark coral flowers. *A. ferox* is a tree aloe with spikes of brilliant red flowers. *A. saponaria* is a small, clumping aloe with yellow to orange flowers arranged in loose heads. This aloe is quite cold hardy. The mainstay of medicinal gardens, *A. vera*, with its spikes of yellow or orange flowers, grows prolifically in the low zones.

Shared Spaces

Mix aloes with other succulents for winter color. Many aloes are tolerant of supplemental watering and can be mixed into perennial or annual beds. Plant them generously near seating areas, patios, or pools both for their long, cool-season blooms and for the humming-birds they attract. Aloes are excellent plants in containers, and the flowering stalks make good cut flowers. Aloes are particularly useful in dry shade.

Cultivation

No soil amendments are needed. Water after planting.

Water every five to seven days for the first month if there is no rainfall. Water established plants carefully and be sure the soil is dry between waterings. Water every one to two weeks in summer, once every two to three weeks in winter if no rainfall occurs during those times. No fertilizer is needed. Remove spent, flowering stalks or dead leaves anytime. Do not prune living leaves of aloes; the wounds invite infection.

Other Species and Cultivars

Aloe humilis 'Hedgehog' has spotted spiny leaves to 20 inches tall that form a rosette. Hardy in Zones 9 through 10, it loves dry, hot conditions, so it should flourish in low desert areas. Spiral aloe, *A. polyphylla*, is hardy in Zones 7 through 9 and likes full sun to partial shade. It forms solitary rosettes reaching 1 foot x 2 feet and rarely blooms. Its leaves form a beautiful spiral pattern as the plant ages. *A. barberae* is a slow-growing tree reaching over 20 to 30 feet tall (Zones 9 through 11).

Blue Chalk Sticks
Senecio mandraliscae

ZONES: 8 through 11
FORM: Fingerlike blue leaves on trailing stems
GROWTH AND MATURE SIZE: Fast-growing evergreen succulent to 1 to 2 feet x 2 to 3 feet
USES: Edging, border, ground cover, mass or drifts, succulent, dry perennial, and dry streambed gardens
SOIL: Well-drained soil is best, but plants will tolerate heavier soils if watered sparingly
PESTS: None

Have you ever seen a powder blue plant? While green, blue-green, and gray-green are common, powder blue is something special, especially when it is the thick, succulent, powder blue leaves of blue chalk sticks. Blue chalk sticks is a perennial succulent from South Africa. It has long trailing stems lined with smooth cylindrical leaves, each 3 to 4 inches long and arranged 360 degrees around a tubular stem. Rub the stem or leaves and you'll see that they are actually bluish green covered in a white waxy coating. Wax coating is a typical water conserving strategy used by plants like this one that has evolved to withstand hot, sunny, and dry environments.

Shared Spaces

Blue chalk sticks makes an excellent ground cover or bed edging. Surround the stout trunk of tall desert spoon with blue chalk sticks; the bright green, upright, succulent leaves of yellow African bulbine; and pink-flowering African daisy. Set blue chalk sticks along the base of a wall or use to soften the edges in borders with succulent spurge. Use it to cascade over the side of a pot of pink, lavender, and teal-leaved hens 'n chicks.

Cultivation

Water well and mulch with a 1-inch layer of pebbles or gravel after planting. For container culture, use a cactus and succulent potting mix or combine standard potting mix with one-third coarse construction sand. Blue chalk sticks is extremely drought tolerant once established. Water twice monthly spring through fall in desert gardens, half as often elsewhere, and none in winters where there is regular rainfall. With more frequent water plants grow quickly—a blessing or a curse depending on the garden. No fertilizer is needed. *Note:* This plant is poisonous if ingested.

Other Species and Cultivars

Blue chalk fingers (*Senecio vitalis*) looks much like blue chalk sticks, but its leaves are slightly greener, more slender, and more graceful. The stems are more upright, giving this species a somewhat refined appearance. *S. serpens* is shorter with smaller gray-blue leaves. In hot dry conditions, the leaf tips sometimes turn purplish. It doesn't like extended periods of temperatures above 100 F.

Flame Flower
Talinum calycinum

ZONES: 4 through 9

FORM: Low-growing colonies with slender stems holding several blooms from late spring through early autumn

GROWTH AND MATURE SIZE: Fairly fast-growing, winter-dormant succulent to 8 inches x 8 inches

USES: Rock, perennial, meadow, dry stream-bed gardens, mass, drifts, edging, borders

SOIL: All but very heavy clay soil

PESTS: Rabbits and quail; new plants rot if overwatered

Flame flower is one of a choice group of cold-tolerant succulents native to the Great Plains and western mesas of the United States. From a modest start of a few fleshy little leaves, a compact cushion of plump foliage on short, pencil-thick stems develops. Every afternoon, drifts of pink-purple flowers float above the plants on slender gold filaments, several flowers per stem. Flame flower looks fragile and ephemeral, yet blooms reliably for several months through the hottest weather, reappearing year after year. It acts like an alpine plant with its tufted form and extreme cold hardiness, it self-sows to form little colonies, and it is at home where the soil is sun-baked and gritty.

Shared Spaces

Because of its preference for good drainage and warmth, flame flower grows well between boulders on gentle sloping soil, in rock gardens, or mixed in beds with other compact xeric perennials. Group flame flowers with desert zinnia, purple ground cherry, iceplants, and small cacti in rock gardens. Use it for edging paths and patios with 'Colorado Gold' gazania and pussytoes.

Cultivation

Flame flower grows from seed pressed lightly into the surface of sharp sand or other coarse, warm soil, and self-sows readily from established plants. Mulch transplants with fine gravel as it keeps the fleshy stems aerated. Water flame flowers to a depth of 18 inches every week or two in summer to keep them blooming. Water them monthly in spring and fall, and once or twice in winter if there is no rain or snow. No fertilizer is needed. Flame flower continues to open new flowers and looks fresh without deadheading through summer.

The succulent tops and dried flower stems can be raked up gently when they collapse after hard frosts.

Other Species and Cultivars

T. calycinum 'Judith's Favorite' is named after author Judith Phillips. It grows vigorously and quickly to 1-foot mounds and puts on a remarkable floral display with its ½- to ¾-inch rose-violet blooms. *Talinum brevifolium* is a little gem that hugs rocky soil with beadlike pale blue leaves dotted with satiny pink flowers.

Giant False Agave
Furcraea foetida

ZONES: 9 through 11
FORM: Large succulent leaves radiate in a "V" shape with flower stalks rising tall from the center
GROWTH AND MATURE SIZE: Slow-growing evergreen succulent to 5 feet x 8 feet; blooms to 25 feet
USES: Centerpiece, focal point, background
SOIL: Well-drained soil
PESTS: None

Giant false agave looks like a giant yucca but it has soft leaves and no sharp spines. Each plant makes a tall, trunkless rosette of sword-shaped leaves, each up to 10 inches wide and 7 feet long. After a few years in the ground, a 25-foot flower stalk rises from the center of the plant. The stalk is lined with small cream, ivory, or pale green flowers that hang like little bells. Each fragrant flower is soon replaced by a tiny green plantlet, which develops for a while and then drops off the stalk to root in the ground alongside the mother plant. The mother plant dies about a year later, leaving a colony of offspring behind.

Shared Spaces

Give giant false agave plenty of room. It can be used as the centerpiece of a dry garden along with silvery leaved feathery senna; colorful flapjack plant; succulent yellow African bulbine; tall, wispy shoestring acacia trees; and succulent echeveria. Giant false agave makes a wonderful container plant as well. Use it in a grouping of potted succulents chosen for their sizes, leaf colors, and textures.

Cultivation

Set plants in the ground an inch or so higher than they were in their containers. Mulch with rock or stone. In climates where winter temperatures regularly dip below freezing, grow in a ceramic pot and move to a protected area. Keep watered through the first summer until established. After that, in the hottest desert gardens water weekly in summer and monthly in fall and spring. In other areas, water every three weeks to once a month in summer and half as often in fall and spring. Do not fertilize in-ground plants. Feed container-grown plants with organic fertilizer; follow label directions. Prune to remove the flower stalk once plantlets drop.

Other Species and Cultivars

Furcraea foetida 'Mediopicta' is a variegated form of giant false agave reaching 5 feet x 8 feet. Its sword-shaped leaves are striped green with white. 'Mediopicta Sport' has yellow central variegation. *F. macdougali* has rosettes of toothed leaves atop a 10-foot-tall stem. *F. bedinghausii* reaches 12 to 16 feet tall with 3- to 4-foot-long bluish green leaves.

Hardy Iceplant
Delosperma species

ZONES: 5 through 11
FORM: Low-trailing, small fleshy leaves covered with daisylike flowers in spring and summer
GROWTH AND MATURE SIZE: Moderately fast-growing, winter-dormant succulent to 2 to 4 inches x 24 inches
USES: Foreground, border, ground cover
SOIL: Gritty, infertile soil but adapts to most soils if not kept too wet
PESTS: Root rot in wet soil; protect from rabbits

Hardy iceplants are carpet-forming succulents that thrive from the cold winters of the high desert all the way down to the coast. Their fleshy leaves are clustered densely on the prostrate woody stems. Daisylike flowers are brilliantly colored and so profuse that at times they hide the foliage. Their modest aboveground growth belies their deep, shrublike roots once established. Purple iceplant (*D. cooperi*) spreads up to 24 inches wide in just a few summers; it is one of the most cold tolerant and easy to grow. Its flowers are 1-inch, deep magenta daisies with yellow stamens. In mild climate gardens, the foliage is evergreen.

Shared Spaces

Iceplant is often overused as a large-scale ground cover. Instead, use it as a reliable filler in medium-sized spaces, growing around taller perennials, shrubs, and trees. Grow with blue and purple flowers such as giant four o'clocks, blue mist, salvias, buddlejas, Texas and Russian sages, and lavender. Yellow iceplant blends well with pineleaf penstemon, rue, and partridge feather.

Cultivation

Purple and red iceplant flowers most profusely in full sun. Yellow iceplant is more vigorous in partial shade. Use gravel as mulch because it stays drier on the surface while maintaining moisture in the soil. Iceplants thrive on deep watering two or three times a month when temperatures are 90 F or above, and monthly or less during cool weather. No fertilizer is needed. Plants do not bloom as well in nitrogen-rich garden soil. Trim away any leggy growth or withered leaves in spring to rejuvenate plants.

Other Species and Cultivars

'Lesotho Pink' blooms midspring with bright fuchsia pink blooms. Yellow iceplant (*D. nubigenum*) grows only an inch high, spreads two feet wide, has bright green leaves that turn vivid red in winter, and yellow flowers in late spring and summer. 'Gold Nugget' has bright sunshine-yellow blooms in early spring. 'Red Mountain' has bright red blooms with white centers all summer. 'Lavender Mist' is soft pinkish lavender. *D. ashtonii* 'Blue' blooms all summer long with bright purple blooms.

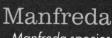

Manfreda
Manfreda species

ZONES: 8 through 11
FORM: Low-growing rosettes with tall stalks holding blooms in May and June
GROWTH AND MATURE SIZE: Moderate-growing evergreen or deciduous succulent to 4 to 6 inches x 6 to 18 inches
USES: Dry gardens, succulent gardens, border, foreground
SOIL: Well-drained, fertile soil; moderately moist soil; as well as rocky, native soil.
PESTS: Ants and mealy bugs; spray with insecticidal soap

With their spotted, soft but brittle leaves, and almost clownish blooms, manfredas feature low-growing rosettes and thrive in dry, shady locations in low and intermediate deserts, and in part and full sun down to the coast. These agave relatives have tall flowering stalks in spring, but plants do not die after bloom. Fragrant flowers are unusual with blooms in chartreuse, maroon, red-brown, or creamy pink, often opening at night. Diminutive *M. maculosa* has evergreen, thin leaves marked purple with fragrant, white flowers that fade to dusky pink. A vigorous form, *M. variegata*, has long, folded, light green, evergreen leaves with purple spots and chartreuse flowers.

Shared Spaces

Mix manfredas with small succulents such as aloes, gasterias, dudleyas, or sansevieras. Plant manfredas generously to form a low, succulent border for a shady desert garden, or along a dry walkway. In beds with very well-drained soil, manfredas can be mixed with perennials such as salvia, penstemon, red justicia, and plumbago. Their striking foliage and small size make manfredas especially useful in large containers or planters.

Cultivation

Water thoroughly after planting. Water weekly through the first summer. Manfredas require no fertilizer. Water established plants weekly in summer, more often if the weather is exceptionally hot or dry. Water evergreen species twice a month or less in winter; rely on natural rainfall for deciduous species. In well-drained soils, manfredas are tolerant of more water, especially in summer. Remove spent, flowering stalks as soon as they dry out. Lift and divide clumping species in early summer.

Other Species and Cultivars

Only the deciduous *Manfreda virginica* is cold tolerant (hardy to Zone 4). Leopard manfreda has rosettes of smooth, 18-inch-long bluish green leaves heavily spotted with maroon markings. *M. sileri* is narrow-leaved with tubular white fragrant blooms. 'Macho Mocha' grows 4 to 6 feet wide with gray-green leaves densely covered with brown-purple spots. A reddish flower stalk rises from the center and blooms white. 'Bloodspot' grows to 1 foot x 2 feet and has 1-inch-wide gray-green leaves with maroon edges dotted with spots of the same color.

181

Red Yucca

Hesperaloe parviflora

ZONES: 5 through 11
FORM: Short, thin leaves forming clumps with tall arching stalks blooming spring through early fall
GROWTH AND MATURE SIZE: Quick-growing evergreen to 3 to 4 feet x 3 to 4 feet
USES: Focal point, mass, drifts, border, meadow, wildflower, perennial gardens
SOIL: Well-drained soil
PESTS: None, deter hungry rabbits.

The rosettes of red hesperaloe have a similar profile to yucca and agave but with slender leaves that are more refined and delicate looking. Its stiff dark green leaves arch from the base, each curling inward almost to the point of forming a long tube. As leaves mature, they typically extend to 2 feet long with a bit of white thread that curls off the edges. Starting in late spring, plants develop 5- to 9-foot arching flower stalks bearing coral-red tubular flowers whose petals are yellow inside. Hummingbirds love them. These Southwest natives can survive on natural rainfall but grow faster with some deep summer water. This grass-shaped succulent perennial is tough—*really* tough.

Shared Spaces

Planted *en masse*, red yucca's striking profile complements plants such as barrel cactus, aloe, and agave in desert theme gardens. Alternatively, red yucca can be grown in a field of wildflowers or combined with Mediterranean climate plants such as red-flowered grevillea, blue-flowered and gray-leaved germander sage, and yellow sundrops.

Cultivation

Water well after planting, and mulch with stone or rock. In coastal and valley gardens, water in-ground plants once a month, and in desert gardens water twice a month during summer (more often in the first year while plants are becoming established). Water deeply (down to the roots) and slowly. Established plants can survive on rainfall alone except in hottest desert gardens. No fertilizer is required for in-ground planting. Water containers regularly and fertilize occasionally and lightly with an organic fertilizer formulated for cactus and succulents. Groom to remove spent flower clusters and dried leaves.

Other Species and Cultivars

Yellow yucca (*H. parvifolia* 'Yellow') is a custard-yellow flowered version. 'Dark Yellow' is a deeper, darker yellow. Night-blooming hesperaloe (*H. nocturna*) is a bit larger with greenish white blooms opening at night. Giant hesperaloe (*H. funifera*) has 4- to 6-foot-long leaves that stand straight and greenish white (sometimes purple-tinged) flowers that open at night. Bell flower hesperaloe (*H. campanulata*) is much like the giant hesperaloe but reaches only 3 feet tall and wide.

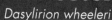
Sotol
Dasylirion wheeleri

ZONES: 6 through 10

FORM: Juvenile growth is long bladed and clumping, maturing to short stubby trunks with raised crown

GROWTH AND MATURE SIZE: Slower-growing evergreen to 5 feet x 6 feet with 10-foot flower stalks

USES: Barrier, focal point, border, mass in large areas, succulent and dry streambed gardens

SOIL: Gravelly or sandy soil; gritty, fast-draining soil

PESTS: None

Sotol grows clumps of slender evergreen leaf blades with margins bordered by fine hooked teeth that angle toward the leaf tips, making the leaves look much like double-edged saw blades. The long, narrow leaves are pale blue or green matte with yellow margins. The crown initially grows at ground level. As it matures, sotol develops a short trunk that elevates the fan of leaves and gives the plant a bold silhouette. Bolder still is the flower stalk, which pushes from the crown skyward 10 or 12 feet, unfolding masses of tiny white florets. *D. texanum*, native to Texas and Mexico, is durable, hardy to Zone 5, and has 8-foot-tall spikes of creamy white flowers.

Shared Spaces
Like all spiny plants, give sotol some extra space as a safety zone. Desert willow, littleleaf sumac, creosote bush, cholla, prickly pear, Apache plume, fairy duster, and turpentine bush are all good companions. Sotol and *Opuntia* species planted together as a border provide a dramatic and formidable barrier.

Cultivation
Mulch with gravel. Speed growth of young plants by watering to a depth of 3 feet once or twice a month, May through August, if you have well-draining soil. Keep plants dry in winter to avoid root rot. A small amount of slow-release fertilizer at planting gets plants off to a strong start, but established plants don't need fertilizing. For a managed appearance, or if you're growing plants near a pool where seed litter is a problem, prune off flower stems immediately after blooming. Trim the oldest basal leaves off as they dry in more cultivated garden settings. In more casual settings or where feeding wildlife is a priority, leave the seedheads until birds have eaten their fill. Use the old seed stalks for fencing around gardens or as habitat for small wild bees that help with pollination.

Other Species and Cultivars
Dasylirion leiophyllum has a shiny green leaf color, and the barbs on the leaf margins angle downward. *D. quadrangulatum* grows larger to 10 feet x 6 to 8 feet and has very narrow and unarmed leaves arranged in whorl around the plant; it's hardy to Zone 10.

Stonecrop
Sedum 'Autumn Joy'

ZONES: 4 through 11
FORM: Upright clumps with sturdy stalks that blooms in mid- to late summer
GROWTH AND MATURE SIZE: Winter dormant, moderately growing to 15 to 18 inches x 24 inches
USES: Taller for midground, focal point, mass, drift, succulent, perennial beds, shorter ground covers
SOIL: Most soils, even heavy clay, as long as it's not too wet
PESTS: Aphids; protect from rabbits

'Autumn Joy' is one of the best of the robust sedums that fare well in the dry heat of the Southwest. Thick, pale green shoots push up from the soil in spring, quickly expanding into clumps of round, fleshy leaves with scalloped margins. 'Autumn Joy' flowers open pale pink, mature to a deep coral, and persist through winter in a rich russet. *Sedum spectabile* foliage is a bit brighter green and its flower umbels are flat-topped rather than crowned. 'Meteor' has burgundy-red flowers, and 'Brilliant' has carmine flowers and bronze foliage.

Shared Spaces

Stonecrop is used in dry flower and shrub borders for late-season color and winter interest, especially to provide contrast with blue oat grass, deergrass, shadscale (*Amelanchier*) lavender sage, or garlic chives.

Cultivation

In perennial beds or borders space plants 15 to 20 inches apart. Mulch with 3 inches of shredded bark, pecan shells, or fine gravel. Water to a depth of 2 feet once a week when temperatures are 90 F or above, every two weeks when temperatures are 70 to 90 F, and monthly during cooler weather in well-draining soils. No fertilizer is needed. To tidy up established plants in spring, cut the past year's dried stems down close to the ground when new shoots begin to emerge.

Other Species and Cultivars

S. middendorffianum, Chinese mountain stonecrop, has short evergreen foliage growing only 4 inches x 12 to 15 inches, with red flower stems holding multicolored yellow to orange-red flower clusters. Other ground cover types are 'Bronze Carpet', fast growing with bronze red foliage and pink blooms; 'Voodoo', with deep mahogany foliage and brilliant red blooms; and 'Cape Blanco', with silvery blue foliage with yellow blooms. Taller ones are 'Autumn Fire' with sturdy stems to 24 inches, spreading to 18 inches and rosy-pink blooms aging to coppery red. 'Mr Goodbud' has very large, dense dark mauve blooms on 17-inch stems.

Yucca
Yucca species

ZONES: 5 through 11
FORM: Spearlike leaf blades form clumps with tall flower stalks in early summer
GROWTH AND MATURE SIZE: Slow-growing evergreen to 3 to 25 feet x 4 to 10 feet
USES: Textural contrast, borders, focal point, dry desert, perennial gardens
SOIL: From moist, heavy soil to well-drained, fertile and rocky, native
PESTS: Occasional borers

Though we think of yuccas as being a western plant, some of our best dry climate yuccas are native to the East Coast of the United States, as well as the forests and plains of northern and central Mexico. Cold hardy, rarely over 10 feet tall, they include *Yucca filamentosa, Y. recurvifolia,* and *Y. aloifolia.* Western species are taller, generally have stiffer leaves, and include the Arizona native banana yucca (*Y. baccata*), soaptree yucca (*Y. elata*), and beaked yucca (*Y. rostrata*). These species are extremely heat and drought tolerant. One of the loveliest yuccas is the Mexican blue yucca (*Y. rigida*) with its powdery blue-green leaves and plumes of bright white flowers.

Shared Spaces

Blend smaller yuccas with perennials or succulents to provide good texture and color contrast. Taller species are outstanding specimen or accent plants. Use native or drought-tolerant yuccas in areas of the garden that receive minimal care, or mix them with succulents such as saguaro, prickly pear, and agaves. Many yuccas grow well in containers.

Cultivation

No soil amendments are needed. Water every four days for the first month. Water established plants every week for eastern species in the low desert, less often in cooler climes and minimally in temperate zones. In summer, water established plants of Western species every two to three weeks, relying on natural rainfall in cooler zones unless the weather is exceptionally warm or dry. Western species need minimal water in winter. Allow the soil to dry completely between waterings. Apply slow-release or organic fertilizer annually in spring to the eastern species. Western species need no fertilizer. Remove spent flowering stalks anytime.

Other Species and Cultivars

Yucca pallida, pale leaf yucca, is native to north-central Texas. It is trunkless, low growing to 1 to 2 feet x 1 to 3 feet, with pale blue-green leaves with light yellow to white striped leaf margins. Hardy to Zone 6, it produces its pure white flowers in late spring.

Annuals

Over the years, annuals have been taken for granted in our gardens. It is common to hear a gardener say, "Oh yes, it's lovely, but it's *just* an annual." In truth, annuals should hold a place of high honor in the garden. They are ever faithful—coming back year after year, demanding little of our time, and blooming throughout an entire growing season. Seasoned gardeners love them and even novices who claim to have a brown thumb can garden with annuals. Little effort, little thought, yet so much in return! Not *just* an annual at all.

Consider the sunflower. Not only is it beautiful, it also has a rich history. Sunflowers were cultivated more than three thousand years ago by Native Americans who ate raw sunflower seeds. They also roasted them, boiled them, and made them into gravy, gruel, and bread. They made what was probably the first power bar ever by molding sunflower seeds into balls that were eaten throughout the day. Folk wisdom tells us that if you cut a sunflower at sunset while making a wish, the wish will come true the next day.

The sunflower's cheerful "sunny" blooms are resistant to strong winds and heat. They also resow themselves. Zinnias are also real toughies in the summer heat. They are drought tolerant once established, put on an outstanding show in the garden and in the vase, and flower from spring through summer and into the first frost. Zinnias bloom atop long, straight stems and come in every color except blue.

In spring, Shirley poppies emerge as gray-green tufts of foliage, and before you know it they send out similarly colored fuzzy stems with buds. Some are so tall they dwarf the young ginkgo trees. As their flowers fade and the petals drop, the seed-pods remain. Some can be used for fall flower arrangements, and others can be left to reseed for the next season.

To plant annual seeds directly in the garden, prepare the bed by roughing up the surface of the soil with a rake. Spread a light layer of slow-release or organic fertilizer and mulch on the surface and rake them in. Broadcast the seed, mixing them with a cupful of sand to help distribute tiny seeds evenly. Cover lightly by raking the soil, or just throw handfuls of compost over the top. Press the soil gently to prevent seed from washing away, and then water the seedbed using a fine spray. In rocky or coarsely mulched areas, broadcast seed over the area and water immediately so the seeds wash down into the crevices between the rocks. You may need to spread bird netting over the seedbed until the seedlings have three or four sets of leaves, or just sow extra seed and share some of the seedlings with hungry birds. When the seedlings have three sets of leaves, thin so they are four to six inches apart.

To plant annuals from six-packs or nursery packs, remember to avoid planting the young seedlings any deeper than they were in their containers. Planting them deeper causes their quick demise. Most of the water-wise annuals in this book neither need, nor like, rich garden soils. That means a labor and money savings for you, and the plants are happier for it. Mulch annuals whenever possible, starting with an inch or so of bark chips, shredded bark, or pebbles depending upon the annual.

African Daisy
Dimorphotheca sinuata

FORM: Blooms grow above the low-growing green foliage in early winter or early spring
GROWTH AND MATURE SIZE: Quick-growing, self-seeding annual to 4 to 12 inches x 4 to 8 inches
USES: Ground cover, slopes, mass, drifts, foreground, meadows, wildflower gardens
SOIL: Any, even rocky, native soil, but grows larger and faster in well-drained, fertile soil
PESTS: None

African daisy is an outstanding and reliable spring annual in the Southwest that reseeds year after year. This hardiness makes it capable of growing in wild areas without a gardener's assistance. Be careful not to use it near parks, preserves, or other wild places where it might become a problem. In cooler zones, plants are not quite as aggressive. In the low desert, seeds germinate in early fall, and by January, plants bloom in shades of yellow and gold-orange. In cool zones, flowering begins in May. Since African daisy one of the first springtime flowers, many gardeners in the Southwest desert cover their entire front yard for its explosion of color.

Shared Spaces

Sow in mass plantings for spectacular effect around pools, walkways, or patios. Mix with other wildflowers such as tidy tips, desert bluebells, or Mexican poppies. African daisy is suitable for planters or large containers, either individually or combined with other annuals, shrubs, trees, and perennials for colorful displays. Their short blooming season allows them to be used in succession with other flowering annuals and perennials.

Cultivation

Sow seed in fall in all but the coldest zones. In those areas, sow as early as soil can be worked in spring. Water every two to three days until seeds germinate, then water every five to seven days. Once there are five leaves on each plant, reduce watering to once a week or less depending on temperatures. Plants are susceptible to collapse if overwatered. Water weekly when plants are in bloom. To reduce aggressive reseeding, deadhead as soon as they finish blooming and begin to fade. No fertilizer is needed.

Other Species and Cultivars

The closely related *Dimorphotheca pluvialis* has white rays with a violet disc, and hybrids are common between the two. Seed mixes include 'African Moon', which grows to 14 inches tall with blooms of white, pink, and salmon; 'Passion Mixed' blooms in hues of purple, lavender, and white; 'Pastel Silks' is buff, cream, orange, yellow, and white. Single colors are *D. aurantiaca*, a dwarf with salmon and apricot blooms.

Annual Coreopsis
Coreopsis tinctoria

FORM: Deeply cut foliage with wiry stems holding blooms from late spring to summer
GROWTH AND MATURE SIZE: Quick-growing to 2 to 3 feet x 1 to 2 feet
USES: Mixed borders, mass, drifts, succulent, wildflower gardens
SOIL: Well-drained, fertile soil or rocky, native soil; no rich soils
PESTS: None

Coreopsis is one of those flowers that just makes you smile. The flat-ray flowers are banded yellow and brown or maroon and held on whisper-thin stems above delicate, finely cut leaves. Their slender appearance entirely belies how rugged this plant is for low-desert gardens and how enduring it is for all the Southwest gardens. Coreopsis is best planted in mass groups and given some room, for plants can grow up to 3 feet tall. Best of all for Southwest gardens, it blooms late, beginning in May and lasting well into July. There are also dwarf and double forms. Coreopsis can be grown as a perennial in southern California gardens.

Shared Spaces
Mix coreopsis with summer-flowering perennials such as salvia, gaillardia, or verbena. Coreopsis is particularly effective in the back of a bed where its flowers are visible but other plants cover its sparse foliage. Because it appreciates dry soil, annual coreopsis can grown with agave, cactus, or other succulents for late- spring color. Sow generously for best effect; the wiry stems make plants seem sparse when they are isolated. It's excellent mixed with other annuals in large containers or planters or around pools, patios, or seating areas.

Cultivation
Sow seed in fall in all areas except high elevation deserts where seeds are sown as early as soil can be worked. Water every two to three days until germination, then water every five to seven days depending on the heat. Water once a week while plants are blooming and if temperatures are hot. No fertilizer is needed. Plants may be floppy if grown in too much shade or if crowded when young. Stake or support plants, but it is better to give them adequate light during their long growing phase instead.

Other Species and Cultivars
'Mardi Gras' is stunning with starlike blooms in gold and red. 'Quills and Thrills' has needlelike foliage with red, gold, and yellow pinwheel blooms. Perennial *Coreopsis* x 'Sienna Sunset' has burnt-orange blooms growing 16 to 20 inches tall in Zones 5 through 9. 'Redshift', also perennial, has red petals, lightening to cream with red streaks at the tips, hardy in Zones 4 through 8.

California Poppy
Eschscholzia californica

FORM: Gray-green ferny foliage with blooms on wiry stems in spring
GROWTH AND MATURE SIZE: Quick-growing and self sowing to 12 to 18 inches x 12 to 18 inches
USES: Wildflower, annual, meadow plantings, mass, slopes, border
SOIL: Any type of soil
PESTS: None

State flower California poppy is one of California's most beautiful and easily recognized wildflowers. California poppies have ferny, gray-green leaves that emerge from the base of the plant, forming a 12- to 18-inch mound. Flower stalks rise from the center, each with a pointed green bud at the tip. The green sepals split to reveal four furled, golden-orange petals. California poppies were once pollinated exclusively by native beetles. But today, European honeybees also pollinate them. After a flower is pollinated, seeds start to develop. The subsequent seedpod dries out and splits, sending tiny black poppy seeds shooting out in all directions.

Shared Spaces

California poppies work in every Southwestern garden, from a wild meadow to a Mediterranean border. Scatter seed on a steep hillside, parking strip, or vacant lot. California poppy is also the perfect flower for a school garden. In areas where California poppies are native and perennial, plant locally grown seed only. Seeds from a garden center or other outside sources cross-pollinate with the local poppies, weakening and ultimately leading to the loss of native populations. In other states, buy seed from reputable sources.

Cultivation

In fall or winter, sprinkle fine seed over a sunny garden bed. Plant just as winter rains or snow begin so there's no need to water. There is no need to fertilize. Very little water is needed after they sprout. Occasional deep water to saturate soil 6 to 8 inches deep promotes longer bloom and lusher foliage. Wait until the soil is dry several inches deep before watering again. For a second bloom, cut leaves to the base once flowers fade and foliage turns dingy gray. Water well; in a few weeks a set of shorter leaves will sprout. Flowers will soon follow, though they too will be shorter.

Other Species and Cultivars

'Apricot Chiffon' has creamy yellow, double-flowered poppies with intense coral-orange edging. 'Thai Silk Formula' is a mix with semidouble flowers with a silky chiffon texture from sunny yellow to magenta. 'Mission Bells' are bicolored in orange, red, white, and gold. 'Red Chief' is crimson with a dark center.

Cowpen Daisy
Verbesina encelioides

FORM: Gray-green foliage with leafless flower stalks blooming July to October
GROWTH AND MATURE SIZE: Reseeding, quickly growing 1 to 4 feet x 1 to 4 feet
USES: Slopes, pasture, meadow, prairie plantings, along driveways, borders, wildflower gardens
SOIL: Not fussy about soils
PESTS: None

This summer-blooming member of the large clan of native yellow daisies gets its name from its tendency to colonize corrals. It also grows along roadsides and fencerows where the soil is disturbed seasonally and extra moisture is likely to accumulate. The lower portions of the stems are hidden by triangular gray-green leaves 2 to 4 inches long and half as wide. The flower stalks are leafless with a single 1-inch bloom per stem. Both the toothed ray petals and the discs are yellow. Cowpen daisy begins to show color in July, but it is most impressive in late summer when it has reached its maximum size and forms a mass of golden flowers.

Shared Spaces

Coarse and a bit rangy, cowpen daisy is best in naturalized areas mixed in shrub borders for summer color among sumacs, Apache plume, fernbush, and junipers. Grow along a driveway, road, or drainage channel. Songbirds harvest the seeds, and mixed with sand lovegrass, little bluestem, or sideoats grama, cowpen daisy is a colorful way to reclaim roadsides, septic leach fields, and drainage swales.

Cultivation

Sow seed in fall or early spring while the soil is still cool. One ounce of seed covers 200 square feet of soil. Rake the seeds into a depth of ½ inch and tamp the surface lightly. If fall-sown seeds don't sprout, scratch the area with a rake and water deeply a few times before reseeding in spring. Cowpen daisy thrives with no extra watering even at northern elevations of 7000 feet. Occasional deep watering is necessary in hotter, drier locations, especially when plants start flowering. In clay loam or decomposed granite soils, no fertilizer is necessary. Water weekly in light sandy soils. Add slow-release fertilizer at planting time. Mow down frost-killed stalks. If litter is left as mulch, cowpen daisy reseeds. If the stalks are cleared, lightly rake and reseed each spring, although sometimes raking alone aerates the soil and induces dormant seeds to sprout.

Other Species and Cultivars

In the foothills of the southern mountains, *Verbesina rothrockii* is a perennial crownsbeard with orange-yellow flowers in summer.

Creeping Zinnia
Sanvitalia procumbens

FORM: Mats of deep green oval leaves with low blooms summer to frost

GROWTH AND MATURE SIZE: Self-sowing, quickly growing, spreading to 4 to 6 inches x 18 inches

USES: Mass, ground cover, foreground, filler, color beds, edging, understory

SOIL: Prefers well-drained soil, adapts to alkaline clay as long as it is not too wet

PESTS: None

Creeping zinnia is a heat-lover that grows best at lower elevations, is naturally trim and tidy, and blooms for months. Native to California, Texas, and Mexico, where it has crept into gardens from roadsides, creeping zinnia brightens the gaps between paving stones and tumbles over edges of stone walls. The mat of small, green, oval leaves is dotted with, ½-inch daisies. 'Mandarin Orange' has bright orange flowers and is a bit more mounded, growing 8 inches tall and twice as wide. 'Golden Carpet' has pumpkin-yellow flowers, and 'Yellow Carpet' is lemon yellow. Creeping zinnia's balance of bright flower color and attractive foliage is charming.

Shared Spaces

A great filler between boulders or flagstones, creeping zinnia is also used as living mulch at the base of shrubs, especially in new gardens where it adds color and a lush look until shrubs become established. It grows well in pots if watered regularly. Because of its low profile, creeping zinnia needs bedfellows that are self-contained such as pineleaf penstemon, hardy African daisy, or rue.

Cultivation

Sow outdoors in spring or as soon as frost is past. Seeds are small and require light to germinate, so press them onto the surface of loosened soil. Germination takes a week or two when the temperature is 75 F. Well-suited to heat and drought, creeping zinnia makes a more attractive garden plant if it is watered deeply every week or two, especially while blooming. In very sandy soils, work in slow-release fertilizer at planting, but at half strength. Too much nitrogen produces leggy growth and fewer flowers. Once established, these zinnias cover densely enough to exclude most annual weeds, but weed while the plants are small.

Other Species and Cultivars

'Irish Eyes' are single flowers in light orange with green centers growing just 4 inches tall. 'Orange' and 'Yellow Sprite' both grow to 12 inches with double orange blooms and singles with orange-yellow blooms and a dark center, respectively. Disease resistant, *Z. elegans* 'Zahara Starlight Rose' is bicolor with pink-yellow centers and hot pink petals dipped in white.

Desert Bluebell
Phacelia campanularia

FORM: Mounding with deep green leaves and loose flower heads in spring

GROWTH AND MATURE SIZE: Self-sowing and quick growing to 6 to 12 inches x 6 to 15 inches

USES: Wildflower, color beds, ground cover, foreground, mass

SOIL: Any soil, including rocky, native soil, or well-drained fertile soil

PESTS: None

Desert bluebell is one of the easiest of all wildflowers to grow. It is a lush, thick plant with dark, gray-green, heart-shaped leaves dimpled along the surface and crimped along the edge. These charming leaves are the backdrop for the brilliant deep purple to indigo blue flowers held in loose heads above the foliage. Plants are tidy, looking like a bouquet in the garden. Look for lacy phacelia (*Phacelia tanacetifolia*) that, as the name suggests, has finely cut foliage, grows to 3 or more feet tall, and has long clusters of lavender to purple flowers. The native scorpion weed (*P. crenulata*) has fingers of purple flowers that curl much like a scorpion's tail.

Shared Spaces

The classic wildflower combination in Southwestern fashion is to mix desert bluebells with Mexican gold poppies or California poppies in large wildflower beds, small corners, or in containers. The color contrasts are stunning. This species reseeds freely, especially in rocky soils, and plants tend to find their way to charming locations at the base of rocks, near doorways, or in nooks of a patio. Use as a filler in containers with succulents for extra spring color or plant generously so that the rich blue flowers cover barren spots.

Cultivation

Sow seed in fall in mild climate zones, and as early as soil can be worked in colder or higher zones. Water every two to three days until seed germinates, then water every five to seven days. Desert bluebells do not need fertilizer and will grow excessive leaves at the expense of flowers under conditions that are too rich. Water once a week through the blooming season, although those planted in rocky locations or in partial shade will require less frequent watering. This is one of the easiest of all wildflowers to grow and enjoy and requires no special care.

Other Species and Cultivars

P. bolanderi, caterpillar flower, grows 18 inches x 24 inches with green-toothed leaves having purplish stems and blue-purple, dime-sized blooms. *P. grandiflora*, giant flowering phacelia, grows to 3 feet tall with large blooms, having lavender petals fading to white centers veined in purple. It grows naturally below 2000 feet in sandy soils.

Gazania
Gazania species

FORM: Mounds of green foliage with short stems hold large blooms in summer

GROWTH AND MATURE SIZE: Quick-growing to 6 to 12 inches x 12 to 24 inches

USES: Ground cover, foreground, mass, drift, color and dry streambeds, borders

SOIL: Any well-drained soil, including good garden soil that's not too high in organic matter

PESTS: None

Everything about gazania is appealing. The large 3- to 4-inch flowers are held on stout leafless stems just above the leaves that are green on top with silver undersides. Flowers open during the day and close at night. 'Mini-Star' is 8 inches tall and wide with 3-inch self-cleaning flowers. 'Tangerine' is an orange selection, and 'Sunshine' is a mix of bicolor blooms in a range of colors, including rust with an olive green band near the center. Trailing gazania (*Gazania rigens* var. *leucolaena*) makes a mat of silver foliage topped with yellow flowers. *G. krebsiana* 'Tanager' has large apricot-orange flowers and overwinters if the soil is kept fairly dry.

Shared Spaces

Grow gazanias in flower borders along paths and patios, or in large pots. We like them where their amazing detail can be fully appreciated, but they are equally beautiful planted *en masse* in drifts planted with creeping sedum, desert zinnia, or purple verbena.

Cultivation

Since young seedlings develop rather slowly, young gardeners may prefer to transplant instead of sowing seeds. Space plants a foot apart for mass planting, or tuck a few in between other annuals or perennials in beds and borders. Water weekly to establish new plants and while plants are in bloom, every two weeks the rest of the growing season. No additional water is needed in coastal California once plants are established. If grown in unamended sand or decomposed granite soil, work a slow-release fertilizer into the soil at planting time, or fertilize lightly a few times in summer. Trim off old stems and leaves when necessary. Gazania persists as a short-lived perennial in the warmest areas.

Other Species and Cultivars

Award-winning series 'Daybreak' Pink Shades (*G. rigens*, var. 'Pink Shades') has larger blooms in bright pink to fading powder pink; 'Red Stripe' has yellow petals with vivid red stripes. 'Fiesta Red' has an orange center with petals of orange with rust stripes. 'Sun Gold' has 2- to 4-inch blooms in yellow. 'Yellow Trailing' spreads and has fuzzy coated leaves, green on top and white on the undersides, with yellow blooms.

Mexican Hat
Ratibida columnifera

FORM: Open-branched with deeply cut foliage and tall, stiff stems holding blooms summer through early fall
GROWTH AND MATURE SIZE: Moderate-growing, self-sowing to 1 to 3 feet x 1 to 3 feet
USES: Mass, midground, meadow, wildflower, and dry perennial or streambed gardens,
SOIL: Any kind of well-drained soil
PESTS: None

Think Mexican hat is a strange name for a flower? You'll understand once you see this black-eyed-Susan relative whose rounded, gold, or gold-edged mahogany petals form a drooping "sombrero" brim around a tall, brown, central cone. These Great Plains native plants puts on a real show in late summer and early fall when their many flowers float above clouds of feathery green foliage. In times past, Cheyenne Indians valued a brew of Mexican hat leaves to draw the poison from rattlesnake bites. Technically a perennial, it is typically grown as a self-seeding annual. Grow both gold and mahogany flowering plants, and the next generation may include all sorts of variations.

Shared Spaces

Mexican hat is right at home in a planted meadow, wildflower, or other dry garden. Plants look best *en masse*. Add purple-flowering penstemon, apricot-flowering anise hyssop, grass like orange-leaved *Carex testacea* or its bronze-leaved cousin, leather-leaved sedge. Native California fuchsia is a good companion as well. For texture, add taller grasses such as silver grass. Plan for flowering sequences by combining Mexican hat with California poppy.

Cultivation

In frost-free gardens, direct-seed in fall. In colder areas, start seeds once the ground warms in spring. When seedlings have two sets of leaves, thin to 1 to 2 feet apart. Or start seeds in pots in spring and transplant later at same spacing. Stake plants if they flop later in the season. Or, just let them grow naturally. Keep the seedbed moist (not wet) until seedlings are several inches tall. Then let the soil dry out between waterings. Once established, they require only occasional deep watering. No pruning is necessary.

Other Species and Cultivars

'Buttons and Bows' (2 to 2½ feet x 2 to 2½ feet) has mahogany petals with golden edges and brown centers. 'Red Midget', listed as a hardy perennial, is shorter growing, to just 1 foot tall. Yellow cone flower (*Ratibida pinnata*) is perennial, has summer and fall flowers on 4-foot-tall plants with long, bright yellow petals that flex away from a deep gray, cone-like center. Hardy to minus 30 degrees F.

Mexican Sunflower
Tithonia rotundifolia

FORM: Tall, thick stems with thick, soft leaves are topped with blooms in late summer to frost
GROWTH AND MATURE SIZE: Moderate-growing to 4 to 6 feet x 3 to 4 feet
USES: Background, border, mass, drift
SOIL: Any well-drained soil
PESTS: None

Late summer brings the brilliant bloom of Mexican sunflower, a 6-foot-tall annual in the sunflower family. Mexican sunflowers' tall central stems are topped with 4- to 5-inch flowers with petals that are bright orange and centers that are golden yellow. The flowers, which bloom until frost, are actually made up of many, many small flowers that produce seeds much beloved by goldfinches. Monarch butterflies seek out Mexican sunflowers for their nectar. Gardeners like them not just for their bright-colored flowers but also for their velvety soft stems and leaves. Seeds are widely available, and starting these plants by seed is easy. Plants reseed themselves.

Shared Spaces

Mass plant Mexican sunflower with colorful zinnias, purple-flowering Mexican bush sage, shrubby blue hibiscus, and yellow-flowering Mexican marigold. To harvest flowers for bouquets, cut the stems well below the flowers. The stalk at the base of the bloom is hollow; with too much handling it will collapse.

Cultivation

Start Mexican sunflower from seed in early spring. Plant seeds ½-inch deep, 2 to 3 inches apart, and in rows 12 inches apart, or simply sprinkle over an existing flower bed and cover with compost. Once seedlings have two sets of leaves, thin to 1 to 2 feet apart. Keep seedbed and seedlings moist but not wet. Once plants have several sets of leaves, reduce watering frequency to let the soil dry out more and more between waterings. No fertilizer is needed. Pruning is not necessary, but pinch off fading flowers to prolong bloom. Stake tall plants if they begin to lean.

Other Species and Cultivars

'Aztec Sun' has yellow flowers. 'Torch' has deep red-orange blooms. Shorter varieties (to 2 feet) need no staking: bright orange-flowered 'Fiesta del Sol', deep red-orange flowered 'Sundance', and mango-yellow flowered 'Yellow Torch'. Bolivian sunflower (*Tithonia diversifolia*) is perennial and grows as a loose shrub, 12 to 16 feet x 6 feet or more, with golden yellow daisylike flowers, 6 to 7 inches across, in late summer. It's hardy to 30 F.

Moss Rose
Portulaca grandiflora

FORM: Low-trailing succulent leaves with stems lined with blooms all summer
GROWTH AND MATURE SIZE: Self-sowing and quick-growing to 4 to 6 inches x 8 to 10 inches
USES: Rock garden, color border, mass, understory (open branching overhead), hanging baskets
SOIL: Infertile, well-drained soil
PESTS: Protect from rabbits and quail

Moss rose is a compact Brazilian native that has enjoyed a hallowed place in the bedding plant palette for at least a hundred years. It is low spreading with succulent stems and plump little cylindrical leaves. Moss rose flowers open in the sunlight, one at a time at the ends of the stems, and close at night. They are 1 to 2 inches in diameter, single or double, and come in a rainbow of jewel-bright colors in red, rose, coral, pink-orange, yellow, and white. There are many cultivars such as 'Sundance', 'Sunglo', and 'Sundial', reminders of its favorite position in the garden. 'Afternoon Delight' has flowers that stay open longer in late afternoon.

Shared Spaces

Southwestern exposures in rock gardens, along paths, and between paving stones are appropriate places to grow moss rose. They are also good for edging xeric flower borders, in cactus gardens for extra color, and in containers on sunny patios. The jewel-like colors contrast the silver foliage of many of the artemisias and Mexican blue sage, and since the leaf canopy of screwbean mesquite is so sparse, moss rose can be grown as a ground cover beneath it.

Cultivation

Moss rose prefers hot sunny spots, so the season is quite short for gardens above 8000 feet in elevation, longer at lower elevations. Sow seeds or transplant greenhouse-grown plants in spring, after the last frost. If transplanting from containers, loosen the soil well when digging the planting holes, and backfill with unamended soil. Thin seedlings or space transplants 6 to 12 inches apart. Fine gravel is the best mulch to encourage self-sowing. Plants may need weekly watering in lower deserts, but otherwise needs little extra watering in cooler and low water gardens. Too much fertilizer or organic matter in the soil reduces flowering, so don't pamper moss rose. Other than occasional watering and weeding, moss rose is undemanding and blooms continuously.

Other Species and Cultivars

'Peppermint' has large double flowers in white with pink streaks. 'Margarita' hybrids are compact and bushy. Look for 'Fruit Splash' mix that includes tropical orange, strawberry, and red.

Mullein

Verbascum bombyciferum

FORM: Long leaves form rosettes with tall flower stalks in summer

GROWTH AND MATURE SIZE: Self-sowing biennial, moderately growing 3 to 6 feet x 1 foot

USES: Midground, mass, drifts, cottage, perennial, meadow gardens

SOIL: Lean, unamended

PESTS: None

Mullein is a Mediterranean plant valued for its basal rosettes of foliage with unusual color and texture. Most species are biennial, producing bold leaves the first season and prominent flower and seed stalks the following summer. 'Arctic Summer' has foot-long silver leaves and 1½-inch clear yellow flowers. Fine white down cloaks the thin, 4-foot-tall stems. *V. undulatum* have large velvety leaves with wavy margins in rosettes 2 feet across that look as if they were frosted with gold. If grown in good garden soil with ample water, they lose their distinctive character, so be sure to grow them dry, lean soils and in full sun.

Shared Spaces

Mullein poses a design dilemma; the first-year foliage rosettes are too striking for the back of the border, but the following year's tall flower stems are out of place in front. Clustering the plants in the middle ground seems the best compromise. Use a group of 3 to 7 plants as a focal point occupying the same space a shrub might; or scatter groups of 3 to 5 plants through a new ground cover planting of cotoneaster or prostrate sumac to add interest until the shrubs fill out.

Cultivation

Seeds germinate when daytime temperatures are 75 degrees Fahrenheit. Transplant seedlings after the last frost. Space a foot apart in groups of three or more. At higher, cooler elevations and along the coast mulleins need little or no supplemental watering. In warmer, lower deserts and inland valleys, regular deep watering is required, especially while plants are blooming. Limit irrigation to once weekly or less. No fertilizer is needed. Like penstemon, mulleins produce copious amounts of seed. Species and varieties cross-pollinate with abandon, so to produce true seed they must be placed far apart. To avoid self-sowing, trim off the spent flowers routinely.

Other Species and Cultivars

'Southern Charm' blooms the first year from seed. A repeat bloomer, it sends out tall stalks of flowers in creamy golden, peachy rose, and lavender. Foliage is silvery, clumping to 16 inches. It does not readily self-sow.

Nolana
Nolana paradoxa

FORM: Fleshy leaves on trailing stems covered with funnel-shaped blooms in summer
GROWTH AND MATURE SIZE: Self-sowing, quickly trailing to 10 inches x 18 to 24 inches
USES: Hot summer ground cover; edging, borders, foreground, mass, drifts, hanging baskets
SOIL: Well-drained, infertile sandy or gravelly soil
PESTS: Aphids in seedling stage

Nolana has been cultivated by specialty growers for at least a century and is a welcome introduction to the bedding plant market. Originally from the coastal areas of Chile and Peru where rainfall is scarce and moisture is available mostly in the form of condensation, nolana requires heat and tolerates drought and salty soil. Its trailing stems are covered with fleshy leaves that glisten in bright sunlight. Large patio pots overflowing with its 2-inch funnel-shaped, cool morning-glory-blue with white-throated flowers are a refreshing sight at the height of summer. Unlike morning glory vines, nolana won't self-sow aggressively or get out of hand.

Shared Spaces

Nolana makes a good border plant or filler between shrubs mixed with desert marigold and wildflowers such as bubblegum mint, blanketflower, and desert penstemon. Because it tolerates shifts in temperature, loves heat, and vines enough to cascade over the edge of pots, nolana is well suited for use in large patio tubs and raised beds.

Cultivation

Sow seeds or transplant potted plants in spring after all chance of frost is past and daytime temperatures reach 75 F. Work a small amount of a slow-release fertilizer in at planting to carry the plants through the growing season. A warm microclimate induces abundant blooms. It's less thirsty and more floriferous when it's shaded from relentless afternoon sun. During the hottest weeks of summer, water nolana growing in full sun once a week to a depth of 18 inches; plants grown in afternoon shade can a bit longer between irrigations to the same depth. Plants in pots fewer than 12 inches in diameter may need watering every day or two when temperatures reach 90 F. Water plants in containers until water drains out the bottom. Too much compost, water, or nitrogen produces foliage at the expense of flowers. Seeds develop inconspicuously, and new flowers continue to form without deadheading.

Other Species and Cultivars

Nolana 'Snowbird' is compact and has pure white blooms. 'Bluebird' has deep sky blue blooms. 'Cliffhanger' has blue with pale yellow flowers.

Scarlet Flax
Linum grandiflorum 'Rubrum'

FORM: Spring through summer
GROWTH AND MATURE SIZE: Reseeding and quickly growing to 18 to 24 inches x 6 to 12 inches
USES: Dry annual or perennial bed, background, mass, drifts, filler
SOIL: Any soil, including rocky, native soil; plants are larger, more vigorous, and bloom best in well-drained, fertile soil
PESTS: None

Many annuals promise long-lasting blooms, brilliant color displays, and spontaneous reseeding—all with little or no effort on our part. Few live up to this pledge, but gardeners throughout the Southwest can count on scarlet flax. Plants are tall, with erect stems that branch toward the ends. Among the earliest annuals to germinate, plants emerge in early fall and may begin blooming as early as January in temperate climates. The true species has rosy-pink flowers, but this selection presents one-inch-wide, scarlet red blooms and has now become the most common form. The variety 'Bright Eyes' has white flowers with a dark, red-brown eye.

Shared Spaces

Mix with other spring-flowering annuals such as Shirley poppy, nasturtium, or coneflower. Because of its height, plant flax as a background for flowering perennials such as salvia and penstemon. Plant generously; the spare stems make an individual plant seem sparse, while they are glorious in groupings. Scarlet flax is an excellent choice to use in mass plantings around patios, seating areas, and pools or to fill in barren spots in a newly planted garden.

Cultivation

Sow seed in fall in low desert, inland valley, and coastal zones, and as early as soil can be worked in colder zones. Sow seed at two-week intervals to extend the bloom period. Water every two to three days until seed germinates, then water every five to seven days. Water established plants every week through the growing and blooming season. No fertilizer is needed. Scarlet flax is effortless in most gardens and requires no special care or attention.

Other Species and Cultivars

L. grandiflorum 'Caeruleum' has blue-purple blooms. *L. perenne lewisii*, perennial blue flax, has lacy foliage growing into clumps to 1 to 2 feet tall and 1 foot wide. It has clear sky blue blooms. *L. flavum*, golden flax, is perennial and grows 1 foot tall and wide. It has spring and summer yellow blooms. *L. narbonense*, also perennial and hardy in Zones 7 through 9, grows 2 feet x 1½ feet and has azure blue blooms. Cultivar 'Six Hills' has richer, bluer blooms.

Shirley Poppy
Papaver rhoeas

FORM: Clumps of foliage with tall thin stems and large blooms from spring to summer
GROWTH AND MATURE SIZE: Self-sowing and quickly growing to 2 to 3 feet x 1 to 2 feet
USES: Mass, drifts, borders, dry perennial beds, background, overplanting, filler
SOIL: Any including hot, rocky, native soil or well-drained, fertile soil
PESTS: None

Shirley poppy is perfectly at home in all Southwest gardens. The dark green dissected leaves grow as a low basal plant through fall and winter in the low desert, coastal areas, and inland valleys; early spring in colder climates. Then in late spring, the plant stretches out and the nodding flower buds form on thin stalks. Flowers are large, with paper-thin petals lasting only a day. There are countless forms in a host of colors, but it is the species is pure, deep red with the black cross at the petal's base. Bread poppy (*Papaver somniferum*) is heftier with large, powdery gray-green, cabbage-like leaves and 4-inch flowers in a vast array of bloom colors.

Shared Spaces
Plant generously—Shirley poppies are spectacular in mass plantings. Unlike other poppies, these have multiple flowers on each stalk that open in succession through the season. Because of its height, use as a background for smaller spring-flowering bulbs, penstemons, or salvias, or to cover winter weary summer-flowering plants such as red bird of paradise or lantana. This is an excellent plant choice for hiding barren spots or empty corners in a newly planted garden.

Cultivation
Sow seed in fall or as early as soil can be worked. Water every two to three days until seed germinates, then water every five to seven days unless it rains. No fertilizer is needed. Plants become floppy and bloom poorly if grown with too much fertilizer or too much water. Water established plants sparingly through winter or spring as they are growing. Water once a week or less when the plants are blooming, depending on the temperatures. Shirley poppy grows with minimal care and little attention.

Other Species and Cultivars
'Shirley Double' has double 3- to 4-inch crinkly blossoms in red, salmon, pure white, and light pink. 'Mother of Pearl' has soft hues in gray, rouge, and even bluish pastels. 'Falling in Love' has 30-inch stems with semi-double and double blooms in rose, salmon, and coral.

Sunflower
Helianthus annuus

FORM: Tall upright and branching stems with large blooms through summer
GROWTH AND MATURE SIZE: Fast growing to 2 to 12 feet x 2 feet
USES: Background, screen, focal point, border, mass
SOIL: Any well-drained soil
PESTS: None; birds relish sunflower seedlings and sunflower seeds; cover seedbed with bird netting or hardware cloth.

Sunflowers are true American natives. Native Americans grew them for food. Spanish explorers took them home to grow as ornamentals. Amazingly, the same sunflowers—and their modern relatives—remain a mainstay of our summer gardens. Sunflowers are popular in part because they are easy to grow. A spot in full sun, a bit of soft soil, and some water are about all it takes. Traditional sunflowers have a single row of large yellow ray petals surrounding a center made up of tiny disk flowers, each of which becomes an edible seed. Hybrids bloom in shades of bronze to chocolate, nearly red to cinnamon, and mixed colors.

Shared Spaces

Grow a sunflower house using 'Russian Mammoth' or another tall sunflower and annual vining morning glory. Sow the two seeds in a rectangle 9 feet x 6 feet and leave one side open for a doorway. Morning glory vines climb sunflower stalks as both reach for the sky. Once sunflower buds appear, gently weave twine back and forth overhead to form a "ceiling" for the vines to climb across.

Cultivation

Start seeds indoors in pots in early spring, or in the ground when the nighttime temperature reaches 50 degrees F. Thin according to packet directions. Resow every few weeks through summer for flowers into fall. Sunflowers bloom best if watered whenever the top 2 inches of soil are dry. No pruning is needed. If your goal is cut flowers or seeds, plant twice as many plants as you need—some for you and some for the birds. For cut flowers, harvest flower heads just as they start to open.

Other Species and Cultivars

New cultivars come out seasonally. 'Starburst Panache' is branching and has 4- to 5-inch pollen-free blooms in orange-yellow with dark centers; 'Golden Cheer' is unique with shaggy double flowers in yellow, 6 feet tall and branching; 'Wahooh' is compact to 2 to 3 feet tall, bushy with masses of 4-inch blooms covering the plant. 'Maxmilliana' is perennial, hardy in Zones 4 through 9, blooms in fall, and grows 6 to 8 feet x 4 feet.

FORM: Low growing, compact with dense covering of blooms in spring
GROWTH AND MATURE SIZE: Quick-growing to 4 to 10 inches x 5 to 10 inches
USES: Dry annual, perennial, streambed and succulent gardens, meadows, wildflower gardens, mass
SOIL: Any soil from well-drained, fertile soil, to heavy clay, and rocky, native soil
PESTS: None

Tidy tips are low-growing, spring-flowering California natives that perfectly live up to their name. The light green lance-shaped leaves are entirely covered by the prolific bloom. One of the earliest wildflowers to bloom, tidy tips flowers until the weather becomes very warm. In desert gardens, it blooms through summer. The flowers have yellow rays that are rimmed in white. The disc flowers are light yellow. The flower is so symmetrical and the colors so regular it looks crisp and cool, like a snappy linen suit. These plants are prolific both in the wild and in the garden. *Layia glandulosa*, native to Arizona, flowers prolifically in early spring with pure white blooms.

Shared Spaces

Mix tidy tips with other annuals such as desert bluebells or poppies to provide interest and contrast in a spring wildflower bed. Plant generously to use it as a low border in front of taller perennials or annuals. This species is particularly effective used in mass plantings along a walkway or around a seating area, courtyard, or pool. Look for a place to plant tidy tips where the stunning regularity of the flowers and their bright colors can be viewed from above. Tidy tips mixes well with succulents and adds a splash of color to potted succulents, cactus, or agaves. Tidy tips can be used in containers or planters, either alone or mixed with other annuals or perennials.

Cultivation

Sow seed in fall in low desert, inland valley, and coastal areas; as early as soil can be worked in cooler zones. Water every two to three days until seed germinates, then water every five to seven days. Water every week during the blooming season depending on temperature. No fertilizer is needed.

Other Species and Cultivars

Tidy tips have a strong value in wildflower seed mixes. Specialized flower blends for the Southwest include tidy tips, lupine, Indian blanket, desert marigold, blazing star, farewell to spring, California poppy, and Mexican hat. Dry meadow mixes also include tidy tips for its drought tolerance. Added to the meadow mix are California poppy, prairie flax, godetia, California bluebell, calliopsis, lemon mint, and black-eyed Susan.

Toadflax
Linaria maroccana

FORM: Narrow foliage on thin stems lined with small snapdragon blooms in spring and summer

GROWTH AND MATURE SIZE: Quick-growing to 6 to 24 inches x 6 inches

USES: Meadow, wildflower, dry cottage garden, mass, drifts, midground, succulent gardens, filler

SOIL: Well-drained, fertile, heavy clay, or rocky, native soil; grows larger and blooms more in fertile soil

PESTS: None

With its stunning array of hues, toadflax is a Moroccan species that doesn't seem able to settle on a color scheme. Its stunning color range includes blues, reds, oranges, yellows, and various bicolors all coming up at once. These plants are small and delicate, with thin stalks whose flowers look like miniature snapdragons. The strain 'Fairy Bouquet' grows to only 9 inches tall with large flowers in pastel colors. 'Northern Lights' has flowers in shades of red, orange, yellow, and some bicolor.

Shared Spaces

Mix toadflax with other spring-flowering annuals such as tidy tips, bluebells, or poppies. Toadflax, with its huge array of colors, is outstanding in mass plantings to fill in a barren spot in a newly planted garden, or to line a drive or walkway. Toadflax mixes well with succulents such as cactus, aloes, or agaves, and brings a dash of color to odd corners or small beds near seating areas and pools. It is excellent in containers or planters, either alone or mixed with perennials or annuals.

Cultivation

Sow seed in fall or early spring. Water every two to three days until seeds germinate, then water every five to seven days. Once plants are established, water weekly through the blooming season. Water more frequently if the weather is exceptionally hot or dry. No fertilizer is needed. Some strains continue to grow and bloom through summer if they are grown in partial shade or at low elevations. Toadflax requires no special care or attention to grow and bloom successfully.

Other Species and Cultivars

'Enchantment' has fragrant magenta and gold blooms in late spring to early summer and grows to 16 inches tall. *L. purpurea* is perennial toadflax, growing to 18 to 36 inches x 6 to 12 inches, with bluish gray leaves and purple blooms early to late summer, hardy in Zones 5 through 9. *L. canadensis* is the California native, an annual to biennial blooming with blue-violet flowers.

Verbena
Verbena species

FORM: Mounds of small leaves with wiry stems holding flower clusters from spring to frost
GROWTH AND MATURE SIZE: Sometimes lasting through two seasons; grows fast to 1 foot x 2 feet
USES: Foreground, filler, mass, drifts, accent, cottage, perennial, dry annual beds
SOIL: Lean, well-drained soil
PESTS: Wash any aphids off with water

South American verbenas are frost sensitive enough to be considered annuals in the coldest parts of the Southwest, and even the natives are erratic and short-lived enough to be thought of as annual plants. They are typically used as perennials in California. But, few flowers bloom as continuously regardless of heat and drought. Verbena's wiry stems are covered quite densely with small rough leaves. 'Imagination Purple' is a luxuriant purple that will not fade in intense sunlight. 'Peaches and Cream' is an apricot and pale yellow variety that is more compact. *V. rigida* is an Argentine native with coarse, thistlelike foliage and deep purple flowers.

Shared Spaces

V. peruviana 'Red Devil' is beautiful interwoven among white zinnia and perky Sue. Verbena is excellent for lining pathways, spilling over the edges of pots and retaining walls, or highlighting entryways. Use it in front of taller perennials or as temporary filler where newly planted shrubs or ground covers need time to grow out. The color stops traffic, especially when planted with 'Moonshine' yarrow, 'Burgundy' gaillardia, or desert penstemon.

Cultivation

Sow seeds when daytime temperatures are 65 to 75 F with frost-free nights. Germination takes three weeks or more. Seeds are fine and need darkness; cover to a depth of 1/16 inch. Set transplants out in well loosened soil in spring after all danger of frost has passed. A mild fertilizer such as bloodmeal or slow-release types worked into the soil at planting sustains blooming. Avoid overwatering or too much nitrogen. In the hottest garden, water verbena once a week; in more temperate spaces water every two weeks except when temperatures soar to the 90s. Removing spent flowers prolongs bloom. If plants start to flag in extreme heat, trim stems back to encourage new growth. Cut plants down to the ground in late fall. Some plants persist for two or three years.

Other Species and Cultivars

Heirloom series includes Apple Blossom with soft white and pink-tinged blooms; Blue Shades includes bicolored blooms with shades of purple, blue, and white; Mango is hues of orange, tangerine, and pale peach.

Wallflower 'Bowles Mauve'

Erysimum linifolium 'Bowles Mauve'

FORM: Compact mounded plants with stiff spikes of blooms midspring through summer
GROWTH AND MATURE SIZE: Quickly growing to 18 to 24 inches x 18 to 24 inches
USES: English or cottage gardens, midground, mass, accent
SOIL: Loosened, well-drained soil
PESTS: None

'Bowles Mauve' wallflower rewards very little work on the gardener's part with whorls of narrow, silver leaves that grow in starburst patterns on compact, mounded plants. The crisp, ever-gray foliage is offset by the many stiff spikes of vibrant pink-purple flowers, starting in midspring and continuing through summer. 'Bowles Mauve' has proven to be too short-lived to be considered more than biennial, although plants may enjoy a third year of strong color. Replanting every few years may seem like a disadvantage, but the reason for the biennial lifespan is that 'Bowles Mauve' blooms so long and intensely that exhausted plants need replacing after their brief show.

Shared Spaces

Its uniform, mounded form lends itself well to small manicured gardens, but it is equally at home in more informal settings. It combines best with yellow and white flowers, and other red-toned purples. The pale foliage contrasts nicely with dark green plants. A few apt partners are creeping germander, yellow pineleaf penstemon, Jerusalem sage, desert zinnia, and rosemary.

Cultivation

Set out plants in spring after danger of hard freezes is past.

When planting in late spring and summer, keep transplants from getting too dry, especially when they are in bloom. Work a few inches of compost and slow-release fertilizer into the planting area, spacing plants 24 to 30 inches apart. Water to a depth of 24 inches once a week when temperatures are 85 degrees F or above, every two weeks when temperatures are 65 to 85 F, and monthly during cooler weather. Too much winter moisture at high elevations or too little winter moisture in the desert weakens plants, so the best approach is moderation. Trim spent flower

stems back to the leaf clusters when they start to look weathered. By the end of their second summer when plants fade substantially, it's time to pull them up and start over again in spring.

Other Species and Cultivars

'Citrona Yellow' is fragrant, reaches 12 inches x 10 inches with bright yellow blooms. Mountain wallflower (*Erysimum capitatum*) has blood-orange and maroon flower spikes that are often obscured by butterflies sipping nectar throughout the summer.

Zinnia
Zinnia elegans

FORM: Tall, stiff stems lined with coarse leaves holding blooms from summer to frost

GROWTH AND MATURE SIZE: Quick-growing to 1 to 4 feet x to 4 feet

USES: Color beds, borders, cutting garden, background, mass, drifts, accent

SOIL: Well-amended soil

PESTS: Powdery mildew; water the ground, not the leaves; choose mildew-resistant varieties

Few flowers shout "summer!" like bright-colored zinnias. Remember zinnias from your childhood? In the heat of summer, their simple, daisylike flowers bloomed in shades of papaya, lemon, and raspberry. But as the summer progressed, they inevitably succumbed to powdery mildew. Today's zinnias are taller and more floriferous than their predecessors, and even more exciting in the garden. Modern zinnia flowers come in double pom-pom blooms in luscious shades of lemon, cream, melon, lime, raspberry, cherry, lilac, and bicolors. Breeders have created many wonderful mildew-resistant varieties that bloom happily almost until frost.

Shared Spaces

Create a cutting garden of colorful zinnias; purple-flowering tall verbena; red-, blue-, or purple-flowered sages; brilliant orange-flowered Mexican sunflower; tall yellow sunflowers; and bronze-leaved fountain grass. Zinnias blooming alongside reed orchids bring color to the tropical garden long before the gingers and canna flowers kick in.

Cultivation

In spring, direct seed onto moist soil or start in pots, ½-inch deep, 2 to 3 inches apart. Thin sprouted seeds or transplants to 1 foot apart. Start more seeds every few weeks for a long season of bloom. Water well and mulch. Water deeply when soil is dry, 2 to 3 inches deep. Apply all-purpose organic fertilizer according to directions on the label. Flower buds form at branch tips; so before buds develop, pinch branch tips. Once flower buds appear, stop pinching. Cut faded flowers to extend bloom.

Other Species and Cultivars

These cultivars are less susceptible to mildew: 'Oklahoma Mix' grows tall, with cutting stems to 30 inches and extended vase life blooms in yellow, pink, scarlet, salmon, and white; 'Purple Prince' grows 3 feet tall with vivid purple blooms; heirloom 'Old Mexico' is deep mahogany red edged in bright gold-to-orange shades; 'Benary's Giant' series includes salmon, lime, and orange selections. Bold-colored zinnias include 'Zowie' with orange-red centers tipped in bright yellow; 'Swizzle' with double flowers in cherry red with white tips; 'Inca' is fiery orange; 'Envy' is chartreuse green. The choices are endless.

Edibles

Then farewell to the city with its
glamour and strife,
I am going to seek some rural scene and lead the simple life.
I want to be a farmer and with the farmer stand,
With hayseed in my whiskers and a
pitchfork in my hand.

"Getting Back to the Farm" from *Poetry in Kansas*
ALBERT STROUD

Maybe you're not ready to join Albert Stroud in pulling out the stops to become a farmer, but more and more people are digging up their front lawn and dumping out pots of Italian cypress to grow their own food, and cities are uprooting large expanses of concrete to make room for Victory Gardens. Eating healthy is one reason and economics certainly plays a role and there is something to be said for the sheer therapy of getting your hands dirty by digging in the soil.

Many people ask whether growing edibles is water wise. The answer is yes, and no. Like all gardening, it depends on what you are growing and how you care for it. Our best course of action is to combine plants with similar water and cultivation needs and to use water-wise irrigation systems. Even if water bills increases a bit during the growing season, you are spending money (and water) on something that feeds you. The beauty of growing an edible garden and a water-wise one is that you can have it all—a gorgeous landscape with water-wise plants that share resources and produce some edible parts, too.

While selecting water-wise plants favored by our author-gardeners, we found a great many trees, shrubs, perennials, and vines that are beautiful in the landscape and do double duty by being edible, as well. There are enough plants in this chapter to frame a garden with shade trees (olive, persimmon, fig), to enclose a garden room with shrubs (bay laurel, pomegranate, artichoke), screen a garden (jujube), climb an arbor (grape), fill a scent garden (curry, oregano, sage, thyme), and anchor a slope (rosemary, bay, oregano). Some of these same plants work well in small places. A beautiful urn, for example, planted with a shrub, small tree, or an herb becomes a garden in itself. Small pots of your favorite water-wise herbs easily become a window garden, beautiful to look at and edible as well.

As it is with our other water-wise plants, the edibles listed here all have very simple cultural requirements with well-drained soil being key. Most are not picky about nutrients and are perfectly happy with what is offered by the native soil, though a few prefer a bit more fertilizer than water-wise ornamentals. Unfortunately, some also attract a few more bugs and critters—they just go along with the territory when it comes to edibles.

Pests can be your biggest challenge with growing your own food, especially if you'd like to grow organically. Fortunately, some edible plants repel bugs while others critters just don't care for them. Nasturtiums deter aphids. Rosemary deters cabbage moths, some beetles, flies, and mosquitoes. Lavender thwarts moths, aphids, and fleas. Thyme and yarrow attract beneficial insects. Artemisia planted as a border can discourage munching rodents.

If your garden has poor, slow-draining soil, the best course of action is to build raised mounds or berms out of native soil mixed with topsoil or compost. To build your own berm, you need space, and scale and slope are critical. The higher the berm, the wider and broader you must make the base.

Shade is a valuable commodity for Southwest gardeners. For some of the water-wise edibles you may notice a full sun and a part shade symbol. In low desert warmer regions, those plants actually enjoy a break from the hot afternoon sun and their production will still continue.

So, who knows? Maybe the decision to plant a water-wise edible garden instead of a conventional landscape will lead to the "grow your own" fever. Before you know it, you might find yourself venturing outside with hayseed in your whiskers and a pitchfork in your hand.

Artichoke
Cynara scolymus

ZONES: 8 through 11
FORM: Jagged, arching gray-green leaves forming wide clumps with tall stalks holding 3- to 6-inch flower buds
GROWTH AND MATURE SIZE: Summer dormant perennial quickly growing to 3 to 5 feet x 3 to 5 feet
USES: Border, focal point, mass
SOIL: Well-amended, well-drained soil
PESTS: Slugs, snails, aphids, and ants; use organic controls

Artichoke is a tri-purpose plant: It is a delicious vegetable eaten for its lovely hearts and meaty, leaflike bracts; it is a perennial with long, jagged-edged, gray-green leaves that emerge like fountain sprays from the base; and it is also a beautiful cut flower. Its flower stalks emerge from the plant's center to form numerous buds at the tips. Those unopened buds are the delicacies we eat. Harvest them large, or small as baby "chokes." If they're left on the plant, buds open up to reveal beautiful thistle-like flowers in shades of rose to purple to blue. Just don't try to eat the flowers!

Shared Spaces

Artichoke's gray arching leaves serve as a sculptural accent in the garden. Plant in permanent garden beds with other Mediterranean climate plants such as rockrose, lavender, and rosemary.

Cultivation

Plant bare-root artichokes in late winter or as soon as the ground is thawed. Set roots 6 inches deep and 5 to 6 feet apart. In colder climates, grow as an annual from seed started in August. Transplant seedlings at 4 to 5 inches tall and from 1-gallon pots anytime soil is workable, at the same spacing.

Water regularly to keep soil moist (not wet), and feed lightly with a balanced organic fertilizer each month during the growing season. After flowering, withhold water to force summer dormancy. Resume watering when leaves resprout at the base. Remove spent leaves. To harvest buds, cut the bud stalk in the crotch above the uppermost set of leaves. Plants produce side shoots that produce more buds. For cut flowers, wait until buds are nearly open and then cut the stalk. After flowering, plants decline and go dormant. Cut all remaining stems back to

3- to 4-inch stubs. Before cooking artichokes, submerge them in a bowl of water with a few drops of dish soap and vinegar. Swish them to remove hitchhiking aphids and then rinse.

Other Species and Cultivars

'Imperial Star' seed produces buds in 95 days, and is good as an annual in colder zones. 'Violetto' from Northern Italy has violet-colored buds (hardy to Zone 6).

Bay Laurel
Laurus nobilis

ZONES: 8 through 11
FORM: 4- to 5-inch long, leathery deep green leaves forming bushy rounded shrub
GROWTH AND MATURE SIZE: Evergreen shrub, moderate grower to 15 to 25 feet x 10 to 20 feet
USES: Background, screen, focal point, hedge
SOIL: Tolerates poor soils that drain well
PESTS: Black sooty mold from scale, whitefly

Bay laurel is more than a dried-out leaf that sits in a can on your pantry shelf. It is a wonderful, aromatic evergreen shrub or tree that is extremely versatile in the garden— and convenient for making marinara sauce or chicken Marbella. Bay laurel is native to the Mediterranean, where long-ago ancient Greeks wove its branches into wreaths to crown their heroes. Grow bay in a container and provide shelter during the winter in colder climates. Like most herbs, bay is far stronger used fresh than used dry. To harvest, choose a leaf from the interior of the plant (so its absence won't be noticed). Simply pick the leaf, rinse off any dust, and get cooking!

Shared Spaces

Bays are beautiful, vertical garden elements at their full size. Plant them in rows and prune for wall-high hedges as they do in Europe. Plant two rows of bays in opposing semicircles to create an intimate outdoor dining room within a larger garden. Keep in scale by regular pruning. Bay is also quite happy in a medium-sized pot on a condo patio.

Cultivation

Plant in spring in colder winter gardens, fall through spring in temperate climates. After planting, water thoroughly; then mulch. Saturate the soil several feet deep to keep the root zone moist (not wet) from the first spring into early fall. Once established (after 2 years), water only once every few weeks in summer (more often in hotter gardens). Let Mother Nature water your bay the rest of the year— unless rains are sparse. Keep container-grown bay moist, but not wet. For faster growth, apply all-purpose organic fertilizer once in spring. Once branches are a few feet long, pick leaves as you need them. Wash well before using.

Other Species and Cultivars

'Saratoga' has rounded leaves and grows fast to is lush and fast growing, to 10 to 25 feet tall. Crushed leaves are slightly sweeter. Hardy to 20 degrees F 'Saratoga' is a cross between European bay and *Umbellularia californica*, California bay. This slow-growing tree reaches 50 feet. Chemical compounds from California bay leaf litter inhibits weeds!

Curry Plant
Helichrysum angustifolium

ZONES: 5 through 11
FORM: Small mound of silvery white foliage with small flowers in summer
GROWTH AND MATURE SIZE: Quick-growing evergreen to 1 foot x 2 feet
USES: Borders, accent, mass, drift
SOIL: Any infertile soil; prefers heavier, clay-based soils that dry between waterings
PESTS: None

Curry plants have two adaptations to hot, dry Southwest gardens: their soft sage green color and their small leaves, which reduce the amount of surface area from which water can evaporate. Silky hairs that cover the leaves reflect sunlight. Umbels of tiny flowers stand several inches above the foliage, adding a golden halo above the pale silver cushion. The leaves' rich aroma may spark sudden cravings for East Indian food. Amazingly, true curry is a mixture of several spices, none of them being curry plant, but these leaves can be used in foods for a bit of the spicy currylike taste.

Shared Spaces
Space curry 3 or more feet apart in groups of 3 to 5 surrounded by oregano, or cluster plants 2 feet apart between larger plants with darker foliage dianthus. Use for strong contrast with green foliage and colorful flowers of Mexican tarragon, superba salvias, torch lily, and veronicas. The repetitious mounding shape contrasts with the bright colors of pineleaf penstemon and turpentine bush (*Ericameria*), creating an interesting rhythm in border plantings. For a more subtle tone-on-tone color variation, mix curry with fernbush (*Chamaebatieria*) and Roman wormwood (*Artemisia*) against a backdrop of silverberry (*Elaeagnus*) to offset bold flower displays.

Cultivation
In higher elevation gardens, transplant curry from spring through late summer; plant from fall through late spring from the low desert down to the coast. No amendment is needed. Water to a depth of 2 feet every two weeks when temperatures are above 80 F monthly in the dry season. In light, sandy soil, water weekly during peak summer heat, especially when plants are blooming. No fertilizer is needed. Trim plants back 4 to 6 inches from the ground in early spring in temperate climates. In colder climes, cover with straw for winter, trim back to new growth in spring. In summer, trim the finished flower stems down below the foliage.

Other Species and Cultivars
More ornamental (but still aromatic) are *H. thianschanicum* 'Icicles' (Zones 9 through 11), which has intensely silver foliage growing to 16 inches x 20 inches.

Edible Oregano
Origanum vulgare

ZONES: 5 through 11
FORM: Low-growing, spreading mat of small leaves with flower clusters in summer and early fall
GROWTH AND MATURE SIZE: Evergreen perennial quickly growing to 8 inches x 24 to 36 inches
USES: Ground cover, foreground, mass, drifts, borders
SOIL: Well-drained soil
PESTS: Protect from slugs and snails

We know oregano is the herb that lends its zip to allk kinds of food. Ancient Greeks, however, believed that the goddess Aphrodite created oregano's spicy scent as a symbol of happiness, so they crowned bridal couples with oregano wreaths. Romance aside, all gardeners and cooks should grow their own oregano, as it is easy to grow and thrives in Southwestern gardens. Oregano forms horizontal stems covered in deep green, almost crinkled leaves. Creeping stems root wherever they touch the ground, so a single plant soon makes a good-sized patch. To harvest, simply snip a branch, rinse off any dirt, then strip the leaves off the stem.

Shared Spaces

If you don't have the room (or the inclination) to plant a dedicated herb garden, plant oregano as a ground cover in any ornamental flower bed. Edible oregano makes a lovely, low, green carpet. Or plant a mixed herb garden in a large container with tall chives or dill and bushy basil or sage and let oregano cascade over the side.

Cultivation

In mild winter gardens, plant fall through spring. In colder areas, plant in spring. Water well after planting and mulch. Water to keep the soil moist down to the bottom of the roots for the first spring through early fall. After that, water deeply once the top inches of soil are dry. No fertilizer is needed. There is no need to prune oregano, but if stems grow beyond the garden bed, snip them off and cook with the leaves, or root to make more plants. If oregano gets too leggy, cut all stems back to the ground in winter or early spring. Water and wait for stems to resprout.

Other Species and Cultivars

Origanum vulgare ssp. *hirtum*, true Greek oregano, (8 inches x 12 to 18 inches) is the primary culinary oregano. Its broad green leaves are covered in fine down. *O. marjorna* is sweet marjoram, frost-tender (Zones 9 to 11), growing to 1 to 2 feet tall, and trailing. Ornamental 'Herrenhausen' (to 16 inches tall) is a prolific bloomer with dark red-violet blooms and reddish leaves in fall.

Fig
Ficus carica

ZONES: 8 through 11
FORM: Low-branched with wide spreading crown
GROWTH AND MATURE SIZE: Fairly quick-growing deciduous tree to 10 to 30 feet x 10 to 30 feet
USES: Shade, groves, espalier, focal point
SOIL: Any; prefers well-drained soil
PESTS: Gophers, rodents; birds

Cleopatra may have loved Marc Anthony, but she adored figs. No surprise, since at 55 percent sugar content, figs are the sweetest fruits, and ones with a long history. Archaeologists have found figs in 7000-year-old archaeological sites. Franciscan friars planted California's first figs at Mission San Diego de Alcala 250 years later. The rest, as they say, is history. Fig trees are deciduous trees with fantastic gnarled branches, white bark, and big, shiny green-lobed leaves. Some varieties have two crops, one in spring and a heavier crop in late summer to fall. Easy to grow, water-wise, and delicious, figs are a garden must-have.

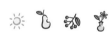

Shared Spaces

Fig trees make spectacular shade trees. They set the tone in Mediterranean gardens, tropical gardens, oasis gardens and Asian-style gardens. Espalier against a sunny wall. While fig trees can be incorporated into garden beds, do not plant beneath the branches. Their roots don't like the disturbance or the competition

Cultivation

Plant fall through spring when soil can be worked Water to saturate soil 2 to 3 feet deep the first year to establish. Year two and after, and in gardens with well-draining soil, deep-water once every week or two in summer, but don't water in winter when trees are dormant. Water slightly more often in desert gardens and less in heavy soils. No fertilizer is needed. Figs can grow in containers that are at least 20 inches in diameter. Fertilize with a balanced, organic fertilizer in spring. Figs ripen *only* on the tree. Pick fruits very soft. Many varieties produce a light crop in early spring and a heavier crop in fall. Prune branches after the fall harvest to remove weak wood, create a strong structure, and encourage the next year's crop. Leave lower branches so fruit is easy to reach.

Other Species and Cultivars

'Conadria' takes intense heat without splitting. 'Brown Turkey' fruits are dark brown with amber flesh and are good for Southern California. 'Panachee' has beautiful, green and yellow striped fruit with strawberry colored flesh. Some varieties are invasive along the rivers and creeks of California's Central Valley.

Garden Sage
Salvia officinalis

ZONES: 5 through 11
FORM: Long, deep green, coarse leaves form upright bushy mound
GROWTH AND MATURE SIZE: Quickly growing evergreen to 1 to 2 feet x 1 to 2 feet
USES: Ground cover, mass, drifts, focal point, border, herb garden, foreground
SOIL: Well-drained soil
PESTS: None

In an 1833 publication, Russian botanist Alexander von Bunge named the genus *Salvia*, which means "to be saved" or "to cure." There are over 900 species of sage, and many have been grown for thousands of years for their medicinal properties. You can grow garden sage for its other attributes. It is a culinary mainstay, both fresh and dried, in the kitchen. It also makes for a lovely garden border, forever green even under a blanket of snow, and flowering beautifully in spring with long lavender flower spikes curving out from the stem tips. It is remarkably durable as it fluffs right back up after the dogs run through it, releasing its lovely scent in the process.

Shared Spaces

Use in a full sun border with pink-flowering currant, midground plantings of 'Blue Fortune' agastache and globemallow, and sage planted in a drift throughout. Plant masses of aromatic sage along a garden path. Use sage planted in groupings in the understory of an Arizona juniper for winter interest. Plant a group of garden sages, green-leaved 'Purpurascens' and 'Tricolor' in a large red-mahogany colored container.

Cultivation

Plant sage in spring as soon as the ground can be worked or in fall in mild weather gardens. Space plants 6 to 12 inches apart in unamended soil. Water deeply and apply organic mulch. Water deeply once a week through the first spring and twice each week during the first summer in hot desert areas. In more temperate climes, water deeply when soil dries out. A monthly watering during winter is only needed if there is no rain or snowfall. After that, established plants need water once each week during the growing season. No fertilizer is needed. Cut back in early spring to just above new growth. Plants may need replacing if they become too woody, after four years or so.

Other Species and Cultivars

'Purpurascens' has purple-gray foliage growing 2 feet x 3 feet. 'Tricolor' has green leaves with pink and white edges. 'Icterina', golden variegated sage, has green leaves with yellow edges and grows 2 feet tall and wide. 'Berggarten' is more compact growing to 16 inches tall and wide with dense growth. It may be longer lived than the species.

Garden Thyme
Thymus vulgaris

ZONES: 5 through 11
FORM: Small-leaved, short-stemmed, and spreading with blooms in spring and early summer
GROWTH AND MATURE SIZE: Quick-growing evergreen to 2 to 12 inches x 5 to 12 inches
USES: Edging, drifts, ground cover, filler between pavers, rock garden, dry streambed, herb garden
SOIL: Well-drained soil
PESTS: None

No herb garden is complete without a patch of thyme, an herb popular in many cuisines. It is a major component, for example, of French fines herbes, along with chervil, parsley, bay, French tarragon, and a handful of others. Culinary thyme has a surprisingly pungent aroma for its tiny leaf. Several scented thymes are good to cook with: lemon thyme, lime thyme, orange balsam thyme, and caraway thyme. Thyme can be a creeping plant, shorter than twelve inches tall. Its tiny pointed green (sometimes variegated) leaves line creeping stems. Flowers are rosy lavender, dark pink, or white. Its diminutive size may be why European folklore has long associated thyme with fairies.

Shared Spaces

Thyme can be upright or low and spreading. Traditional culinary thyme is an upright type that can be planted as an edging in the garden, particularly in an herb garden. Creeping thymes, on the other hand, are good for low profile, water-wise ground covers planted between pavers (they handle light foot traffic), around the base of other plants with similar cultural needs, or to cover a temporary bare spot while woodier plants fill in. Both upright and creeping thyme can be grown in a pot.

Cultivation

Plant from fall through spring in mild winter gardens and in spring in cold winter areas. Water well after planting, and mulch. Culinary thyme prefers weekly water from spring through fall. If winter rains are normal, let Mother Nature cover winter irrigation. Otherwise, water to completely saturate the root zone every few weeks in winter. No fertilizer is needed. Cut culinary thyme back by a third of its height after bloom unless you use it often. Every time you snip a piece, you have pruned your thyme. Lower-growing ground cover thymes need no pruning.

Other Species and Cultivars

Golden lemon, Doone Valley, and silver thyme are all variegated. 'Elfin' is the lowest growing, to a diminutive 1 to 2 inches tall, with pink flowers. Silvery leaved woolly thyme is the most drought tolerant. Other flavored thymes include pinewood, coconut, and *T. thracicus*, a scented blend of lavender and thyme.

Grape
Vitis species

ZONES: 5 through 11
FORM: Large deeply lobed leaves on winter dormant/deciduous vines with grapes ripening in summer
GROWTH AND MATURE SIZE: 20 to 30 feet long
USES: Arbors, vineyard, pergola, fences, garden walls
SOIL: Deep, well-drained soil
PESTS: Mildew; four-legged and winged critters

Vines emerge from rough twisted trunks and sprout broad, shiny green leaves that turn fall colors and drop in winter. Their fruits (really, berries) develop in clusters on vines that grow long and fast. In the warmest summer, a grapevine can grow 10 to 12 inches in a week! There are both edible and ornamental grapes, but from a gardener's standpoint, they all grow the same way. As is typical of plants that have been cultivated for millennia, there are a staggering number of grape varieties. Some have seeds, others are seedless; they are green, blue, black, yellow, or red. Some are best for eating, others for making juice, wine, or raisins.

  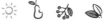

Shared Spaces
Grapevines are beautiful and functional as garden plants. Train them onto walls, over fences, or onto arbors for fast summer shade and warm sunshine in winter. Grapes can be grown in large pots, too. Use cut grapevines to weave wreaths.

Cultivation
Purchase and plant grapes as dormant rooted "whips" in winter or as potted leafed-out vines in spring. If your soil drains poorly, plant on a mound. Mix in balanced organic fertilizer. Mulch with a 3-inch layer of compost. Water deeply the first three summers to encourage deep roots. Established grapes are extremely drought tolerant and produce best on a low-water diet. Early farmers grew grapes on rainfall alone. Fertilize minimally, if at all. Too much nitrogen makes for lush foliage at the expense of fruit. There are several methods for training grapevines, all of which are designed to prevent vines from tangling, keep fruit off the ground, and ensure both good ventilation and sunlight penetration. Prune in early spring, just before new growth starts. Since grapes fruit on year-old wood, learn to identify fruiting wood before you start cutting.

Other Species and Cultivars
Grapes exist for nearly every microclimate of the Southwest: 'Reliance' is a seedless, pinkish red table grape that ripens midseason; 'Lakemont' is a seedless green table grape; and 'Swenson' is an early-season red grape (with seeds) suitable for table, juice, and wine.

217

Jujube
Zizyphus jujuba

ZONES: 6 through 9
FORM: Dense foliage and thorny stems form thickets with blooms in summer followed by fruits
GROWTH AND MATURE SIZE: Quick-growing deciduous tree to 20 to 30 feet x 10 feet
USES: Screen, windbreak, barrier; single specimen as a tree
SOIL: Jujube grows well in most soils; tolerates alkaline soil
PESTS: None

Jujube, called "Chinese date" for the sweet fruit it produces in autumn, has been cultivated for so long that its native origin is debated. The Chinese developed cultivars but jujube may actually be native to the Mediterranean. It forms thickets, creating a grove of thorny stems where songbirds find inviting cover. Its stems arch and curve stiffly downward; branches zigzag at the plentiful spines. Plant far away from walkways and wear protection when you harvest. Jujube has small, glossy, light green leaves that turn a clear, pale yellow in autumn. Inconspicuous yellow-green flowers are wonderfully fragrant, and the datelike fruits provide an interesting contrast.

Shared Spaces

Mix jujube with evergreens in screen, windbreak, or barrier plantings where its rootsprouting will be an asset. Their dormant silhouette is attractive highlighted against a high wall. Mexican evening primrose, yerba mansa, and prairie sage are good companion ground covers.

Cultivation

Rooted offshoots and nursery-grown cultivars can be transplanted in spring or autumn. Either plant in large open spaces where it can rootsprout and form a grove, or contain it by surrounding the planting with a wide band of unirrigated, compacted soil such as a wide path. For the first two or three years, water jujubes to a depth of 24 inches weekly in summer in sandy soil, half as often in clay; monthly or less in winter. Once established, water to a depth of 30 inches once a month in dry months. Plants bear well without fertilizer. Plant where there is space available for a grove, letting it grow naturally. For a single tree, remove all the twiggy growth within several feet of the ground and cut rootsprouts and suckers out in early summer, exposing more of the trunk as the plant gets taller and the bark thickens. Use a double layer of landscape fabric under 4 inches of mulch to suppress root sprouts.

Other Species and Cultivars

'Li' and 'Lang' are the two most common varieties. 'Georgia 866' is extremely sweet. It grows well in the Southwest, producing 2-inch-long red fruits in September. Graythorn (*Zizyphus obtusifolia*), a native of North and Central America, grows slowly to 6 feet tall and produces small blue fruits that birds favor.

Lavender
Lavandula species

ZONES: 5 through 11
FORM: Small leaves on a small woody perennial or subshrub with flower spikes in spring or summer
GROWTH AND MATURE SIZE: Evergreen and moderately growing to. 1 to 3 feet x 5 to 6 feet
USES: Herb, perennial, cottage, Mediterranean gardens, border, low hedge, single focal point, drifts
SOIL: Well-amended, well-drained soil; tolerates poor soils
PESTS: None

Lavender is for more than perfumes and sachets; some varieties can be used in cooking. Cookies and cakes made with lavender are slightly sweet, slightly spicy, slightly resinous, and very aromatic. Baked goods made with English lavender (*Lavandula angustifolia*) have a sweet fragrance, while those made with hybrid lavender 'Provence' (*Lavandula* x *intermedia*), are a bit milder. Not all lavenders are edible and not all are grown for their fragrance. Spanish lavenders (*L. stoechas*), are grown for their large purple, pink, white, or chartreuse-yellow flowers. Lavenders claim their spot in the garden with their full, lush mounds and beautiful flower spikes.

Shared Spaces
Plant lavender in herb gardens, cottage gardens, Mediterranean style gardens, and even knot gardens. Use them as a low, fragrant hedge or to edge a flower border. Grow in containers as well.

Cultivation
Plant early fall through spring in areas where winter temperatures don't fall much below freezing. In colder areas, wait until spring. Water well after planting, and mulch. French lavender, Spanish lavender, and other North African lavenders are more drought resistant than the English lavenders and their hybrids. Water all lavenders at least weekly through their first growing season to thoroughly moisten the root zone so they become established. After that, allow lavender to dry between watering. Overwatering can cause fatal root rot. Fertilize in early spring with a balanced organic fertilizer. Prune to control lavender's size and to increase longevity. Harvest flower wands as they reach their brightest and fullest color, severing them where they emerge from the foliage. Prune branches back by a third to promote bushiness and refresh foliage. Unpruned lavender grows heavy and woody after a few years, often splitting in the middle.

Other Species and Cultivars
'Mitcham Gray' has blue-gray foliage with vivid deep violet-blue blooms. 'Royal Velvet', a rapid grower, is covered with long-stemmed dark navy blue and lavender flower spikes. 'Hidcote Superior' has a compact habit and deeply colored violet-blue flowers. 'Provence' has light purple blooms.

Olive
Olea europaea

ZONES: 8 through 11
FORM: Small leaves on a rounded crown, scented flowers in spring followed by small fruits in fall to winter
GROWTH AND MATURE SIZE: Slow-growing evergreen tree to 20 to 30 feet x 20 to 30 feet
USES: Grove, screen, espalier
SOIL: Well-drained or poor soils
PESTS: Ants, black scale, and sooty mold; other pests in different regions (Consult local Master Gardeners)

It is hard work, but after you taste homegrown pressed olive oil, you might want an olive tree of your own. Olive is originally from the hot and dry Mediterranean region, so it's no wonder that olive trees are widely grown for their drought and heat tolerance. Add to that the sheer beauty of the tree with its rounded crown, the scented flowers that adorn it in spring, and its small, green oval fruits in fall. You'll have a beautiful tree to enjoy for its graceful structure and soft green leaves, if not its fruits and oil.

Shared Spaces

Gnarled branches that reach gracefully toward the sky, smooth gray bark, and gray-green leaves make olive trees valuable landscape plants. Olive trees are adaptable to a wide range of situations and tolerant of extreme neglect. Full-sized specimens are defining features of many garden styles. Plant as a grove, screen, or espalier. Plant dwarf, fruitless olives as hedges, borders, or container plants.

Cultivation

Plant in early fall or early spring. Keep away from sidewalks and other structures that could be damaged by surface roots. To grow several trees, space 20 feet apart. Water deeply and mulch after planting. Water young trees deeply once a week through the first summer and less often in spring. Established trees are extremely drought resistant, but to produce olives, water deeply, and monthly in summer. Avoid overwatering, which causes root rot. Apply all-purpose organic fertilizer before spring flowers appear. In early spring remove dead or diseased wood. Prune fruiting olives to a vase shape for good light penetration, air circulation, and to keep fruit accessible. Fruiting starts after about four years in the ground. For lye curing, harvest olives when they turn from green to straw-colored. For salt, sun, or oven drying, pick olives when they're black.

Other Species and Cultivars

For olive fruits, plant 'Manzanillo' or 'Mission' and to cross-pollinate, plant 'Sevillano'. To make olive oil, try Tuscan 'Leccino' or 'Maurino' in cool winter areas.

Persimmon
Diospyros species

ZONES: 5 through 10
FORM: Broad crown with fall foliage, followed by fruit ripening in late fall and winter
GROWTH AND MATURE SIZE: Deciduous tree growing slow to moderate to 25 feet x 25 feet or wider
USES: Specimen, grove
SOIL: Deep, well-drained, but tolerates poor soils.
PESTS: Ants, mealybugs, and scale; bigger problems are birds, possums, gophers, and even coyotes

The cooler shorter days of autumn bring edible color to the garden. Pomegranates turn ruby red and persimmons turn from bright green to red, orange, or gold. Persimmons grow on handsome trees and in mild winter gardens, their large, shiny green leaves turn fall colors before they drop, around the time of Thanksgiving. In colder gardens, leaves drop with the first frost. Either way, the tennis-ball-sized fruits hang around a bit longer. Their round, oblong, flat, square, or acorn-shaped silhouettes dangle from bare branches like enormous Christmas ornaments against the blue winter sky. Some are eaten hard and others must be soft as jelly to be palatable.

Shared Spaces

Plant persimmon trees as specimens to show off their fantastic fall and winter display. Leave the ground beneath the branches bare rather than planted with perennials or other plants.

Cultivation

Plant fall through spring. Do not kink or coil the long taproot. After planting, cut the main trunk to 3 feet high. New branches sprout to form a nice structure. Paint trunks with one part latex paint mixed with three parts water to prevent sunburn. Water to wet the entire rootball when soil is dry—three inches down for the first two years. After that, water deeply but infrequently during spring and summer (more often in desert gardens). Fertilize with citrus and avocado food, following avocado recommendations. If too much non-fruiting wood develops, cut back fertilizer. Trees fruit after a few years with heavy and light crops alternating years. Thin fruits to one per shoot. Prune damaged wood and shape when dormant. Do not to cut back too far, as trees fruit on one-year-old branches. Plan to share with wildlife or pick fruit before it ripens. Ripen in a paper bag or freeze overnight. Thaw to eat.

Other Species and Cultivars

"Astringent" persimmons are inedible until the jelly is soft and translucent. 'Hachiya' (self-pollinating) has astringent, acorn-shaped, deep orange, very sweet fruit. 'Saijo' is cold hardy to minus 10 degrees. Non-astringent persimmons are sweet and edible—apple hard or tomato soft. 'Jiro' (self-pollinating) has non-astringent, flat, round fruit with orange skin.

Pomegranate
Punica granatum

ZONES: 6 through 11

FORM: Shiny small leaves form bushy shrub with spring flowers, followed by fall foliage and fruits

GROWTH AND MATURE SIZE: Deciduous, moderately growing 12 to 20 feet x 10 to 15 feet

USES: Background screen, mass, focal point, hedge

SOIL: Deep, well-drained, fertile soil or rocky, native soil; not moist, heavy, or poorly drained soils

PESTS: None

Pomegranate is the tree of many colors. In spring, the dark green, glossy leaves coat the stems, and the plants look cool and refreshing. Then the tree is covered in flaming red-orange, yellow, apricot, or white flowers that give way to large, round fruit with its characteristic flared end, like the mouth of a marine creature. Fruits stay on the plant for months and deepen in color to a rich wine red. Finally, in fall leaves turn a blazing yellow before they fall, leaving the bare stems holding the red globes of fruit. The fruit and seeds are delicious. 'Wonderful' has rich, red fruit and red-orange flowers. 'Chico' and 'Nana' are dwarf varieties with colorful, decorative fruit that is not edible.

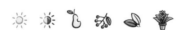

Shared Spaces

Pomegranate makes a spectacular espaliered plant. When grown as a shrub, it makes a good visual screen hedge either alone or mixed with other shrubs. Plants trained as a small tree make good specimen or accent plants for small patios or courtyards. Pomegranate also grows well in a large container.

Cultivation

Plant in winter or early spring while plants are dormant. Mulch the root zone generously, but do not allow mulch to touch the bark. Water thoroughly and continue to water deeply every three to four days for two or three weeks. Water newly planted trees every week for the first year. Apply slow-release or organic fertilizer in fall and spring. Established plants should be watered every ten days in summer; monthly in winter. Although pomegranate is quite drought tolerant, it has better quality and quantity of fruit when it's regularly watered. Prune in winter while the plant is dormant to remove suckers, crossing branches, and dead or damaged wood. Plants are easily trained to a single trunk or even an espalier by removing suckers and unwanted branches annually in early spring.

Other Species and Cultivars

'Utah Sweet' is the most cold hardy to Zone 6, has pink-orange flowers, and pink pulp and skin. 'Angel Red' matures in early September (Zones 7 through 10) and has the highest juice content. 'Grenada' has deep red blossoms and fruit ripens in August, earlier than 'Wonderful'. 'White' has whitish pink fruit, transparent white flesh, and is very sweet, ripening early September.

Rosemary
Rosmarinus officinalis

ZONES: 5 through 11
FORM: Needlelike foliage densely covers branches, forming upright bushy to low and trailing; covered with small blooms from March to May
GROWTH AND MATURE SIZE: Quick-growing evergreen to 3 to 6 feet x 3 to 8 feet
USES: Borders, hedges, topiary, ground cover, mass, drifts, slopes
SOIL: Rocky, alkaline soil; fails entirely in heavy, clay soil
PESTS: None

Many gardeners only know rosemary for its culinary qualities, but it is a valuable addition to ornamental gardens throughout the Southwest. The deep green, evergreen leaves are covered with sticky, resinous oil. It is this oil that produces the sharp, clear fragrance when the leaves are touched and the rich flavor when they are cooked. The light or dark blue, purple, white, or pink flowers of rosemary are small and crowded on the stems. Beekeepers prize the honey made from these blossoms. There are many cultivars identified for their upright, trailing, or bushy forms, for flower color, and for taste. Taste before you buy; there is an astounding range of flavors.

Shared Spaces

Plant rosemary as a low hedge or border plant. Its deep green color makes it a stunning background for bulbs, perennials, or annuals. Its heat tolerance makes it a good choice against a hot wall, around a pool or patio, or other areas where reflected heat is intense. Many of the trailing forms are reliable ground covers for erosion control. Place near a walkway, where the foliage can be brushed often to release the fragrance.

Cultivation

Plant in fall in the low desert; in spring as soon as soil can be worked in colder zones. Water thoroughly and mulch after planting. Water every three to four days for two or three weeks, then water every seven to ten days. No fertilizer is required. Water established plants every two to three weeks in summer in the low desert, less frequently in higher elevations. Water every three to four weeks in winter in low elevation zones; rely on natural rainfall in high elevation zones. Prune late fall or early spring, removing dead or damaged wood. Prune to a foot or two from the ground every two or three years to rejuvenate the plant.

Other Species and Cultivars

'Irene' is a ground cover (1 to 2 feet x 4 feet) with blue-violet blooms, larger and more profuse than others. 'Tuscan Blue' is upright (3 to 6 feet tall and wide) with good culinary traits. 'Roman Beauty' is compact, with arching stems (16 inches x 12 inches) and violet-blue blooms.

IRRIGATION

By now, you probably realize that choosing low-water plants is only one component of having a successful, water-wise garden. One of the most important ways to support those plants is to water them appropriately. All plants, low-water or not, need regular water their first year or two in the ground until their roots are established. After that, you can cut back watering.

This section is all about irrigation technologies that deliver water to plants more efficiently, more directly, and more appropriately than old-fashioned spray heads that sprayed the garden, the sidewalk, the neighbor's garden, the driveway … you get the picture.

New generation irrigation technologies borrow from the agriculture industry and gardening practices in Israel and other regions where water is even more scarce than it is here. These technologies are more efficient, "smarter" than ever before and, fortunately, not any more complicated to use.

All irrigation systems, regardless of the type, have some common features. Unless you are on a well, water probably enters your property from the street through a water meter. From there, pipes carry the water into your house and to your garden, ideally (but not always) on separate lines. Some of that water goes to your hose spigots, and some goes to irrigation valves that turn the water on and off as it flows through pipes into your garden. Each valve controls a "zone" of irrigation that runs independently from the others. They number of zones your garden has or needs depends on how large the space is, the water requirement of the plants in each zone, how much water pressure you have, and so forth.

The lines that carry water from your valves into the garden ultimately connect to the devices (sprinklers, drip irrigation, and so forth) that deliver water to your plants. That's a very generalized description of how water gets to the garden. Our major focus in this section is that last part: how water gets from the irrigation lines to your plants.

NEW MINI-ROTOR SPRINKLERS

In the mid-2000s, the irrigation industry saw a new type of overhead sprinkler head come into its own. These mini-rotors are matched-precipitation heads that operate at a lower pressure than old-fashioned spray heads, but they are not considered to be drip irrigation. They are best used for beds of low-growing ground covers, turf, or meadows where plants are all about the same height.

These nozzle-sized rotors have several water-saving features, including bigger, heavier drops that are less likely to evaporate into the air. Each rotor sprays multiple streams of water, each of which projects a slightly different distance. This pattern eliminates "donuts" of dry, brown plants surrounding the risers. In addition, they adjust the amount of water they spray according to the distance of the streams. Traditional sprinklers, in contrast, spray a set number of gallons, whether over 8 feet or 28 feet.

Irrigation systems designed for these new rotors are essentially the same as designing systems for an old-fashioned sprayers. Each rotor head is positioned and adjusted so its spray reaches all of the adjacent heads. This "head-to-head" layout ensures that the entire area is watered by two or more spray heads.

Swapping out traditional spray heads for new matched-precipitation rotors is as simple as screwing the old one off and the new one on. They cost a bit more, but many water agencies offer rebates. Check with your local agency to see the kinds of rebates that are available.

LOW-FLOW, "DRIP" IRRIGATION

Low-flow, "drip" irrigation gets its name for the rate at which drip systems release water. These systems operate on the scale of *gallons per hour* rather than the *gallons per minute* used by the older, overhead sprinklers and mini-rotor sprinklers. In fact, water delivery rate is so slow that water percolates down into the soil, rather than running onto your driveway or otherwise being directed away from its target. Because water is aimed directly at plant roots—which is where plants need it—no water is sprayed into the air, so virtually no water is lost to evaporation.

That deep-water penetration encourages deep, drought-resistant roots. Drip-irrigated gardens are also blessed with fewer weeds. Why? Weed seeds need water to germinate. Without water sprayed over broad, unplanted areas, weed seeds don't get enough water to sprout.

JOE LAMP'L (*The Green Gardener's Guide*/GGG) also points out the value of drip irrigation in saving water in your landscape.

Drip systems in non-turf areas can save from 25 to 75 percent of the amount of water used by in-ground sprinkler systems, depending upon the local climate and the types of plants being irrigated. Most studies show savings in excess of 50 percent.*

*EPA, www.epa.gov/watersense/water/why.htm

Convert to soaker hoses or drip irrigation where feasible. Watering directly at the soil level is the most efficient way to irrigate, for two reasons. First, it cuts down on wasted water tremendously as water is delivered directly to the soil. There's no drift or evaporation; all water is utilized right where the plant needs it most—at the roots. Furthermore, the water isn't deflected away or suspended on the foliage where it is exposed to wind and sun, the two biggest culprits of rapid evaporation. By watering at the soil level, the foliage stays dry, thus minimizing plant diseases. That's an important point when it comes to water conservation because a healthy plant requires fewer resources to keep growing strong.

Drip irrigation, also, known as micro-irrigation or trickle irrigation, is a popular system for applying water at or just under the soil level. It may not be as appropriate for lawn areas, but for the most precise and efficient watering of individual plants (such as trees, shrubs, ground covers, perennials, vegetables, and containers), drip irrigation is the ideal way to go. In fact, it's so efficient that many water municipalities exempt landscapes watered with drip irrigation from restrictions during drought.

Drip systems are flexible and adjustable systems that can be connected to the pipes coming out of valves or, with a small garden, connected to a hose bib. These low-flow systems operate at low pressure, typically lower than your household water.

So, when the irrigation system goes on, there are no surprises for the family member who happens to be in the shower.

Drip irrigation comes in several "flavors." Residential drip systems typically consist of microsprayers, drip emitters, or drip lines. There are tubes and fittings that fit together with a minimum of tools and no pipe glue. Think of them as big Tinkertoys®. They are nearly as easy to put together!

Microsprayers (also referred to as **microsprinklers**) are small plastic spray heads that shoot out fine jets or fans of water over an area of just a few feet. Some spray full circles, some half or quarter circles, while others water long, narrow strips like you'd find along a walkway. Most microsprayers have two parts. A spray head attaches to a stem or stake that stands six to twelve inches tall. Spray heads are rated for different amounts of water, from less than a gallon per hour to as much as 20 gallons per hour, and some have adjustable flow rates.

Microsprayers are valued for their even coverage over a relatively broad area. Irrigation experts often recommend using several microsprayers beneath the canopy of a tree or large shrub to water the entire rootzone. They are also useful for watering plants in the cracks between walkway pavers. Each spray head attaches to a piece of narrow, flexible, "spaghetti" tubing, which is attached on the other end to flexible, half-inch-diameter tubing that is, in turn, connected to irrigation pipes.

Drip emitters emit water drop by drop, or dribble by dribble. Some are shaped like buttons, others like flags. One or more emitters is positioned around the base of an individual plant. The variety and styles of emitters can be a bit staggering, but they all do about the same thing. Again, their flow rates are so slow that runoff is eliminated. Look for emitters that are self-flushing or easy to take apart and clean if they happen to clog.

Drip lines (also called **dripper lines**) are long plastic tubes with what look like holes poked into them, every foot or two. The tubing is flexible, except at the holes where it is thick and rigid. That rigidity comes from an emitter embedded *inside* the line. If you cut the line open, you would see the tubular emitter with tiny channels snaking through it. Those channels are designed to keep the emitters from clogging as the water flows. They work surprisingly well.

Drip lines have many advantages over installing individual emitters at each plant. Since the emitters are *inside* the tubing, they are very well protected. Maintenance is easy. There are no little parts to break off or clog or come unscrewed or disappear amidst the mulch. In fact, drip lines can be covered by mulch in situations where you don't them to be visible.

The drip line is also quick and easy to install. Simply lay parallel lines through the garden bed, or a grid across the garden, or snake the line through the garden, wrapping it around the base of trees and large shrubs. Most companies produce drip lines that are roughly a half-inch in diameter, the perfect size for ornamental garden beds. Narrower, quarter-inch-diameter lines with emitters spaced every six inches are perfect for vegetable gardens.

Don't confuse laser-drilled tubing with emitter tubing. Laser-drilled products are simply that—tubes with holes in them. They clog easily, and you'll have no idea how much water drips out of each hole.

INSTALLING A DRIP IRRIGATION SYSTEM

Converting your irrigation from overhead spray to drip isn't very difficult. Irrigation supply houses sell all the parts you need, including pressure reducers and filters. The specifics about how to make that conversion or to design a brand new drip irrigation system from scratch is beyond what we have room for here, but a savvy do-it-yourselfer can create a pretty good design with a bit of research. Community colleges, water districts, and irrigation supply stores often offer classes on irrigation system design, installation, and maintenance. The amount you can save in water and money will far outweigh the cost of a class and the time you invest.

JOE LAMP'L (GGG) explains the ease of installing a home irrigation system:

The basic drip irrigation equipment needed for the typical home system makes installation quick and easy.

1. Connect the flexible plastic supply line to the spigot, just as you would with an ordinary garden hose.

2. Run the supply line along the path that will deliver the water to the area needed. Once you have enough length laid out, cut the end, and then bend it back and secure to crimp.

3. Next, determine where along the supply line you want to insert the microtubes that will supply the water to the base of your plants. A puncture tool makes the hole in the supply line for insertion of the microtubing.

4. Connect the desired emitter to the end of the microtube, and you're finished.

In permanent systems, a backflow prevention device is installed at the beginning of the line to prevent contaminated water from being sucked back into the water source, should a reverse-flow situation occur. Attach an automatic timer to the system for a carefree, low-cost, highly efficient watering system. Note that micro-irrigation lines are subject to occasional clogging, so periodically inspect the lines and system to ensure more efficient operation. Also note that because the supply line and microtubes are along the soil surface, care should be taken for maintenance of plants around the system.

Of course, you can always hire a professional. The advantages? Your system will be installed more quickly, more efficiently, and hopefully with less trial and error. And if there are problems, the contractor is responsible for troubleshooting and fixing them. There are irrigation contractors in every state who specialize in drip systems. Do your homework and be an educated consumer so you know how to evaluate that professional and what he or she proposes for your garden.

IRRIGATION CLOCKS

As much as you might think you will remember when and how much to water your garden, an irrigation clock does a better job. Irrigation clocks turn your irrigation valves on and off on a regular schedule that you can set or, if you are using one of the new "smart clocks," on a schedule that the clock determines based on current weather conditions, where you live, the kind of soil you have, the type of sprinkler system, and the types of plants each zone waters. In other words, it gives your garden exactly the amount of water it needs, when it needs it, and no more than it needs.

When set and managed properly, irrigation clocks are extremely consistent and reliable. For details about irrigation clocks, see page 27 in the introduction.

MAINTAINING THE WATER-WISE IRRIGATION SYSTEM

"Efficient irrigation involves more than just making sure you're watering at the right time and with the right method. It also means making regular inspections of your system to ensure that it is operating properly and is leak-free. Consistent inspections, tune-ups, and repairs can yield substantial water savings. Over time, even the best irrigation systems will succumb to cultural and environmental pressures (normal wear and tear, lawn mowers, foot traffic, and of course the car or delivery truck that drives over them). Generally, most irrigation problems are easy to identify and repair. But without regular inspections, thousands of gallons of wasted water can be lost."

JOE LAMP'L

In addition to proper installation and control, your irrigation system needs to be maintained. No irrigation system, regardless of the type, is maintenance free.

Check once a month, with the system on, one zone at a time. Run water through each zone long enough to inspect it for leaks, sprung lines, separated joints, broken heads, heads that point in the wrong direction, and so forth. As you walk through the garden, listen for leaks; that sound is often your first clue that there is a problem.

Wilted plants are another sure sign of a problem. One possibility is that the zone doesn't deliver enough water to keep those plants going. If most of the plants in a zone are fine, and those that are wilted are all the same kind, then most likely that kind of plant is thirstier than the others and should be moved. Another possibility is that the drip emitter to those plants was kicked away or clogged, or the spray head that should be watering them is blocked by a plant that has grown up between the plants and the spray head. Or, maybe your spray head is spraying at the wrong angle. Use your powers of observation to troubleshoot the situation.

Overhead spray systems can also develop leaks at the heads. If you see water spurting out around a spray head, unscrew the head and check out its innards.

SOMETHING YOU SHOULD KNOW

Most irrigation system leaks are hard to detect because they're underground. But even a tiny leak can waste a lot of water. A $^{1}/_{32}$-inch hole in a water line under 60 pounds of pressure wastes 6300 gallons of water in a month—that's 75,600 gallons a year!

JOE LAMP'L (GGG) describes additional maintenance issues with overhead sprayers:

Another common problem leading to wasted water is a clogged nozzle. Again, nozzles can easily be unscrewed and inspected. Most of the time they can be cleaned with a blast of water or a thin piece of metal. You can suspect a clogged nozzle if the spray pattern is warped, the volume is reduced, or if areas of your yard or garden appear to be dry from lack of moisture in the zone in question.

An easy fix, and one that will save you a lot of water, is to readjust heads that overspray and are misdirected, so the water only goes toward its target. That means not on the driveway, sidewalk, street, or your neighbor's yard! Tilted heads should be straightened so that water delivered to the ground is even from side to side. Sunken heads that have been overgrown by surrounding vegetation confine the water to a very small area around the head. Similarly obstructed heads prevent water from getting to its intended target zone. The result is overwatering near the obstruction and insufficient water beyond it.

Watch for wet spots in the ground from leaks in underground pipes. Dig down to uncover the pipes and look for obvious problems. If you don't find the leak, hire an irrigation professional to troubleshoot and repair the system.

Before you finish with monthly maintenance, adjust your irrigation clock for the amount of water your plants need at that time of the year. How much water do plants need? That varies between Hardiness Zones, from plant type to plant type, from season to season. If you live in Southern California, you can create a customized, monthly watering schedule using an online landscape watering calculator. For details, see page 241. Ultimately, your goal is to keep the soil damp around roots, not necessarily at the soil surface. This is one reason that mulch is so incredibly important; it is an insulating layer that keeps water from evaporating from the surface of the soil into the air.

If you use drip irrigation in a cold winter climate, you will need to winterize your lines. A freeze sensor installed between the valves and the irrigation clock prevents the valves from turning on when temperatures fall below freezing. You can install a small, automatic drain valve at the low point in the system, so when the valves turn off, any water remaining in the lines drains out. If you prefer the low-tech method, simply open the end of the lines to drain them before freezing weather approaches. You can blow out any residual water with an air compressor.

When spring arrives, turn your irrigation back on, zone by zone, and inspect the lines for splits and ruptures. Always keep extra parts and pieces on hand for quick repairs.

It isn't possible to give you all the information you need to select, design, install, and maintain your low-water-use irrigation system within these pages. There are, however, many other sources of information easily available to you. For more water-saving ideas, see page 239.

One final note: After all of your hard work selecting water-wise plants, planting them appropriately, mulching the garden, and upgrading your irrigation system, resist the temptation to give established plants more water than they need. Some people operate on the idea that if a little is good, a lot is better. There may be a situation where that works well, but a garden isn't one of them. These plants are not only accustomed to surviving on little water, more water can actually hurt them! In fact, ask anyone who works in a nursery, and they will tell you they more often see plants their customers have killed by overwatering than by underwatering.

Not that we don't want you to be nice to your garden, just be nice in a different way. Overwatering isn't good for plants, it isn't good for your bank account, and it isn't good for the Southwest's limited water resources!

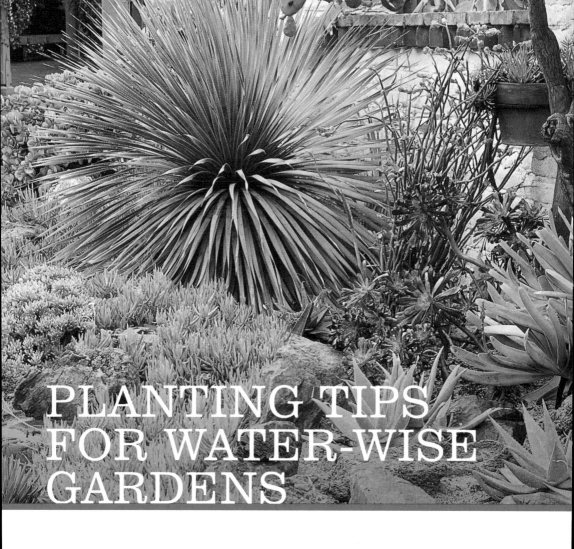

PLANTING TIPS FOR WATER-WISE GARDENS

HOW TO PLANT BARE-ROOT TREES, VINES, AND SHRUBS

If your bare-root plants arrive before you can plant them, set the roots in a container of dampened sawdust or construction sand and place them in a shaded location.

- When you're ready to plant, soak the rootball for several hours.

- Dig a hole twice as wide and half again as deep as the size of the rootball. Fill the hole with water and allow it to drain completely. If it takes more than a few hours to drain, build a planting mound or raised bed of well-draining soil. Dig a hole in the mound and fill the hole with water as described.

- If fertilizer is specified, add a balanced, organic fertilizer to the backfill soil and incorporate thoroughly. It is important that concentrations of fertilizer don't touch plant roots. Check the label for instructions on the amount of fertilizer to use.

- Whether or not fertilizer is called for, throw in a few handfuls of worm castings.

- Set the plant in the hole so the roots can spread out. If you have to twist or crush roots to fit the hole, the hole is not wide enough.

- Check the trunk of the tree or shrub for the dirt line. This line shows you how deep the plant was buried before it was dug up and the soil washed from the roots. Make sure that your hole is deep enough so that the tree will sit an inch or so above the dirt line once the hole is refilled.

- Set the plant in the hole. Gently scoop soil back into the hole, tamping it down around the roots. Wet the soil as you go if you'd like. Once the soil is level with the ground, build a watering basin and water deeply.

- Apply 3 or 4 inches of mulch to the soil surface, making sure that the mulch covers the entire rootball area. Make sure no mulch touches the trunk, so stop applying the mulch at least 3 inches away from the trunk.

HOW TO PLANT TREES, VINES, AND SHRUBS FROM NURSERY CONTAINERS

- Water the plant in its pot thoroughly the day before you intend to plant. Dig a hole just as deep as the pot is tall and 1½ to 2 times as wide as the pot.

- Fill the hole with water and allow it to drain completely. (See directions under the "How to Plant Bare-root Trees, Vines, and Shrubs" section.)

- Most of the plants in this book are best planted into native, unamended soils. For those that require amended soils, mix amendments into the soil that was dug out of the hole.

- Add a few handfuls of worm castings to the bottom of the hole.

- Refill the bottom of the hole with enough soil so the plant will sit at the same level it was in the pot. When planting natives, set plants an inch higher than they were in their pots.

- Step on the soil in the bottom of the hole to pack it down.

- Lay the pot on its side and squeeze the sides gently to loosen the plant from the pot.

- Grab the plant at the base of the trunk and carefully pull it from the pot.

- Check the roots. If they circle the rootball, gently loosen them unless they require minimum root disturbance. Remove any roots that are broken or dead.

• Set the plant into the hole. Refill with soil, tamping it as you go to eliminate air pockets. Before you reach the top, water the soil to settle it, then continue adding soil.

• Make a watering basin.

• Apply 3 or 4 inches of mulch to the soil surface, making sure that the mulch covers the entire rootball area. Make sure no mulch touches the plant, so stop the mulch at least 3 inches away.

TO BUILD A RAISED MOUND OR BERM

If your garden has poor, slow-draining soil, consider building raised mounds or berms out of native soil mixed with topsoil or compost. To build a berm, you need space, and scale and slope are critical. The higher the berm, the wider and broader you must make the base. The rule of thumb is that the slope should never be greater than one foot for every two feet in height. So if you have a berm standing 3 feet tall, you want your base to be 6 feet across. Plant the taller plants on top of the berm, midground growers in the middle, and use the lower base of the berm that collects water runoff for thirstier plants.

STARTING WATER-WISE PLANTS FROM SEED

Prepare the bed by roughing up the surface of the soil with a rake. Spread a light layer of slow-release or organic fertilizer and compost on the surface and rake them in. Mix fine seed with a cupful of sand to help distribute tiny seeds evenly. Broadcast and cover lightly by raking the soil, or just throw handfuls of compost over the top. Press the soil gently to prevent seed from washing away, and then water the seedbed using a fine spray. In rocky or coarsely mulched areas, broadcast seed over the area and water immediately so the seeds wash down into the crevices between the rocks. You may need to spread bird netting over the seedbed until the seedlings get to a size having three or four sets of leaves, or just sow extra seed and share with hungry birds.

PLANTING FROM CONTAINERS OR NURSERY PACKS

Dig a hole two to three times wider than the plant's container and about as deep. Remove the plant from its container and, with your pruners, cut an inch thick slit into the rootball, slicing from top to bottom. Make a few slits around the rootball. If the plant is potbound and roots are thicker than a pencil, lay the rootball on its side, then use your pruners or a sharp knife to cut about an inch wide slice off the bottom of the roots, just as if you were cutting a slice off a loaf of bread. Then make the slits down the sides with your shears. Set the plant in the hole just slightly higher than it sat in the container. Fill in around the plant with unamended soil, then press gently around the base to remove air pockets. Apply several inches of mulch, and water the soil deeply.

PLANTING WATER-WISE LAWNS

To prepare a new area for sod, seed, or plugs, level, clean, and thoroughly water the area, then let it dry for two days. Apply any recommended amendments (which depends upon the turf type) and lawn fertilizer according to preplant directions. Turn the soil, working in the amendments to a depth of 10 or 12 inches, then rake smooth and level. Water to a depth of 4 inches and let it dry for three days. Roll the area with a water roller, then rake to level out undulations. Water lightly just before planting. When laying sod, be sure the mats touch edges so they knit together quickly to avoid drying at the edges. If seeding or plugging, sprinkle on a thin layer of topdressing of sawdust, sand, or topsoil to protect the seed or plugs from drying out and from hungry birds.

Water two to four times a day for the first two weeks (don't allow the seedbed to dry out), then once a day for the next two weeks or until established. Then water every other day while increasing the depth of watering. During the first summer, you may need to continue watering every two days. If you are mowing your lawn, wait until the blades just start to bend before the first mowing.

PLANTING WATER-WISE BULBS

Dig a hole or trench that is up to two inches deep in well-drained, fertile soil. Apply a thin layer of bonemeal or organic fertilizer to the hole. Set bulbs in the hole or trench to about twice their height and cover completely. Alternately, rototill the area, rake it clean, then put the bulbs in a box and toss them out in the bed. Then plant them where they land, making sure their growing tips are facing up before burying.

HOW TO DESIGN CONTAINER PLANTINGS

Container planting is an art form. Don't let that put you off, however, as containers offer a huge range of design options.

You can create container plantings using a single large specimen or by planting combinations: annuals with perennials, shrubs, grasses, and so on. The most beautiful combinations include plants of different shapes, textures, and sizes—tall narrow spikes or sword-shaped leaves surrounded by broad leaves and a ground cover or trailing plant to spill over the edges. Plan your flower and leaf color combinations as well. This is a lot of fun.

HOW TO MATCH PLANTS WITH POTS

Whether you choose the container first or the plants first, look for complementary colors, shapes, and sizes. Gray-green leaves, for example, look stunning in a terracotta pot, one with a burgundy glaze, or even a deep green glaze. But put that same plant into a pot with a light green glaze and chances are it will look quite sickly.

Choose a pot that is large enough for the ultimate size of the plant and the root mass. It's better to err on a slightly larger size rather than a smaller size. In terms of sizes, place a tall plant into a tall pot that balances its proportions and accommodates its roots. Tiny plants are lost in a large pot but look very much in proportion if placed in a small pot.

Choose unglazed pots for plants that prefer to grow on the dry side. Without the glaze, the pot surface "breathes," that is, it allows water to evaporate readily from the surface. Plants that prefer moist conditions are best planted in glazed ceramic or plastic pots, which hold moisture longer.

Drainage holes

Be sure the pot has several ½-inch or larger drainage holes in the bottom. If there are no holes, drill some. Many pottery stores will drill holes for a small charge. Cover any holes in the bottom of the pot with a small square of fiberglass window screen. The screen lets water flow freely but keeps soil from falling out the hole and critters from crawling in.

Potting mixes

When it comes to potting mixes, you truly do get what you pay for. Cheap ones are not worth the money. For most plants, an all-purpose potting mix is fine, but there are special well-draining mixes for plants such as cactus and succulents. Orchids, *Epidendrum*, and *Epiphyllum* do best in mixtures that include small chunks of bark.

Choose a good granular fertilizer (preferably organic) to mix into the potting soil while planting. Some gardeners also add biodegradable water-absorbing granules that swell when they're wet and release water slowly as the roots need them. Add worm castings, too.

CREATING A WATER-WISE GARDEN

This section is devoted to providing guidelines for establishing your own water-wise garden and to share additional references, suppliers, resources, and professionals that Southwestern gardeners can go to for more information.

CREATING A WATER-WISE GARDEN

1. **Planning and Design:** Start with a plan based upon a water-wise approach.
2. **Irrigation:** Install a well-designed efficient irrigation system.
3. **Lawns:** Limit lawn space to what you need and plant water-wise grasses.
4. **Plant Selection:** Choose water-wise plants.
5. **Soil Management:** Provide well-drained soils.
6. **Mulch:** Cover the soil and surround the plants with mulch.
7. **Maintenance:** Practice good maintenance to grow healthy plants.

STEP ONE: PLANNING AND DESIGN—START WITH A PLAN BASED UPON A WATER-WISE APPROACH

Books

Landscaping on the New Frontier: Waterwise Design for the Intermountain West by Susan E. Meyer, Roger K. Kjelgren, Darrel G. Morrison, William A. Varga, Utah State University Press

Natural by Design: Beauty and Balance in Southwest Gardens by Judith Phillips, Museum of New Mexico Press

Native Gardens for Dry Climates by Sally Wasowski with Andy Wasowski: Clarkson Potter Publishers

Residential Landscape Architecture, 5th Edition by Norman Booth and James E. Hiss: Prentice Hall

Southwestern Landscaping with Native Plants by Judith Phillips: Museum of New Mexico Press

Water-Wise Gardening: America's Backyard Revolution by Thomas Christopher: Simon and Schuster

Internet

www.the-landscape-design-site.com/xeriscapedesignideas.html

The Landscape Design Site offers free do-it-yourself advice for all sorts of design tips and resources for homeowners. Specific designs are presented, addressing challenges such as water-wise designing for sloped areas, Southwest Xeriscape ideas for a square-foot front yard, and more. The site has an extensive listing for other services and resources involving basic landscape design principles, design aids, and plant selection, including a page devoted to consulting a designer for specific questions.

Consult a Professional

American Society of Landscape Architects (ASLA)

A national professional association for Landscape Architects, representing approximately 17,000 members nationwide. Log on as a visitor to find a landscape architect in your area.

36 Eye St. NW

Washington DC 20001

888.999.2752

www.asla.org

Association of Professional Landscape Designers (APLD)

4305 North Sixth Street, Suite A

Harrisburg PA 17110

717.238.9780

www.apld.com

A nationwide organization with a membership of landscape designers from around the United States. The Web site offers a handy "Find a Designer" page that lists certified and member landscape designers by each state.

STEP TWO: IRRIGATION—INSTALL A WELL-DESIGNED, EFFICIENT IRRIGATION SYSTEM

Books

Drip Irrigation for Every Landscape and All Climates by Robert Kourik: Independent Publishers Group

Sprinklers & Drip Systems: The Right System for Your Yard by Lisa Stockwell Kessler: Sunset Books

Internet

www.irrigationtutorials.com

Free irrigation design and installation tutorials and reference guides, trouble-shooting information, and product reviews.

www.netafimusa.com

Offers homeowners a downloadable guide, "Right Solution for Beautifying Your Yard," and a frequently asked questions section (FAQ) on drip irrigation and how to design, install, and find products. Click on "Landscape and Turf" on the homepage, then look on the FAQ drop-down menu.

www.rainbird.com

Offers homeowners information, manuals, support, and parts for irrigation systems.

www.toro.com

Offers information and design services for homeowners for new drip systems, retrofits, and upgrades. Look for the "Homeowner" tab on the homepage, then go to "Irrigation" at the bottom of the page.

WATER HARVESTING

From *The Green Gardener's Guide*, **JOE LAMP'L** offers more water-wise tips.

RAIN BARRELS

Harvesting rainwater from your roof is convenient and free.

Rain barrels are an easy way to harvest rainwater from your roof. They provide a convenient (and free) supply of water whenever you need it or when water restrictions make your normal sources unavailable. In fact, you might be surprised to know just how much water can be harvested from the roof of even a modest-sized home. Ready-made rain barrels are available from a wide range of sources, including gardening catalogs, Internet sources, and some garden centers and home improvement stores.

Internet

www.harvestingrainwater.com; www.harvesth2o.com; www.rainwater.sustainablesources.com; www.sandiego.gov (water conservation link); www.twdb.state.tx.us; www.zonagardens.com

Consult a Professional

The Irrigation Association

6540 Arlington Blvd.

Falls Church, VA 22042

703.536.7080

www.Irrigation.org

Find a Certified Irrigation Professional in your area. From the homepage, find the pull-down menu "Certification." Select "Certified Professionals," and enter your zip code.

THE ONLINE WATERING CALCULATOR

The amount of water your plants need depends on the type of plant you are watering, your garden soil, your growing region, your microclimate, and your type of watering system. With so many different variables, precise watering directions are impossible. There is, however, a great online tool to help you determine how often and how long to water each zone of your garden every month of the year. The online Watering Calculator uses your zip code, soil type, the kinds of plants you grow, and the kind of watering system you use (drip, bubbler, sprinkler, and so forth) to generate a customized monthly irrigation schedule for each of your garden watering zones.

The online Watering Calculator is available for all areas of Southern California. If you live in San Diego County, go to http://apps.SanDiego. gov/landcalc/. If you live in Santa Barbara County, go to www.SantaBarbara.gov/WaterCalc/. If you live in any other part of Southern California, go to www. BeWaterWise.com/ calculator.html.

For those not living in these areas, www.h2oconserve.org provides an online water calculator as well as a section called "Water Saving Tips, Education, Issues and Solutions."

STEP THREE: LAWNS—LIMIT LAWN SPACE TO WHAT YOU NEED AND PLANT WATER-WISE GRASSES

Books

The Encyclopedia of Ornamental Grasses by John Greenlee: Rodale Gardening

The Everything Lawn Care Book: From Seed to Soil by Douglas Green: Adams Media Corporation

Gardening With Grasses by Michael King, Piet Oudolf: Timber Press

The Impatient Gardener's Lawn Book by Jerry Baker: A Ballantine Book

Internet

www.lawncare.net

A site devoted to lawn care and maintenance, including seasonal maintenance schedules. "Katie's Column" covers specifics on lawn care and common problems related to specific regions.

www.penningtonseed.com

Pull down "Knowledge Center" toolbar for the lawn care center that gives maintenance, fertilizing, and watering tips and FAQs.

www.turfgrasssod.org

Turfgrass Producers International (TPI) official Web site representing the voice of the turfgrass sod industry. Click on "Consumer" for tips on lawn care, installation, maintenance, or buying turfgrass.

www.yardcare.com

Expert advice on grass selection, lawn diseases and pests, maintenance, and water conservation. Also has information on related tools and equipment.

Consult a Professional

Cooperative Extension System Offices: www.csrees.usda.gov/Extension

This Web site will help you find your nearest Cooperative Extension office. The Cooperative Extension System is a nationwide, noncredit educational network. Each U.S. state and territory has an office at its land-grant university and a network of local or regional offices. These offices are staffed by one or more experts who provide useful, practical, and research-based information to agricultural producers, small business owners, youth, consumers, and others in rural areas and communities of all sizes.

Master Gardeners

Visit the American Horticulture Society Web site at www.ahs.org, and click on "Master Gardeners" to find a program in your area. Master Gardeners have become a vital part of the Cooperative Extension's ability to provide consumers with up-to-date, reliable information.

Professional Landcare Network (PLANET) "The Voice of the Green Industry"

A nationwide network of green industry professionals, providers, suppliers, associations, and student chapters. Offers "Homeowners Resources" from tips on hiring a professional to finding a licensed provider in your area. Visit www.alca.org.

Professional Grounds Management Society (PGMS): www.pgms.org

Use the Web site to locate a professional grounds manager in your area.

STEP FOUR: PLANT SELECTION—CHOOSE WATER-WISE PLANTS

Books

Arizona Gardener's Guide by Mary Irish, Cool Springs Press

California Gardener's Guide, Volume II by Nan Sterman, Cool Springs Press

Nevada Gardener's Guide by Linn Mills and Dick Post, Cool Springs Press

New Mexico Gardener's Guide by Judith Phillips, Cool Springs Press

Rocky Mountain Gardener's Guide by John Cretti, Cool Springs Press

Dale Groom's Texas Gardener's Guide by Dale Groom, Cool Springs Press

Trees and Shrubs of the Southwest by Mary Irish, Timber Press

Xeriscape Plant Guide, Denver Water, American Water Works Association, Fulcrum Publishing

Internet

www.abcwua.org—click on "Xeriscape" to view extensive plant list

www.ci.gilbert.az.us/water/waterwise.cfm—plant lists, water-wise tagging program, and landscape examples

www.h2ouse.org—garden guide, plant lists, plant search, and garden gallery

www.sdcwa.org—click on "Conservation," "Nifty 50 Plants for Watersmart Landscapes," rebates

www.snwa.com—click on "Landscapes" to order a comprehensive CD that includes
a plant search database

www.waterwiseplants.utah—plant lists with a nursery water-wise tagging program

Water-Wise Plants

For complete nursery directories for each state, go to www.manta.com

Arizona

www.azna.org for retail nursery outlets throughout the state

www.desert-tropicals.com for nursery listings throughout the state

Moon Valley Nurseries, visit www.moonvalleynursery.com for three locations

Mountain States Wholesale: 800.840.8509 for retail nurseries carrying MSW products

Treeland Nurseries Inc.: 2900 S. Country Club, Mesa, AZ

California

Armstrong Garden Centers, 33 locations in California, www.armstrong.com

California Flora Nursery, 2990 Somers St., Fulton, www.calfloranursery.com

Las Pilitas Nursery, two locations, mail-order, www.laspilitas.com

Living Desert Nursery, 47-900 Portola Ave., Palm Desert, www.livingdesert.org

Nevada

Moana Nursery, three locations in Reno, www.moananursery.com

Nevada Division of Forestry, two locations, 775.849.0213
    http://www.forestry.nv.gov/main/seedbank01.htm

Plant World, locations in Nevada and Utah, www.plantworld.com

Star Nursery, locations throughout Nevada and Utah, www.starnursery.com

New Mexico

Bernardo Beach Native Plants, 1 Sanchez Drive, Veguita

Osuna Nursery, 501 Osuna Road NE, Albuquerque, www.osunanursery.com

Plants of the Southwest, two locations, www.plantsofthesouthwest.com

Tooley's Trees, PO Box 392, Truchas, www.tooleystrees.com

Texas

For a complete listing, www.helpfulgardens.com

Covington Nursery, 1905 Bingle Rd., Houston, www.covingtonnursery.com

Magnolia Gardens Nursery, locations throughout Texas,
    www.magnoliagardensnursery.com

Rancho Lomitas Nature Plants, www.rancholomitas.com

Utah

Ballards Nursery, 691 N State St., Hurricane

Big Trees, 240 N. 100 E., Kanarraville, www.bigtreesnursery.net

Elim Valley Tree Nursery, 1095 South 3325 West, Hurricane,
    www.elimvalley.com

Wildland Nursery, 370 E 600, Joseph, www.wildlandnursery.com

More Places for Water-Wise Plants

Search the Internet for online ordering

American Meadows, Annie's Annuals & Perennials, Busiani Plant Farm, JuJube Tree Nursery, Logee's Tropical Plants, Park Seed, S & S Seed, Seedman, Seedsource, Simply Succulents, Southern Bulbs, Streamback Gardens, Sunny Gardens

STEP FIVE: SOIL MANAGEMENT— PROVIDE WELL-DRAINED SOILS

More from **JOE LAMP'L**, GGG

Get Worms! *Let earthworms do the work for really healthy soil.* When it comes to manure and compost, there's one combination that works so well, it has its own name: vermicompost. Worms are quite resourceful, both in what they do to our soil and what they do in our soil. As they move through the surface and underground, they do great things to decompose the organic matter. The tunnels they leave behind while mining for sustenance aerate the soil while at the same time improve drainage (especially in clay and compacted soil). Worms consume massive amounts of organic matter on and in the soil. As the material passes through the worm's gut, the output, or castings, are more nutrient rich than before, as much as seven times richer in phosphate, ten times higher in potash, five times higher in nitrogen, three times higher in usable magnesium, and one and a half times higher in calcium.

Internet

www.vermicompost.net

Benefits and techniques for worm composting

www.bae.ncsu.edu/topic/vermicomposting/vermiculture

A list of vermicomposting publications

Field Museum, www.fieldmuseum.org

A tutorial for learning how to determine the composition (texture) of your soil by performing a texture test. If you want more in-depth information, visit the Web site and click on "Zone for Teachers."

Master Composters, www.mastercomposter.com

Visit the Web site for information on building compost piles, composting equipment, worm composting, and other composting methods, references, books, classes, and CDs. Also discusses why we compost and includes surveys and studies about compost, with links to more composting education.

National Resources Conservation Service, www.nrcs.usda.gov

Visit the Web site, and click on "Homeowners" for links to composting techniques (Your Own Backyard); conserving while landscaping (Conservation Where You Live); lawn and garden care (Home & Garden Tips); soil science education (Teach Your Children); and Earth Team, a volunteer organization that promotes conservation.

National Sustainable Agriculture Information Service, www.attra.ncat.org

The service provides an extensive list of soil testing labs and services offered, including sampling procedures, testing, diagnosis, and recommendations.

STEP SIX: MULCH—COVER THE SOIL AND SURROUND THE PLANTS WITH MULCH

Books

Better Homes New Garden Book: Meredith Books

The Green Gardener's Guide by Joe Lamp'l: Cool Springs Press

Rodale's Low-Maintenance Gardening Techniques: Rodale

Sunset Western Garden Book: Sunset Publishing

Internet

www.the-organic-gardener.com, www.gardenguides.com, www.planetgreen.discovery.com

Finding Mulch

Arizona—http://phoenix.gov/GARBAGE/landfill.html

California—www.ciwmb.ca.gov/organics/compostmulch

Nevada—http://ndep.nv.gov/BWM/landfill.htm

New Mexico—www.newmexico.wm.com

Texas—www.garden-ville.com

Utah—www.slvlandfill.slco.org/

STEP SEVEN: **MAINTENANCE—PRACTICE GOOD MAINTENANCE TO GROW HEALTHY PLANTS**

Books

All New Square Foot Gardening by Mel Bartholomew: Cool Springs Press

Bulbs for Warm Climates by Thad M. Howard: University of Austin Press

California Gardener's Resource by Bruce and Sharon Asakawa:
    Cool Springs Press

Carrots Love Tomatoes by Louise Riotte: Storey Publishing

Garden Color: Annuals & Perennials: Sunset Books

Growing Fruits & Vegetables by Richard Bird, Hermes House: Anness Books

Guide to Rocky Mountain Vegetable Gardening, Robert Gough and Cheryl
    Moore-Gough: Cool Springs Press

Modern Arboriculture by Alex L. Shigo: Shigo and Trees, Associates

Month-by-Month Gardening in the Deserts of Arizona by Mary Irish:
    Cool Springs Press

Month-by Month Gardening in the Deserts of Nevada by Mary Irish:
    Cool Springs Press

Month-by-Month Gardening in New Mexico by John Cretti: Cool Springs Press

Month-by-Month Gardening in The Rocky Mountains by John Cretti:
    Cool Springs Press

Succulents by Terry Hewitt: The New Plant Library

Texas Gardener's Resource by Dale Groom, Dan Gill: Cool Springs Press

The American Horticultural Society A-Z Encyclopedia of Garden Plants by
    Christopher Brickell, Judith D. Zuk (Eds.): DK Publishing

MORE WATER-WISE RESOURCES

Water Authorities, Agencies, and Districts

Water authorities, agencies, and districts are public entities charged with administering local water resources. Visit the Web site of your local agency for more information on water conservation demonstration gardens and landscapes, homeowner rebates, drought conditions, conservation methods, educational publications, water education opportunities, and to learn about agency outreach efforts that encourage water conservation both in the home and in the public environments.

Arizona

Arizona Department of Water Resources: www.azwater.gov

Central Arizona Project: www.cap-az.com

Water Conservation Alliance of Arizona: www.watercasa.org

California

California Water Districts and Associations:
    www.lib.berkeley.edu/WRCA/district.html

Metropolitan Water Authority: www.mwdh2o.com

San Diego County Water Authority: www.snwa.com

Nevada

Las Vegas Valley Water District: www.lvvwd.com

Southern Nevada Water Authority: www.snwa.com

Nevada Division of Water Resources: www.water.nv.gov

New Mexico

Albuquerque Bernalillo County Water Authority: www.abcwua.org

USGS New Mexico Water Science Center: www.nm.water.usgs.gov

Texas

Canyon Regional Water Authority: www.crwa.com

North Texas Municipal Water District: www.ntmwd.org

Texas Water Development Board: www.twdb.state.tx.us

West Central Municipal Water District: www.wctmwd.org

Utah

Central Utah Water Conservancy District: www.cuwcd.com

Metropolitan Water District of Salt Lake City: www.mwdslc.org

Utah Division of Water Resources: www.water.utah.gov

CONSERVATION, DEMONSTRATION, AND BOTANICAL GARDENS

Arizona

Southwestern Arboretum
520.883.1380
www.ag.arizona.edu

Desert Botanical Garden
480.941.1225
www.dbg.org

University of Arizona Cooperative
 Extension Demonstration Garden
602.470.8086
www.ag.arizona.edu/maricopa/garden

California

LA County Arboretum & Botanic Garden
626.821.3222
www.arboretum.org

Rancho Santa Ana Botanical Garden
909.625.6787
www.rsabg.org

Santa Barbara Botanical Garden
805.682.4726
www.sbbg.org

The Water Conservation Garden
619.660.0614
www.thegarden.org

Nevada

Acacia Demonstration Garden
702.267.4000
www.cityofhenderson.com/parks

North Lake Tahoe Demonstration Garden
775.586.1610
www.demogarden.org

Springs Preserve
702.822.7700
www.springspreserve.org

New Mexico

Rio Rancho Water-Wise
 Demonstration Garden
505.867.2582
www.ci.rio-rancho.nm.us

Santa Fe Greenhouse Xeric
 Demonstration Garden
877.811.2700
www.santafegreenhouse.com

Texas

Amarillo Botanical Gardens
806.352.6513
www.amarillobotanicalgardens.org

Dallas Arboretum
214.515.6500
www.dallasarboretum.org

Lady Bird Johnson Wildflower Center
512.232.0100
www.wildflower.org

Water Conservation
 Demonstration Garden
www.houstonwatergarden.com

Utah

Central Utah Gardens
801.222.0123
www.centralutahgardens.org

Conservation Garden Park
877.728.3420
www.conservationgardenpark.org

INDEX WATER-WISE PLANTS FOR THE SOUTHWEST

Nan Sterman: Nan Sterman is a horticulturist and well-known garden writer who was the former editor of the *San Diego Home, Garden and Lifestyle Magazine*. In addition, she is an award winning writer for the *Los Angeles Times*, the *San Diego Tribune*, *Sunset Magazine*, *Organic Gardening* magazine, and many others. Nan is the author of *California Gardener's Guide: Volume II*, which is about gardening with low-water-use, climate appropriate plants that are low maintenance and use limited  resources. Nan is an advisor to the San Diego Water Authority and answers the Water Smart Pipeline, a low water gardening hotline for the Water Conservation Garden in El Cajon, California. Nan is well known for promoting the use of California native plants and other plants from low water using, Mediterranean regions of the world. Nan is the co-producer and host of *A Growing Passion*, a television show about real-world, sustainable home gardening.

Mary Irish: Mary Irish has an extensive background in horticulture, having served as an author, lecturer, educator, and garden writer. She is an accomplished gardener who has lived in Arizona for more than twenty years. Irish assisted thousands of gardeners through the years as the Director of Public Horticulture at the Desert Botanical Garden in Phoenix, during which time she managed the botanical garden's Plant Introduction and Sales Programs. Mary  has authored numerous books on Southwest gardening including *Month-By-Month Gardening in the Desert Southwest*, *Month-By-Month Gardening in the Deserts of Nevada*, and the *Arizona Gardener's Guide* for Cool Springs Press. In addition to her frequent contributions to regional and national publications, Irish regularly teaches classes on desert gardening, the use and cultivation of agaves, and the care and cultivation of succulents.

Judith Phillips: Judith Phillips is a landscape designer, nursery grower, university lecturer, and garden writer. As a landscape designer, Phillips has designed hundreds of residential landscapes in New Mexico, many of which have won design awards. Phillips is the author of numerous books including the *New Mexico Gardener's Guide* for Cool Springs Press. Judith has received recognition both for her work promoting native plants and water conservation, as well as for her writing. Her awards include: the City of Albuquerque Water Conservation Award; NPSOT Carroll Abbott Memorial Award for *Natural by Design and Plants for Natural Gardens;* NPSNM Lifetime Membership for contribution to the use of native plants in landscapes; and the City of Albuquerque Award of Merit for Xeriscape Demonstration Garden.

Joe Lamp'l (aka joe gardener®): Lamp'l is the host of two national television shows: *GardenSMART* on PBS and DIY Network's *Fresh from the Garden*. His latest project includes producing and hosting a new series on PBS titled *Growing a Greener World*. He's also a syndicated columnist and author; his latest book is *The Green Gardener's Guide: Simple Significant Actions to Protect & Preserve Our Planet*. Joe's passion and work related to gardening, sustainable living, and environmental stewardship through multiple media platforms has positioned him as one of the most recognized personalities in the "green" sector today. Find out more information about Joe and his work online at www.joegardener.com.

Diana (Dee) Maranhao: Dee Maranhao has been a professional in the horticulture industry for over thirty years, serving as a nursery production specialist, horticulture department manager and as a college horticulture instructor in xeriscape principles and design, plant identification, plant propagation, and greenhouse management. She has served as Horticulture Editor and Copyeditor for Cool Springs Press, *Garden Compass Magazine*, Ball Publishing, and as Project Editor for the Irrigation Association. Dee and her husband Steve garden intensively at their Apple Valley, Utah, home where she works as a horticulture editor, copyeditor, and garden writer. Ms. Maranhao authors a gardening column and assists in the production of *Southwest Trees and Turf* magazine, a monthly publication that caters to arboriculture, turf, and landscape industry professionals.